NORWAY
THE COMMANDOS
DIEPPE

This volume has been written at the request of H.M. Government as one of a series designed to furnish the general reader with a short military history of the Second World War, 1939–45, pending the publication of the Official Histories. The author has been given access to official documents and sources of information: for the presentation of the material, for the statements made, and for the opinions expressed he alone is responsible.

*Other Volumes in this Series:*

ARMS AND THE MEN

THE CAMPAIGN IN ITALY

*In preparation:*

THE CAMPAIGNS IN AFRICA

GREECE AND CRETE

IRAQ—SYRIA—PERSIA—MADAGASCAR—
THE DODECANESE

N.W. EUROPE, 1944–45

THE FAR EAST, 1941–45

THE SECOND WORLD WAR, 1939–1945
A POPULAR MILITARY HISTORY BY VARIOUS AUTHORS
IN EIGHT VOLUMES

# NORWAY
# THE COMMANDOS
# DIEPPE

BY
CHRISTOPHER BUCKLEY

LONDON
HIS MAJESTY'S STATIONERY OFFICE
1951

*First published* 1951





LONDON: PUBLISHED BY HIS MAJESTY'S STATIONERY OFFICE
To be purchased directly from H.M. Stationery Office at the following addresses: 429 Oxford Street, London, W.1; York House, Kingsway, London, W.C.2; 13a Castle Street, Edinburgh 2; 39 King Street, Manchester, 2; 2 Edmund Street, Birmingham, 3; 1 St. Andrew's Crescent, Cardiff; Tower Lane, Bristol, 1; 80 Chichester Street, Belfast; or through any bookseller.

Price 10*s*. 6*d*. net. 1951 S.O. Code No. 63-111-1-4*

*Printed in Great Britain under the authority of His Majesty's Stationery Office at The Curwen Press, Plaistow, E.13*

# Foreword

CHRISTOPHER BUCKLEY, who was killed in Korea in August, 1950 while correspondent of the *Daily Telegraph*, revised the first proofs of this volume before his untimely death. In carrying out this revision he had at his disposal the comment and criticism of many authorities including those who had helped him with advice and material when the original typescript was in preparation. As he was able to give his personal attention to these matters the work remains substantially the author's own.

# Contents

# Maps and Illustrations

## MAPS



## ILLUSTRATIONS

# THE CAMPAIGN IN NORWAY

# CHAPTER I

# War Comes to Norway

## 1

### *The Prelude*

THROUGHOUT the long and bitter winter of 1939–40, the period which has won the name of the Phoney War, Germany on the one hand, Britain and France on the other, were each sparring for position. During these months of unnatural lull two regions in Europe appeared to provide possible routes for the 'way round', the line of indirect approach which would enable the Allies to strike at Germany from an unguarded side. One of these was the Balkan peninsula; the other was Scandinavia.

From the very opening of the war Mr. Churchill, as First Lord of the Admiralty, had been impressed with the economic value to Germany of the iron ore from the Gallivare area in northern Sweden. Germany imported some 6,000,000 tons out of the average annual output of 8,000,000 tons from this region. The bulk of it (about four-fifths) was railed down to the Norwegian port of Narvik and thence shipped to Germany. Only a small portion was despatched from the Swedish port of Lulea inside the Gulf of Bothnia. Moreover, Lulea was ice-bound in the winter, when the whole supply passed by Narvik.

Since this iron ore was of great importance in enabling Germany to maintain and expand her war industry, Mr. Churchill, as early as September 1939, had drawn the attention of the Cabinet to the need for taking some action, preferably by means of an extensive minefield, to prevent the German vessels hugging the coast through Norwegian territorial waters. But difficult questions arising out of Norway's position as a neutral were involved. Months were to pass before any action was initiated, and by the time that we were at last ready to take steps to prevent this traffic it was too late.

Meanwhile the attention of the German leaders, and particularly of their naval leaders, had likewise been drawn to the Scandinavian peninsula. They were well aware of their dependence upon the iron ore of Sweden; and the possibility that Britain might block the traffic from Narvik, obtain control of the Norwegian ports (thereby shutting German shipping out of the Atlantic), and finally bring both Norway and Sweden into the war against them, was an ever-present preoccupation.

That the occupation of Scandinavia formed no part of Hitler's original conception is now certain. He stated to the Italian Foreign Minister, Count Ciano, on August 12th, 1939, that he believed that neither antagonist would attack Scandinavia and that the Scandinavian countries would themselves refrain from an attack upon Germany. There is no particular reason to disbelieve this. Unless there were signs that Britain herself intended to extend the war northwards, Germany might be taking a big risk in launching an operation of this nature. It involved a dispersal of force from the main battlefront in the West, where the great decision was to be sought, and it put German communications to a great extent at the mercy of British attacks by sea and air. While the gains that would accrue from success were likely to be considerable, the penalty of failure seemed still greater. So long as the vital traffic in iron ore and nickel could be sustained by the use of Norwegian territorial waters, so long as Nazi strategy aimed, in general terms, at directing the main blow in the West against France, to be followed after the expected victory by a peace offer to England and thereafter by the grand assault upon Russia, so long did Norway remain largely a strategic irrelevance.

Such was Hitler's view. But the naval chiefs were not so easily lulled. On October 3rd, at the time when the last shots were being fired in the Polish campaign, Admiral Raeder, Chief of the Naval War Staff, submitted a memorandum to Hitler regarding the possibility of extending the operational bases of the German Navy further to the north. This might be achieved, he considered, by means of the combined pressure of Russia and Germany upon Norway. Six days later Admiral Doenitz, in a memorandum submitted to Raeder, developed the thesis still further. Any naval base established in Norway, he submitted, must answer three prerequisites. It must be situated outside the Shetlands–Norway straits; it must be ice-free; it must possess rail communications. Only two ports answered all

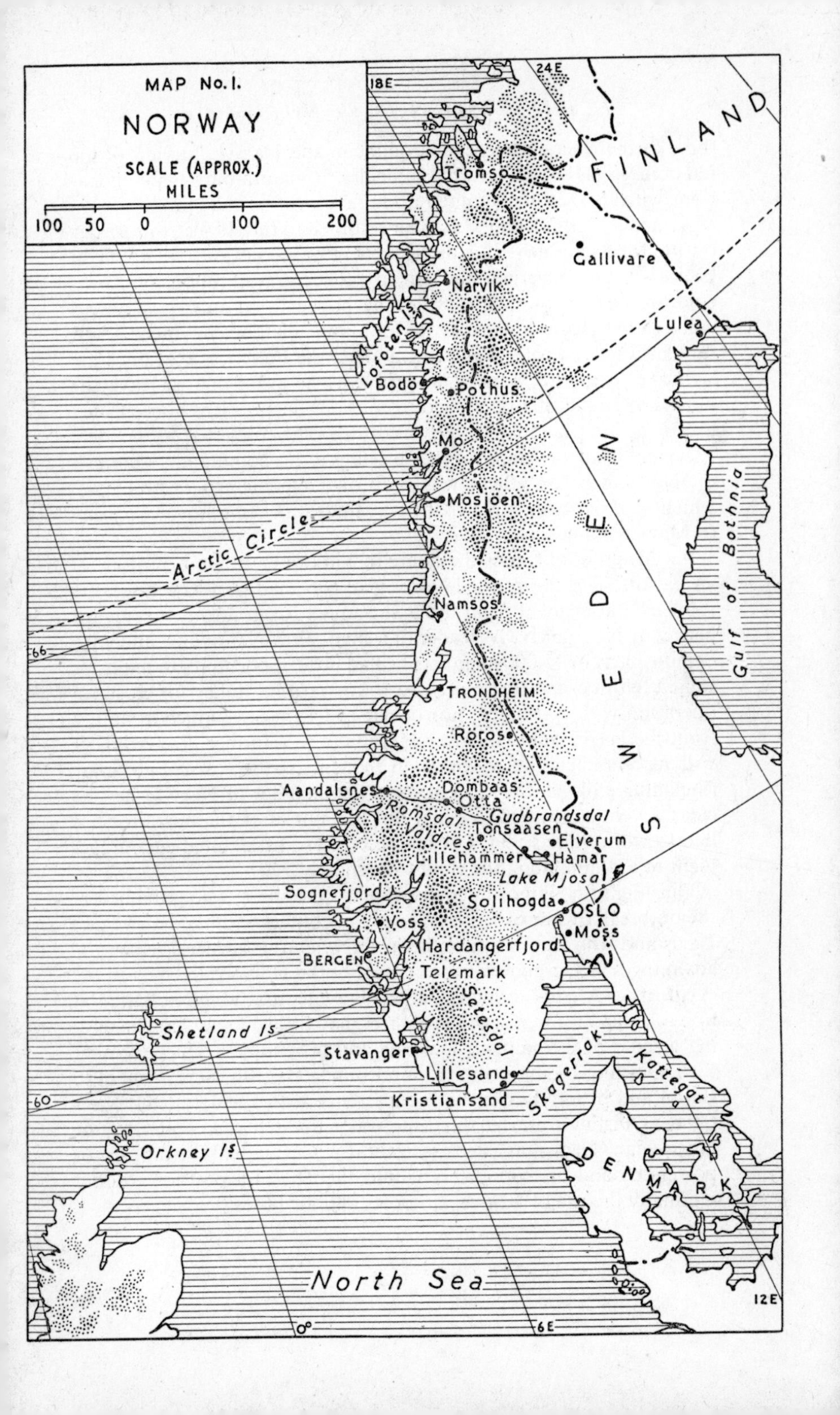
MAP No. 1.
NORWAY
SCALE (APPROX.)
MILES
100 50 0 100 200
18E
24E
FINLAND
Tromso
Gallivare
Narvik
Lulea
Lofoten Is.
Bodö
Pothus
Mo
Mosjöen
Arctic Circle
SWEDEN
Gulf of Bothnia
Namsos
66
TRONDHEIM
Roros
Aandalsnes
Dombaas
Otta
Romsdal
Gudbrandsdal
Valdres
Tonsaasen
Elverum
Lillehammer
Hamar
Lake Mjosa
Sognefjord
Solihogda
OSLO
Voss
Moss
Hardangerfjord
BERGEN
Telemark
Setesdal
Shetland Is.
Stavanger
Lillesand
Kristiansand
Skagerrak
Kattegat
60
Orkney Is.
DENMARK
North Sea
0°
6E
12E

three of these requirements—Trondheim and Narvik. In view of the remoteness of Narvik and the difficulty of maintaining communications with it, Doenitz summed up in favour of Trondheim.

Armed with this opinion Raeder returned to the subject with Hitler on the following day. But the Führer, always cautious where naval projects were concerned and already concentrating upon the forthcoming blow in the West, which he hoped to be in a position to deliver that same autumn, was not immediately convinced. And though Raeder wrote subsequently that 'the Führer saw at once the significance of the Norwegian problem; he asked me to leave the notes and stated that he wished to consider the problem himself', yet it does not appear that Hitler was at this time converted to the idea. It is significant that in his secret briefing to his commanders-in-chief on November 23rd there was only one reference to Scandinavia, which he described, somewhat surprisingly, as being hostile, 'owing to Marxist influences'.

At this point obtrudes the figure of Vidkun Quisling, prototype of all traitors. This disgruntled Norwegian Nazi had vainly been seeking some encouragement from the preoccupied Reich for his scheme for betraying his country. As leader of a small ultra-Nationalist and anti-Semitic party of 15,000 members he had little opportunity to make his weight felt in domestic politics, or to forward his policy for close co-operation with Germany; nor did he at first receive much attention from the Nazi leaders themselves, though as a former War Minister with close association with certain elements in the Norwegian Army (including Colonel Sundlo, garrison commander of Narvik) he was clearly a contact worth nursing. But it is not often that a traitor has had to work quite so hard or has received so little initial encouragement to aid him along the road to perfidy.

Quisling's first important convert was Rosenberg, who, even before the outbreak of war in 1939, had been in contact with the Norwegian Nazis and who bent a sympathetic ear when the former stressed the advantages to Germany of the control of the Norwegian coast in the event of an Anglo-German conflict. Rosenberg, though he failed at first to enlist the interest of the Führer, had little difficulty in persuading Raeder of the value of Quisling and his contacts. On December 11th, Quisling and his principal subordinate Hagelin, were brought to Berlin and promptly went into conference with Raeder at the Navy Office. Quisling's aim at this time was a sudden *coup d'état* by the Norwegian Nazis, assisted secretly by Germany. Having seized power, he and his supporters would then be in a position to offer Germany the use of Norwegian ports and air bases.

All this Raeder reported on the following day to Hitler. Apparently the Führer, his eyes still set upon a winter offensive in the West, remained dubious; at any rate he affected reluctance to see Quisling in person. Two interviews, however, took place, on December 16th and 18th respectively, at which Quisling outlined his plan once more. At these meetings Hitler emphasised repeatedly that the most desirable attitude for Norway as well as for the rest of Scandinavia from his point of view would be one of complete neutrality. He stated that he had no intention of enlarging the war and drawing other nations into the conflict. If, however, the enemy were preparing an enlargement of the zones of war with the aim of further threatening and strangling Germany, he would of course be compelled to arm against such steps.

This categorical statement seems to have been to some extent a smoke-screen. Hitler, by this time, was at least partially convinced. The Russian war against Finland had already started, and if Anglo-French sympathy with the Finns were to crystallise in the form of direct assistance the Allies were bound to seek footholds in the peninsula, whereupon the whole war would swing north in the direction of the Baltic. In that case Hitler must arrive first.

Accordingly the Führer, while stressing German military disinterestedness, promised Quisling financial assistance for his movement and 'for the purpose of combating increased enemy propaganda'. And that same day he gave orders for a planning staff to be set up to work upon a hypothetical campaign in Scandinavia, to be undertaken if the political coup of the Norwegian Nazis failed to materialise. Quisling had achieved more than he can at first have realised as the result of his meeting with Hitler.

As Hitler had foreseen, the new development in Europe had drawn the attention of Britain and France northwards and was powerfully to influence their planning for the ensuing phase of the war. On November 30th, Soviet Russia, following abortive negotiations during which she had demanded territorial concessions to strengthen her position in the Baltic against attack, declared war on Finland. Sympathy in the West with this latest victim of aggression was sincere and widespread. But sympathy was one thing; effective action was quite another matter.

The Allied Supreme War Council decided on December 19th, at a time when the first Russian attacks had been most vigorously repulsed, in favour of all possible assistance to Finland. A force of 100,000 was to be prepared for operations in that country, and the acquiescence of Norway and Sweden to the passage of the troops was to be sought. Thus, from the early days of January 1940, planning with a view to possible operations in Scandinavia and in the Baltic area generally was being carried on concurrently both by the Germans and by the Western Allies. And the point of intersection of the two plans was the Norwegian port of Narvik.

But from the first there was a divergence of view between the French and British with regard to the real objectives of any northern expedition. The French plan, formulated about mid-January, involved the landing of British and French forces at Petsamo, the Finnish port in the far north on the Arctic Ocean. Such an operation would automatically mean war with Russia, since Petsamo was now in Russian hands. The British attitude was at once more cautious and more realistic. At the inter-Allied military conferences held on January 31st and February 1st, our representatives showed themselves less interested in the Petsamo project than in the possibility of denying the Germans the iron ore of northern Sweden from the mines around Gallivare. In the British view the securing of Narvik should become the major operation, and only a part of the force should be passed on to Finland. The British representatives showed themselves, also, more alive to the unwisdom of directly provoking Russia.

Of the two schemes, that of the British was much the less impracticable, and it was that which was adopted at a meeting of the Allied Supreme War Council on February 5th. Preparations were thereupon put in hand for an expedition to Scandinavia.

The main objective was to be Narvik, which fulfilled the double prerequisite of being admirably situated both for the purpose of interrupting the iron ore traffic with Germany and also as a base for passing on troops and material to Finland. Supplementary landings, however, were to be made at Trondheim, Bergen, and Stavanger. We would endeavour to procure the concurrence and, if possible, the co-operation of the Norwegians and Swedes. At no time did either Government contemplate landing and moving their forces across to Finland in face of opposition from either Norway or Sweden. It was hoped that Finland could be persuaded to issue an SOS appeal to the world and that Britain and France, invoking the Covenant of the League of Nations, might use this appeal as a lever to persuade Norway and Sweden to permit the transit of troops to Finland.

In view of the geographical situation of Scandinavia in relation to the two Allies, in view of the important role which would necessarily fall to the British fleet, and in view of the French commitments and responsibilities in the West, it was decided that the supreme direction of the force should be British.

Meanwhile in Germany planning for an operation against Norway (under the code name of 'Exercise Weser') had been begun during January and was being carried on concurrently with the planning for the great offensive in the West. But Hitler was still reluctant to commit to a campaign in Scandinavia forces that might be required for the far more important operation against France. And so through January and February the question of priority remained in abeyance.

The decision to undertake the invasion of Norway before opening the offensive in the West was brought about by the celebrated *Altmark* incident. In mid-February the *Altmark*, a German auxiliary ship, carrying as prisoners 299 officers and men of British merchant ships previously sunk by the *Graf Spee*, was proceeding down the coast of Norway on its homeward course, keeping within Norwegian territorial waters. By February 15th it had reached Josing Fjord, almost at the south-western extremity of the coast, where it was discovered by a Hudson of R.A.F. Coastal Command.

The Admiralty had ordered that the vessel should be hunted down and searched, even if this involved entering neutral waters, and that any prisoners found on board should be liberated. Captain P. L. Vian in H.M.S. *Cossack*, therefore sailed into the fjord and, after some parley with the local Norwegian commander, who appeared convinced that there were no prisoners on board the *Altmark*, engaged the German ship, boarded her and released the prisoners.

This action, breaking the long monotony of the period of the Phoney War, aroused immense enthusiasm in England and was not without its effect upon neutral opinion, which was beginning to grow comprehensibly dubious about the desire or ability of the Allies to undertake any really bellicose action. On Hitler its effect was decisive. He appears to have been genuinely convinced that this action represented the preliminary to an Allied operation in Scandinavia. Reports of the probable Norwegian attitude in face of such a development were conflicting; for while the German Legation in Oslo was convinced that the country would remain strictly neutral, Quisling and Hagelin wrote of the increasingly Anglophil tendencies in the Government and people and described the *Altmark* incident as 'a prearranged affair' between the British and Norwegian Governments. About this time it began to be apparent to Hitler that the chances of a successful political coup by the Norwegian Nazis could be ruled out. Quisling had over-called his hand from the first, and it was clear that so far from Germany merely lending secret help to bring about a successful political coup, a full-scale invasion would now be necessary.

On February 21st, Hitler placed General von Falkenhorst in charge of the preparations for 'Exercise Weser'. But right up until the end of the month it remained an open question whether it should be given priority over the attack in the West. If the Norwegian campaign were undertaken first, would it overlap chronologically the invasion of the Low Countries? In fact, the vital part of this operation—the fighting in southern and central Norway—was to end with just a week to spare before the German armies crossed the frontiers of Holland and Belgium for the great sweep to the Channel. The timing could scarcely have been bettered.

On March 1st, Hitler issued his positive directive for the attack upon Denmark and Norway. He emphasised that 'the operation should prevent a British encroachment upon Scandinavia and the Baltic, should guarantee our ore base in Sweden and give our Navy and Air Force a wider start line against Britain'.

The force to be employed was to be kept as small as possible, and numerical weakness was to be balanced by 'daring actions and surprise execution in seizing the main cities and forts of the west coast'. As far as possible the operation was to create the appearance of a peaceful occupation of the Scandinavian States with a view to preserving them from aggression.

Seven divisions (69th, 163rd, 181st, 196th, 214th, 3rd Mountain and, later, 2nd Mountain, together with some territorial tank units) were eventually allotted for the occupation of Norway; three to take part in the assault phase and the remainder for the follow-up. The ports to be attacked were Oslo (against which four companies of parachutists would be employed in addition to the seaborne troops), Kristiansand, Stavanger, Bergen, Trondheim, and Narvik. In view of the strength of the British Home Fleet it was decided to commit every serviceable unit of the German surface fleet to escorting the transports and covering them from attack. This was one of the most gigantic gambles of the war. No naval units, however, could be left to support the troops once they were ashore; protection would then become the task of the Luftwaffe.

Two divisions and a motorised brigade were allotted for the land invasion of Denmark.

Even now it was not all plain sailing for the planners. No satisfactory unification of command could be achieved. Falkenhorst had only conditional command of the supporting naval forces and only temporary command of the Luftwaffe units involved. Of a conference of the Commanders-in-Chief held on March 5th, Jodl noted in his diary:

'Field-Marshal (Göring) in a rage because not consulted until now. Won't listen to anyone and wants to show that all preparations so far made are worthless.'

There was also the gigantic conundrum of the Soviet Union to be taken into account. Russia was at this time in the process of bringing the protracted 'incident' of Finland to a conclusion, and it was uncertain how she would react to a German aggression against a state which possessed a common frontier with Finland in the extreme north. Under the circumstances Raeder favoured buying the Russians off with the Norwegian port of Tromsö. 'Better the Russians sit in Tromsö than the British' he commented. But Hitler felt, and quite rightly from the point of view of his future plans, that no further concessions to Russia were either necessary or desirable in this quarter, and the proposed offer was never made.

The strategic necessity for the operation was overriding. Germany must secure her access to the iron ore of Scandinavia and could not afford to see British troops installed in the Norwegian ports. But the risks involved were fully realised. Raeder, while concurring in the necessity, was fully alive to the risks and summed up as follows:

'The operation in itself is contrary to all principles in the theory of naval warfare. According to this theory, it could be carried out by us only if we had naval supremacy. We do not have this; on the contrary we are carrying out the operation in face of the vastly superior British fleet. In spite of this the C.-in-C. Navy believes that, provided surprise is complete, our troops can and will successfully be transported to Norway.

'On many occasions in the history of war those very operations have been successful which went against all the principles of warfare, provided they were carried out by surprise. The critical moment is the penetration of the harbours while passing the coastal fortifications. It is to be expected that this will succeed if carried out by surprise, and that the Norwegians will not make the decision to fire quickly enough, if they decide to do so at all.'

There was much anxiety among the German war leaders during the next week or two. Not only was the forthcoming operation appreciated as the gamble it was, but the danger that the Allies might anticipate the attack upon Scandinavia by a landing of their own could not be ignored. And so, while the planners pushed ahead with the final preparations, German propaganda set to work to deter any corresponding Allied movement. It was presumably with this purpose in view that the representative of the German Foreign Office informed the American correspondent William Shirer on March 13th that Hitler had stated to both Oslo and Stockholm that, had Allied troops set foot in Scandinavia at a time when they were planning assistance to Finland, Germany would immediately have invaded the north to cut them off.[1]

Meanwhile, as the German preparations hastened towards their conclusion, the slow-moving plans of the Western Allies were at last beginning to mature. By the beginning of March the first stage of the plan was ready to be put into operation—always assuming the consent of the Norwegian and Swedish Governments. The French were prepared to commit 50,000 volunteers and 100 bombers to the aid of Finland, and the first contingent of this expeditionary force, a brigade of Chasseurs Alpins, was actually embarked at Brest on March 1st. Further British and French units were to follow. This aid for Finland was designed primarily as a means of tightening the blockade and cutting Germany off from a vital source of raw materials rather than as a way of opening up a new front against her in the north.

On March 2nd the Allies notified Norway and Sweden that they were prepared to act in response to the expected Finnish appeal for aid. They based their expectation on the information earlier received from Marshal Mannerheim that he would not require additional troops before the spring, provided that he could receive munitions and, above all, medical stores. With the spring at hand, it seemed reasonable to suppose that he would readily welcome the Franco-British force.

The Allies stated in their Notes to Norway and Sweden that, if the answers to their proposals were in the affirmative, their troops would be in a position to land in Norwegian ports from March 20th onwards. Four and a half divisions would be employed in the first phase, with a subsequent build-up. In view of the fact that the first contingent was already on board ship at Brest when the Notes were delivered one may suppose the date, March 20th, was named with a view to misleading the German Intelligence regarding the state of our preparations.[2]

The reply of the Norwegian and Swedish Governments to the Allied Notes took the form of a firm refusal to countenance the use of their territory for direct aid to Finland. In the interval since the initiation of the plan the incident of the *Altmark* had occurred, the immediate consequence of which had been to harden Norway's determination to defend her neutrality, while Sweden was equally definite in refusing to permit the transit of troops, as distinct from volunteers and

[1] Shirer, *Berlin Diary*, pp. 234–5.
[2] But see Churchill, *The Second World War*, Volume I, p. 453.

war material, through her territory. And scarcely had these refusals been received than the news came that the Finnish Government had opened negotiations for peace.

The Finns had hesitated to issue their appeal until they could obtain some indication of the attitude likely to be adopted by Sweden and Norway. The discouraging replies to the Franco-British *démarche*, following close upon the final breach of the Mannerheim Line, had convinced their Government of the hopelessness of further resistance. A delegation left for Moscow on March 6th, following news of the refusal of the Swedish Government to allow the transit of troops. Negotiations opened on the following day, and an agreement for the cessation of hostilities was reached on March 13th.

A new and embarrassing situation now faced the Allies. Their preparations for the expedition were already well forward when the primary justification ceased to exist. In the light of this development there appeared no adequate reason for keeping the expeditionary force together, and it was accordingly dispersed.

But the impetus once given could not easily be reversed. The tide of war was still flowing towards the Baltic. Britain remained predominantly interested in the necessity for drawing tighter the blockade around Germany, while the French Government thought rather in terms of opening up a new front. The basic objective of the Norwegian campaign, in French eyes, was subsequently expressed by Paul Reynaud in terms distinguished rather by their optimism than by their sense of reality. It was 'to create a new theatre of war in which the Germans would use up their men, their material and in particular their air force, and, above all, their reserves, especially of petrol'. How far these desirable objectives were to be attained by a small Allied force operating far from its bases and exposed to overwhelming enemy air superiority in the narrow mountain-bound valleys of Norway was far from clear.

A decision was taken at a meeting of the Allied Supreme War Council on March 28th. The habitual violation of Norwegian territorial waters by German vessels engaged upon the iron ore traffic could no longer be tolerated. Norway and Sweden were to be informed by a Note handed to their Ministers in London and Paris on April 1st that measures were being taken to tighten the blockade against Germany. These measures would take the form of the laying of mines in Norwegian territorial waters.

It was assumed, not without logic, that the act of mine-laying would not, in itself, provoke Germany to invade either of the Scandinavian States. But, in the event of Germany reacting in this manner, a force was to be held in readiness to counter any enemy initiative. Under the title of 'Avonmouth', the equivalent of a British division[1] commanded by Major-General P. J. Mackesy, was to stand by for a landing at Narvik and the three southern ports of Trondheim, Bergen and Stavanger. At the same time, the French Alpine division, which had, by the earlier plan, been destined for Narvik, would be employed for the same purpose.

Our purpose was to obtain a strategic 'jump' on the Germans by the laying of the minefield. If the Germans did not react—well and good. We should have stolen a march on them. But if their reaction took the form of an invasion of Norway, then we should be in a position to bring immediate direct aid to the victim of aggression.

The written instructions issued to General Mackesy on April 6th indicate that the British landing would be made only by agreement with the Norwegian Government following German aggression. It was not intended that our troops should fight their way through Norway.

The object of the expedition was defined as 'the port of Narvik and the line of communications inland as far as the Norwegian-Swedish frontier. Subsequently, should an opportunity arise to go on to Gallivare, the task of the force would then become a denial of the Gallivare ore fields to the enemy.'

There was some postponement of the intended time-table. The Notes were to have been delivered on April 1st. Actually, they were not handed to the Norwegian and Swedish Governments by Lord Halifax and M. Reynaud until April 5th. The next stage, the mining of Norwegian territorial waters, was to have begun on April 5th. Actually, it did not occur until April 8th.

The main points made in these Notes were that the two Allied Governments could not permit a new attack upon Finland either by Russia or by Germany and would take appropriate measures to bring aid to Finland whether or not they were granted facilities by the two Scandinavian States. They would regard as unfriendly the conclusion of any exclusive political agreement by either country with Germany or any attempt on the part of the Soviet Union to obtain from Norway a base on the Atlantic coast. Finally, in view of the fact that the Allies were waging the war as much in the interest of the small nations as in their own, they declared that they reserved the right to take such measures as they might deem necessary to hinder or prevent Germany from obtaining in Sweden or Norway resources from which she might, in the conduct of the war, derive advantages to the detriment of the Allies.

[1] 49th (West Riding) Division, including the 24th (Guards) Brigade.

The laying of mines in Norwegian territorial waters was to be undertaken with a view to forcing the German ships, which loaded up with iron ore at Narvik, out into the open instead of permitting them to creep down, as they had hitherto done, within Norwegian waters and under the shelter of the fringe of islands which cover the coast. Three zones were selected for the minefields. The most northerly would be situated off Bodö, about 150 miles south of Narvik. The others were off Bud and Stadtland, much further south, between Trondheim and Bergen. Such a disposition of minefields, while it certainly constituted a technical violation of Norwegian neutrality, was calculated not to interfere with her own port to port coastal trade.

It was hoped that the laying of the minefields, though it would necessarily provoke a formal protest from the Norwegian Government, would persuade them that we could no longer allow Scandinavian neutrality to be weighted against us by fear of Germany.

## 2

### *The Assault*

On April 4th the German ships destined for Narvik were preparing to put to sea. And on the following day the German Minister in Norway, Dr. Braüer, invited members of the Norwegian Government to witness at the German Legation a film entitled *Baptism of Fire* which dealt with the German invasion of Poland and culminated with the picture of the bombing of Warsaw.

The German plan aimed at the rapid occupation, with quite small forces, of the six main ports of Norway in order to achieve a *fait accompli*. Though ten divisions were ultimately committed, the preliminary forces were very small. At no point did the initial wave exceed 2,000 men, but these were picked troops who knew exactly the task that lay before them. Considerable risks were of course taken in landing such small forces at widely divergent points where mountain barriers prevented the possibility of any quick link-up between the different landing parties. Against an enemy who was both powerful and prepared such a method must almost certainly have spelt disaster, for the various small parties might have been counter-attacked and overwhelmed in detail. But the Norwegians were neither powerful nor prepared, and any attempt on the part of the British to assist them would be accompanied by considerable risk.

While the Germans owed something of their success to the treachery which paved the way for them, as in the case of Vidkun Quisling at Oslo and Colonel Sundlo at Narvik, they depended much more upon the sheer bewilderment of the Norwegians who, unwarlike and unprepared for war, found themselves without resource in the face of the German *blitzkrieg*. There was much talk of the achievements of the Fifth Column, and the name of the despicable Quisling has earned a shabby immortality as the prototype of the traitor from within; yet the extent of actual Fifth Column activity was certainly exaggerated at the time in Britain and France. If there had not been a single quisling in Norway the country would still have been overwhelmed by the German armed forces. It would have taken longer—but not much longer.

The instructions given to the German forces were that they were to act swiftly and sharply, taking over the necessary strategic points not as a hostile force but as protectors who came to secure Norway against an attack from England. They were not to treat the Norwegians as enemies unless the latter opposed their entry, and it is quite clear that many of the German troops were genuinely surprised and pained when the Norwegians opened fire upon them. The purpose of the invasion, it was explained in a memorandum submitted to the Norwegian Government, was to anticipate the expected Anglo-French initiative and to prevent the Western Allies from transforming Scandinavia into a theatre of war. Even if the Norwegian Government had the desire to resist the aggression of Britain and France, it was stated, she had not the means. All attempts at resistance would be crushed by the German forces and could only result in useless bloodshed.

Finally, the German Government declared that their action involved no present or future attempt against the integrity or political independence of the kingdom of Norway.

It was on April 6th that the first detachment of the German fleet put to sea. The sailings were carefully synchronised to ensure that the transports with their escorting warships arrived as nearly as possible simultaneously off Oslo, Kristiansand, Stavanger, Bergen, Trondheim, and Narvik. At the same time, as a preliminary and necessary corollary to the conquest of Norway, German troops were to cross the Danish frontier and take that small country under the 'protection' of the German Reich.

The German surprise succeeded, though only by a narrow margin. On April 8th, about midday, the Polish submarine *Orzel*, cruising in the Skaggerak, sighted and sank a large German transport ship,

*Rio De Janeiro*, off Lillesand, while another German transport, *Posidonia*, was sunk on the same day in the outer fjord of Oslo.

About one hundred and fifty survivors of *Rio De Janeiro* were picked up and brought ashore. Without exception they were all found to be wearing uniform and admitted to having been armed. One of them further stated that the ship also carried tanks and aircraft for a landing operation.

And the world had just twenty-four hours to meditate upon the significance of that fact and decide whether or not it was a *canard* before it woke to even graver and more sensational news.

Meanwhile information had been received by the British Admiralty from aircraft reconnaissance that a portion of the German fleet was at sea and heading north. The direction of the German movement left plenty of room for speculation. It might imply an armed attack upon some part of Scandinavia, but it might equally mean no more than a commerce raid in considerable force. It might even mean that a determined attempt was being launched against our own country. Or again it might be a challenge which would lead to another Jutland.

With such information as it possessed, the Home Fleet put out to sea from Scapa on the night of April 7th. Conditions were just about as bad as they could be for bringing an enemy to action, for a high sea was running and poor visibility and blinding snow-storms hampered our reconnaissance. Nevertheless, there seemed reasonable hope that we might bring the Germans to battle, since later reports confirmed that, contrary to expectation, the bulk of the German vessels appeared to be heading in the direction of Narvik. The first and almost the only encounter, however, occurred as the result of chance. The destroyer *Glowworm*, on her way to take part in the mine-laying operation, had become separated from the remainder of the expedition. On the morning of April 8th she sighted the German heavy cruiser *Hipper*, and though hopelessly outmatched succeeded in ramming her and tearing a hole 120 feet wide in her bows. She was subsequently set on fire and sunk, but not before she had given the alarm to the Home Fleet.

The hunt was now up, but in default of further detailed information and in the appalling weather conditions that prevailed the Home Fleet failed to make contact. The old battle cruiser *Renown* had been covering the mine-laying operations in the Bodö area and was proceeding northward when, upon a sudden break in the clouds, she caught sight of the German battle cruisers, *Scharnhorst* and *Gneisenau*, which had just completed their task of escorting the expedition to Narvik. *Renown* went into action against both ships at a range of 18,000 yards and scored hits on *Gneisenau*, but both the German ships, helped by the poor visibility and intermittent snow-storms, made off successfully at top speed. With better weather conditions and a little more information regarding the precise localities of the main German convoys it is possible that the enemy operation might have been fatally deranged at the very start.

The basic principles governing the German attack were treachery, bluff, and speed. The way was made smooth by some skilful Fifth Column work on the part of Vidkun Quisling and his adherents, but the decisive factors in the German success were immense technical superiority, the total unreadiness of the Norwegians to deal with invasion, and the inability, for reasons which will become apparent in this narrative, of the Western Allies to render the latter aid on any important scale.

Without any doubt or question the first day of the campaign was decisive. Within twelve hours from the time of the initial landings Oslo, the capital, and the ports of Kristiansand, Stavanger, Bergen, Trondheim, and Narvik, had all fallen into German hands. All the major aerodromes in the country had been secured, including Fornebu, outside Oslo, and the larger airfield at Stavanger. And the railway communications with Sweden were in process of being taken under control.

A heavily escorted fleet of transports moved northwards up the deep indentation of the Skaggerak towards Oslo. It included the pocket battleship *Lützow*, the 10,000-ton armoured cruiser *Blücher*, the 5,600-ton light cruiser *Emden*, a modern gunnery ship, and a screen of mine-sweepers, torpedo-boats, and motor craft.

Against this the only ships of importance lying in Horten harbour at the side of the fjord were the three mine-sweepers *Olav Tryggvason*, *Otra*, and *Rauma*. Two larger ships, *Harald Haarfagre* and *Tordenskjold* were lying at the quayside incapable of combat, and there were four submarines available. This was the force at the disposal of the Norwegians when the news came through, just before midnight April 8th–9th that ships believed to be German were entering Oslo fjord. The three mine-sweepers went into action. One of them rammed the German destroyer *Albatros*, but the fleet passed on and began to approach the Drobak narrows, the last point at which they could be checked before Oslo. It is not true, as was reported at the time, that the commander of the Norwegian warships at Horten obeyed an order which he believed to have been issued by M. Koht, the Minister for Foreign Affairs, instructing him to permit the German ships to pass.

In view of the state of alert, the Norwegian Government had been summoned to meet at 1.30 in the morning, and news began to come through of the strange behaviour of these foreign warships steaming in not only up Oslo fjord but also reported off the approaches to Bergen, Stavanger, and Trondheim. While the Cabinet was still in session the German Minister, Dr. Braüer, presented his ultimatum.

Meanwhile a hard-fought battle was going on in the narrows approaching Oslo. At 3.30 the guns of the Oscarsborg fortress, which commands the final, inmost stretch of the fjord, opened against *Blücher*, setting her on fire with two hits on gun turrets; and subsequently she was hit by torpedoes in the narrows and rapidly sank. With *Blücher* went down her crew of 800, in addition to 1,500 men of the landing-party, a number of staff officers and the Gestapo units who were to have policed the Norwegian capital. A considerable number of survivors managed to swim ashore and were taken prisoner by the Norwegians.

Oslo was not taken by the naval assault, which was well behind schedule in forcing its way up the fjord on Tuesday morning, but by the airborne troops who landed on Fornebu aerodrome in daylight while German bombers circled over the capital almost at rooftop level. A little later, German fighter planes, flying equally low, discharged rounds of machine-gun fire into the streets. After some hard fighting during the morning against the Norwegian Royal Guards, German troops began to defile through the streets of Oslo between two and three o'clock in the afternoon, while the populace, lining the pavement, gazed in bewildered fascination at the invaders and showed at first a complete lack of comprehension of what was going on or why it was happening. That was how an initial force of about 1,500 men was able, after the preliminary encounter on the airfield, to occupy a city of 300,000 inhabitants without bloodshed. It was not much before the third day, April 11th, that the people of Oslo awoke to the reality of the situation and the young men began to make their escape towards the north and the mountains on skis, by car or on foot.

The naval force detailed for the attack upon Kristiansand consisted of the light cruiser *Karlsrühe*, two torpedo-boats and several auxiliary vessels. Owing to thick fog off the approaches to the port the time schedule could not be maintained and it was not until 6.30 a.m. that the German formation entered the fjord. The small Norwegian ships in the harbour and the coastal batteries resisted, and three separate attempts to force the passage were unsuccessful. At about 9 a.m., however, the commander of the Norwegian garrison received a message that French warships were approaching and should be allowed to enter the harbour. Accordingly, when the Germans made their fourth attempt about a couple of hours later the Norwegian batteries did not fire and the German troops landed without opposition and proceeded to occupy the town. It was some compensation that *Karlsrühe*, almost at the outset of her return journey, was torpedoed by the British submarine *Truant*, and sank in the course of the evening.

Stavanger was swiftly taken. A Norwegian torpedo-boat sank a German supply ship but was then sent to the bottom herself, and German forces occupied the town during the morning, while their parachutists got possession of the airfield at a very early hour. Of this important gain they took the fullest advantage. Numbers of troop-carrying planes continued to arrive in the course of the morning, for the Germans assumed that we should strike hard for the recovery of this vital position. They wasted no time in establishing themselves in strength here, and even by that first evening our chances of a successful counterstroke had practically vanished.

At Bergen, as at Kristiansand, a *ruse de guerre* contributed to the German success. A number of supply ships carrying war material were already lying at anchor, flying foreign but friendly flags. At 2 a.m. on April 9th the assault force, led by the cruisers *Köln* and *Königsberg* entered the fjord. *Köln* was picked out by Norwegian searchlights and promptly made the recognition signal in English 'H.M.S. *Cairo*, proceeding to Bergen for a short visit'. It was thereupon allowed to proceed. The ruse was later detected, and Norwegian coastal defence guns in the forts of Kvarven and Hellen kept up a fire for some time, scoring three hits on *Königsberg*. Norwegian mines also caused a two-hour delay to the invaders. But the forts were presently overpowered, and German troops were in occupation of the town soon after dawn. The first of them entered with white flags tied to their bayonets and announced that they came as friends. Mobilisation of the Norwegian forces in the Bergen area was, however, carried out fairly successfully, and the troops fought their way back stubbornly towards Voss before being transferred to the Gudbrandsdal to help stem the German drive up from Oslo.

*Königsberg*, unable to put out from Bergen after the damage it had received from the shore batteries, was attacked and sunk the next morning by dive bombers of the Fleet Air Arm.

Trondheim, the most important German objective after Oslo, was defended at the entrance to the fjord by the two forts of Brettingen and Hysnes on the eastern shore and by the fort of Hambaara on the western. At each of the two former forts there was a battery of 210-mm. and a battery of 150-mm. guns, but at Hambaara only a battery of 150-mm. Moreover, for reasons of economy, Hambaara was completely unmanned at the time. Arrangements had actually been made to garrison the fort on April 9th—just twenty-four hours too late for it to be of any use in fulfilling the purpose for which it had been constructed.

The German ships, consisting of one heavy cruiser, *Hipper*, and four destroyers, began to pass the entrance to the fjord at 2.45 a.m. The forts on the east side of the straits having already received information of what was going on in Oslo fjord, opened fire on them, although—a further sign of the tragic unreadiness of Norwegian defence preparations—there was found to be no ammunition for the 210-mm. battery in Brettingen. Moreover, the telephone connection between Brettingen and Hysnes had broken down four days earlier and had not been repaired. One German destroyer was hit by the guns from Hysnes and beached, but visibility was poor and snow was falling steadily, with the result that the remaining ships passed safely on up the fjord. About 300 men were landed on the west shore near Hambaara and about twice that number on the east shore, while some 600 men were put ashore at dawn on Trondheim quay and the town was occupied without further resistance. Sporadic fighting continued between the German troops and the garrison of Hysnes until 5 p.m. when the Norwegian troops surrendered. Brettingen fort surrendered early next day. Rather oddly, while a party of Norwegian troops successfully crossed the straits and removed the breech-blocks from the guns in Hambaara fort, next to nothing was done to put the guns out of action at Brettingen and Hysnes when these two forts were handed over to the Germans.

As a result the Germans had been enabled to occupy Trondheim with very little difficulty, a single cruiser lying off the town and dominating it with its guns, under cover of which the troops went ashore. Their exploitation from this important position, situated at the narrowest part of Norway and therefore providing the best opportunity for cutting the country in two, was to some extent foiled by the heroic resistance of the old fort of Hegra, twenty-five miles to the east. The fort had not been in use since 1926 and much material had been taken away in the interval, but a scratch garrison of troops, 260 strong, who had escaped from Trondheim, under Lieut.-Colonel Holtermann, took control on April 10th. The fort is situated high up on a mountain side with its guns sited with a view to firing not west towards the fjord and the sea but east towards the Swedish frontier. Nevertheless the garrison repulsed two determined attacks made in mid-April and held out for nearly four weeks with a determination which was as courageous as anything in the campaign. It had been hoped that the guns would be able to command the nearby airfield of Vaernes, but this proved to be just out of range, and the airfield passed into and remained in German hands. Nevertheless, Hegra was a continued obstacle to the German exploitation eastwards from Trondheim. It did not surrender until May 5th, three days after the evacuation of the British troops from Namsos, when only one day's supply of food was left for the garrison.

The boldest of all the German landings was that which was carried out at Narvik. The port lies in the far north, over 600 miles from Oslo as the crow flies, and the small force about 2,000 strong, under General Dietl, which landed there took the biggest imaginable risk. It seemed so improbable that an enemy contingent would be flung so far afield, depending on sea communications hundreds of miles long vulnerable to attacks by the full weight of the Royal Navy, that Mr. Chamberlain at first refused to believe the report. He informed the House of Commons that the mention of Narvik was probably a mistake for the small port of Larvik situated just outside Oslo fjord.

On the evening of April 8th there were ten German merchant ships lying at anchor in Narvik harbour or fjord and, in view of the announcement of the laying of the British minefield some hours before, the naval officer in command at Narvik had despatched a signal asking for instructions in the event of British naval units entering the fjord to attack German shipping. At midnight he received orders that all attacks upon Narvik should be met with force, but within a very few hours the situation had radically altered.

About 3 a.m. a force consisting of ten of the newest and largest German destroyers began to penetrate the long and winding fjord that leads eventually to Narvik. Two 4,000-ton Norwegian coastal defence ships, *Eidsvold* and *Norge*, which lay in the fjord, courageously engaged the German flotilla. Both were rapidly sunk, with heavy loss of life, and the way was open for the Germans to continue unimpeded to their destination.

By 5 a.m. German troops were beginning to come ashore in the sleepy little port. They landed at the piers and jetties and marched up into the market-square of the town. Many carried placards with the following reassurances written in Norwegian: 'Be calm. Take things easily. We come to help you against the English.' But the people of Narvik, roused by the shooting in the fjord and peering sleepily from their windows through the thickly falling snow, attached greater significance to the hostile appearance of the machine-gunners who marched on either side of the sandwichmen.

Already when General Dietl came ashore at 8.15, German troops were in control of Narvik and no opposition had been offered by the local garrison. A commandeered taxi was in readiness at the jetty-side when the German commander landed and he drove straight up to the headquarters of the garrison, where he was received by the local commander, Colonel Sundlo.

Colonel Sundlo made a formal surrender of the town and of his own troops to the German commander.

This really settled the issue; for already the German forces—some twelve hundred were ashore, by this time—were spreading out and taking up positions at key points in the neighbourhood of the town and the docks, and rounding up British merchant seamen whom they found ashore. In an hour or two it was all over. About 200 Norwegian troops under the second in command, Major Omdahl, refused to obey the orders of Colonel Sundlo and had fallen out of the ranks. These now made off into the mountains in the north where, joined by others, they were able to maintain themselves and for a week even succeeded in denying the use of the railway from Narvik to the Swedish frontier to the Germans.

This was the situation which the Allied Governments were called upon to face on Tuesday, April 9th. Their first reaction was necessarily a naval one. Narvik seemed the point most sensitive to an immediate counter-stroke, as it was certainly the most remote and isolated and the place which the Germans would find it hardest to reinforce and re-supply. The German garrison around the town itself did not at first exceed 1,200, the remainder having fanned out to the north and east to engage the Norwegian troops. With so many irons committed to the fire in other parts of Norway, the German High Command was not yet in a position to provide any important reinforcement. There was therefore a good chance of a successful counter-stroke at Narvik, provided that it could be made with the utmost speed.

The German destroyers had completed their task when they set General Dietl and his troops ashore at Narvik on the morning of April 9th. Had things gone according to plan they were to have sailed for home the same evening, since they constituted far too valuable a stake to be left in so remote and exposed a situation for a single hour longer than was absolutely necessary. But every one of them needed to refuel, and only one of the expected tankers was found to have arrived in Narvik harbour. Commodore Bonte, who was in charge of the destroyer formation, decided to postpone his departure until the night of April 10th.

This was a stroke of good fortune for the Royal Navy, which helped partially to balance their misfortune in failing to get to grips with the German fleet on its outward course.

On the morning of April 9th the Second Destroyer Flotilla was in the neighbourhood of the Lofoten Islands, not far from the approaches to Westfjord and Narvik, when it received orders to enter the fjord with a view to preventing a landing. No information had at that time been received about the movements of the ten German destroyers, and there was no reason to suppose that the enemy were yet in Narvik. A little later in the day it was learned that a single enemy ship had entered and that only a trifling force had been landed at Narvik. Captain B. A. W. Warburton-Lee, who commanded the flotilla, therefore entered the fjord with his ships only to learn from Norwegian pilots that six large German destroyers and a U-boat had passed up the channel to Narvik and that the approaches to the port were believed to be mined. He signalled back this information, adding 'Intend attacking at dawn, high water'. The Admiralty thereupon left him discretion to act as he saw fit, adding that they would support whatever decision he might make. There were, of course, though this was not known at the time, ten German destroyers (each of 1,800 tons) in the fjords around Narvik. Captain Warburton-Lee's flotilla consisted of five destroyers, *Hardy*, *Hunter*, *Havoc*, *Hostile*, and *Hotspur*, of a lighter displacement (only *Hardy* was above 1,300 tons) and less heavily gunned.

Outnumbered both numerically and in fire-power by the ships he was about to attack, Captain Warburton-Lee on the morning of April 10th led his flotilla in H.M.S. *Hardy* up the gradually narrowing waters of the fjord. It was a decision in keeping with the highest traditions of the Royal Navy.

The surprise was complete. German records attest that they had no indication of the approach of the British ships until the bombardment opened shortly after dawn. One German destroyer was almost immediately hit and began to sink, and among those killed on board was Commodore Bonte, who had been in command of the expedition to Narvik. A second was later sunk, and three more were set on fire. So far all had gone well for the attacking force. But as they swept a third time up the approaches to Narvik they were beset on either flank by further German destroyers emerging from subsidiary fjords to the north and south. The heavier fire-power of the German ships began to tell. *Hunter* was sunk, *Hotspur* seriously and *Hostile* lightly damaged, and the enemy fire concentrated upon *Hardy*. She was hit repeatedly and under this hail of fire was run aground by the one officer who remained unwounded. About 170 of the crew managed to get ashore, but Captain Warburton-Lee himself died of his wounds. For the courage and enterprise which he showed in this action he received the posthumous reward of the Victoria Cross.

Though in this first naval battle of Narvik we had suffered somewhat severely in the latter stages, the balance of advantage remained with us. We lost two destroyers and had another badly damaged, but we sank two German destroyers and seriously damaged five others. In addition we had sent half a dozen enemy supply ships to the bottom, while in the very last stage of the action *Havoc*, while withdrawing from the fjord, sighted the German auxiliary *Rauenfels*, which carried the reserve of ammunition for the destroyers at Narvik. She promptly opened fire and blew it up. The loss of this ammunition ship, on whose arrival the enemy were anxiously counting, was to exercise an important influence on the course of the action three days later.

The decisive fact about the naval engagement that goes by the name of the First Battle of Narvik was that the German destroyer flotilla had been so badly mauled that its immediate return to home waters was out of the question. At the end of the battle not more than three or four of the vessels were actually seaworthy. The initial blow, therefore, had pinned them to the Narvik area and enabled H.M.S. *Warspite* and a flotilla of nine destroyers to force their way into the fjord three days later and destroy the entire German flotilla.

## 3

## *Norway Fights Back*

The land operations in Norway fall naturally into two phases. The first is the period of single-handed Norwegian resistance; the other and longer period is that of Anglo-French intervention. Norwegian resistance was at its most intense during the first week after the German occupation and continued, though on a diminishing scale, throughout the eight succeeding weeks when Allied troops were operating in the country.

The Allied plan for bringing aid to Norway and countering the German aggression was hastily improvised, too frequently changed and came finally to grief because lack of material and above all of air power never made possible the development of the execution in terms of the conception. But in view of the difference in strength between the opposing forces it could under no circumstances have succeeded.

Briefly, the intention was as follows:

One force, of mixed British, French and subsequently Polish troops, was to land in the far north at the entrance to the Narvik fjord, eliminate the German troops in this area and take possession of Narvik itself and the railway leading up to the Swedish frontier. It seemed reasonable at the time to suppose that this could be achieved in a matter of a few days. Admiral of the Fleet Lord Cork and Orrery was to be in charge of the naval and Major-General P. J. Mackesy of the military operations in this sector.

Further forces were to be landed in the neighbourhood of Trondheim. At first a direct assault upon the port was envisaged. This was modified about April 12th when it was realised that the Germans were established there in some strength and an elaborate concentric attack was substituted. One force under Major-General A. Carton de Wiart, V.C., was to be landed at Namsos to the north of Trondheim, while an independent brigade was put ashore at Aandalsnes to the south. While the northern force swung down through Steinkjer the southern would secure the important junction of Dombaas thereby preventing the Germans from reinforcing Trondheim by rail. Then a naval contingent would force the entrance to Trondheim fjord and land troops, under the command of Major-General F. E. Hotblack, to storm the port and city itself.

With Trondheim in our hands we should possess the means at least of sealing off all northern Norway from the enemy and thereby obtain our original objective of denying the enemy the winter route for the iron ore to Germany; and we should have established a footing in north-west Europe with the possibility of expansion southwards to contact and support the Norwegian troops fighting back from the neighbourhood of Oslo.

Within a few days the plan was changed once more. The convergent attack upon Trondheim was abandoned. The southern force was diverted to stem the German advance from Oslo, the seaborne force never sailed, and the northern force was left to advance by itself. Thereafter, with increasing German strength and increasing weight of material being committed, the situation tilted further and further against us.

It is symptomatic and significant of the campaign that the three landings—Narvik (April 15th), Namsos (April 17th) and Aandalsnes

(April 18th)—so far from converging towards a pre-arranged strategic goal, developed along divergent lines, with the result that, for a proper understanding and to avoid continuous shifting of the picture, they will be treated separately in this narrative.

In the second phase of the Norwegian campaign, therefore, the Allies were engaged in three quite distinct operations:

1. The attempt of the force landed at Aandalsnes (known as 'Sickleforce') to link up with the Norwegians fighting around Hamar and Elverum and to contain the Germans in the southern valleys; and, when this latter objective failed, the fighting retreat back up the Gudbrandsdal.

This operation covers the period from April 18th to May 3rd.

2. The attempt of the force landed at Namsos (known as 'Mauriceforce') to fight its way down to Trondheim. This was the only part of the projected three-pronged offensive that ever got going at all, and it was stultified by the fact that the attack of the naval prong in the centre was not proceeded with.

This operation covers the period from April 17th to May 2nd.

3. The combined operations around Narvik by the force bearing the code name successively of 'Avonmouth' and 'Rupertforce'. This aimed at the capture of the port and town by a *coup de main* in the very first days of the campaign, but developed into a wasteful and wearisome campaign of attrition, with the result that Narvik was not actually taken until after its capture had lost all possible strategic importance and after the decision to evacuate the Allied forces from Norway had already been reached.

This operation covers the period from April 15th to June 8th.

The keynote of the German assault had been surprise, rather than 'quislingery'; surprise again, rather than the employment of overwhelming force. Nowhere was this more remarkable than in Oslo, where the original German force, which arrived by air on the Fornebu landing-ground, was extremely small—about 1,500—and its orderly entry into the capital helped to create in the minds of the bewildered citizens something of a sense of a *fait accompli.*

This is how it appeared to an American newspaper correspondent who was in Oslo when the German troops marched in:[1]

'Tens of thousands of persons clustered in the streets and on the pavements, waiting, utterly baffled. We all asked where the British were, but, also, where the Germans . . .

[1] *The Daily Telegraph,* Lord Strabolgi, *Narvik and After,* pp. 48–51.

'Norway's capital in every quarter was a scene of dazed disorganisation, completely without leadership. Apparently even the men who had been called to the colours did not know where to go or simply forgot about it.

'The streets were filled with men of fighting age, all standing watching the German planes, waiting and speculating, but doing nothing and going nowhere . . .

'Shortly before three o'clock two lorries filled with a dozen German soldiers rolled along the street. Soldiers lolled in them with rifles dangling as if they had been assured that they had not the slightest resistance to fear. From the rear of the second lorry two machine-guns poked their noses out straight down the boulevard. Their crews lay prone with intent, hard faces, ready to fire. This was the only show of force and all that was needed.

'At 3.03 a murmur ran through the crowd. We could see two mounted men swinging into the boulevard in front of the palace, then six more, then the head of a marching-column in field-grey. The mounted men were Norwegian policemen actually escorting the German troops who were occupying the capital. We looked on uncomprehendingly. Later I was told that the Norwegian policemen never carry any kind of arms; this also was why they failed to fulfil the Government's order to arrest Quisling.

'The German column marched steadily through a lane of 20,000 or 30,000 Osloans, fully half of whom were men of military age. A tall, broad-shouldered officer, General von Falkenhorst, and two other officers marched directly behind the mounted police. Then came the German regulars in column of threes, as if to make the line look as long as possible.[1] One out of nine carried light machine-guns; all carried compact aluminium kits and bulky shoulder-packs.

'They were hard-muscled stony-faced men. They marched with rifles on shoulders with beautiful precision. Mostly they stared straight ahead, but some could not restrain triumphant smiles in the direction of the onlookers.

'Several times Falkenhorst and the other two officers returned the Nazi salutes of persons in the crowd, who must have been German advance agents and had been busy in Oslo for weeks before this crowning moment.

'From our hotel balcony, two Nazis gave the salute. I noticed in particular the beaming face of a chic, slim blonde German woman whose husband had been very active in our hotel since we arrived the previous Thursday.

'It was a thin, unbelievably short column. It required only six or seven minutes to march past. It was composed only of two incomplete battalions —surely less than 1,500 men in all.

'Norway's capital of nearly 300,000 inhabitants was being occupied by a German force of approximately 1,500 men.

'The last of the German troops went by without a single tear noticeable on any Norwegian face. Like children the people stared. Thousands of young men stood watching this occupation parade. Not one hand or voice was raised. We could discern no sign of resentment upon any face about

[1] In fact, the German troops, like our own, habitually marched in 'threes'.

us. This was the most incomprehensible thing among all the incomprehensible things of this fantastic twenty-four hours.

'Somehow it seemed as if curiosity was the strongest sentiment in the throng of Osloans who watched the Germans come in. No other emotion was betrayed in the countless faces we scanned anxiously. The only indignant people we met or saw that day were foreigners. The Norwegians of Oslo seemed stunned beyond recovery. All acted curiously, like children suddenly given a chance to see a parade of strange creatures out of prehistoric times—something which had no connection with real life.'

With parades up and down the streets and with music in the parks and squares (a Nazi band was playing 'Roll out the Barrel' in the big square in the centre of the city on the morning after the occupation) the Germans strove to create the impression that this occupation was no more than a friendly act of protection and that now they could all be carefree young men together. But meanwhile the German High Command and German diplomacy were acting rapidly.

While the hostile warships were sailing up the sound towards the capital and had already engaged the *Olav Tryggvason* and the coastal defences, but before the first airborne troops had arrived, the German Minister, Dr. Braüer, had called upon the Norwegian Foreign Minister, Dr. Koht, with his memorandum explaining and justifying the invasion, and a nineteen-page Note containing the demands of the German Government. Summarised, these involved the surrender to the German armed forces of all strategic points which the commanders of the German troops might consider necessary to their security. The Germans would also have the control of all railways and steamship services, telegraph, telephone, mails, wireless, and press—in short all means of communication and information within the country. All communications with the west, with America as well as with Britain and France, were to be cut off.

The Foreign Minister had naturally referred this to his Government before being in a position to tender a reply, despite the urging of Dr. Braüer for a speedy answer. There was never any doubt what the reply of the Norwegian Government would be, and by 5.30 (only an hour after the presentation of the demand) Dr. Koht was able to announce to the German Minister the decision of the Government to defend its independence. The light was just greying towards the dawn and the two men talked without candlelight. As the Foreign Minister gave his reply, German transport aeroplanes were beginning to circle down over Oslo bringing the first of the occupation troops.

The Government, following its decision to resist, had agreed upon a hurried evacuation of the Storting to Hamar, on Lake Mjosa, about eighty miles north of Oslo. It was a wise decision, since it was particularly important that they should remain at liberty to take what measures they saw fit; and subsequent actions by the Germans clearly revealed the fact that it was the intention of the invaders to endeavour to get control of the person of the King or, failing him, someone who could be regarded as representative of the Norwegian people, since the German Minister had not at this time been informed that he was to regard Major Quisling as head of the Government. A special train had been ordered to be in readiness for 7 a.m., and it was a remarkable achievement that 145 out of the 150 members of the Storting were able to take part in the meeting that afternoon. They owed much during these crucial days to the courage and determination showed by three men, King Haakon himself, who never wavered in his patriotism and his determination to maintain the honour and independence of Norway, Mr. C. J. Hambro, President of the Storting and Chairman of the Foreign Affairs Committee, whose great influence was throughout thrown upon the side of resistance, and Colonel Ruge, shortly to be appointed General and Commander-in-Chief of the Norwegian Army, to whose energy and inspiration the resistance of the Norwegian troops in countless isolated valleys in all parts of the country was primarily due.

At 12.30 the German Minister had made a further appeal to the Norwegian Government, urging them to give instructions that resistance was to be brought to an end, drawing attention to the action of the Danish Government in similar circumstances and requesting a further interview. Meanwhile Quisling had installed himself in Oslo as Prime Minister. He was at first ignored by Dr. Braüer, who continued to treat the Premier Nygaardsvold as the official head of the Government, until directly instructed in a telephone conversation with Ribbentrop that recognition was to be given to Quisling. Accordingly he altered his request to a demand for a private interview with the King.

But already the situation had passed out of the sphere of diplomacy into that of war. That night a small German motorised force, led, somewhat surprisingly, by the air attaché at the German Legation, had raced north from Oslo towards Hamar in what was palpably an attempt to get control of the person of the King and as many of the Government as possible. On news of the advance upon Hamar the Storting once again adjourned, this time to Elverum, some miles to the east. News of their fresh move, however, seems to have reached the German column, which accordingly changed direction and swung off along the road in the direction of Elverum. A small body of

Norwegian troops, mainly consisting of recruits, volunteers and labourers, was hastily scrambled together, and arms were issued to them. Most of them had had no experience of handling machine-guns; many had never before used firearms at all. About seventy-five, however, after a brief and rudimentary instruction, were stationed at Midtskogen covering the approach to Elverum, behind an improvised barricade. The German force, about a hundred strong, seems to have counted upon rushing Elverum without opposition under cover of darkness. They ran slap into the defence force at Midtskogen and were driven off with considerable loss. Among the casualties was the German air attaché himself, who was mortally wounded. The German force thereupon withdrew, and for more than a week Elverum was secure from the enemy ground forces.

This action was carried out on the night of April 9th–10th, at a time when negotiations had not yet been broken off by Dr. Braüer, the German Minister, who was in fact still hoping for an audience with the King that night. It represented yet another example of the calculated treachery which characterised German action in Scandinavia.

Taken aback by the speed and success of the German landings and by the fact that all the great cities and ports of the country had fallen into enemy hands within twelve hours of the first attacks, the Norwegian General Staff reported on April 10th that resistance was hopeless. Both the Chief of the General Staff and the Commander of the Field Army handed in their resignations. It was a critical moment, and the arguments for a recognition of a *fait accompli* seemed strong. At this point Colonel Ruge was asked for his views. Very frankly, he admitted that the defence of the eastern districts (the lower-lying lands on either side of the Oslo fjord and north towards Hamar and Elverum) would prove very difficult and probably impossible. But he hoped that with adequate assistance from abroad western Norway including the Trondheim area could be held or regained. He even considered that Trondheim and its neighbourhood might be regained by Norwegian troops alone.

This was more encouraging than anything that the Government had yet been told about the military possibilities, and Colonel Ruge was appointed Commanding General on the following day and subsequently Supreme Chief of the whole defence. No better appointment could have been made, for Ruge was generally accepted as both the most capable and the most determined of the Norwegian commanders.

Here is his description of the state of things when he became responsible for mobilisation of the army for the defence of a country all of whose key-points and strategic centres had already fallen and where all means of communication were in the hands of the enemy.

'When I took over the command, what was known at General Headquarters was only this: Around Oslo from Eidsvold in the east to Solihogda in the west dispersed Norwegian units tried to break the German onslaught. At Elverum detachments of the Osterdal regiment were gathering. It was not clear whether or not we had any forces in the Glommen Valley and around Kongsvinger. It was believed that there must be some Norwegian troops in Ostfold, but we did not know and it was impossible to establish any telephone connection. Nothing was known of conditions in Telemark, in the Kristiansand area, at Stavanger, and in the Trondheim area. But we knew that the Bergen Division tried to mobilise at Voss and the Möre Regiment at Romsdal.

'After a lapse of a week—in some cases not until a longer time had elapsed—we were informed in a circuitous way by officers we had sent out that isolated detachments of 1st Division were at Mysen, of 3rd Division at Setesdal and of 5th Division at Storen and around Steinkjer. But we were at a loss as to the numbers of these forces and the amount of arms and ammunition at their disposal.

'While General Headquarters did not know more, you will understand that individual local commanders knew even less. Every kind of rumour was circulated. The Oslo radio systematically worked to increase the confusion; instructions from our Government did not get across the country. Under such conditions it is not difficult to understand that things may have happened which ought not to have happened. But this I can safely say: that in every district where I knew what was going on there was a manifest determination to fight, and this determination waxed more stubborn as the attitude of the Government became known: that we should not give in but take up arms and carry on. This was done.

'In the north of Norway the situation was far more hopeful. The German force at Narvik was isolated. The 6th Division was already to a large extent mobilised under a determined commander. There was no ground for anxiety. But we had no opportunity to render assistance from southern Norway. General Fleischer had to look after himself.

'What we had to do was to keep a firm foothold somewhere in southern Norway, preferably in Tröndelag, where it seemed that the Allies could most easily land. Allied help on a large scale was promised at once. It was our task to keep going and protect Tröndelag from the south. With the weak and improvised forces we had at our disposal, practically without artillery, it was impossible for us to engage in any decisive battle before the Allies came to our aid. All we could do was to hold a position till the Germans became too strong for us, then fall back quickly to some distance and repeat the same game there. In this way we fought our way back through eastern Norway from one position to another—Eidsvold, Harestua, Solihogda—back to Dovre, gradually drawing eastward what we could of the forces in Voss and Romsdal. It was a constant race against time, on one side the Germans pressing even harder, on the other the anxiously waited Allies...

'Remember what kind of an army this was. From Oslo, for instance, came hundreds of men who could not mobilise because the Germans held Oslo. They gathered around some leader and became a "company"; they met other groups of the same kind and became "battalions" under the command of some officer. Casually assembled infantrymen, artillerymen, sailors, and aviators, with cars and chauffeurs, collected from God knows where, became fighting units. A commissary department was improvised, the women on the farms doing the cooking and looking after things. Sanitary service we had none, but it seemed to spring up out of the ground under the hands of energetic and resourceful physicians. I visited one hospital in Gudbrandsdal which was full of wounded and fairly well equipped for its work. The doctor in charge was a civilian who said that he had started at a cross roads near Eidsvold with one box of aspirins in his pocket. Willing hands had done the rest.

'The railway station at Dombaas was bombed every day, burned and laid waste, the railway and telegraph connections broken—but every night it was repaired sufficiently to use. The unknown men who, in great danger of their lives, did this work night after night, seeming never to sleep, will not be forgotten by us who saw them . . .

'The so-called Sörkedal Ski Company consisted of men who had escaped from Oslo and met in the ski hills in Nordmarka outside the city and turned up as a fighting unit thoroughly welded together. Our fliers with their old Moths and Fokkers darted in and out among the fast German planes ready to take any risk. The 4th Division—that of the west—fought a suicidal battle at Tonsaasen for four days, holding back a large German force and thereby easing the situation in Gudbrandsdal while British troops were landing in Romsdal. Hegra, an old abandoned fort, held out for a month, manned by casually assembled people who simply would not give up.'[1]

For the most part the hastily mobilised Norwegian forces had to carry on the struggle in isolated detachments with little opportunity for mutual support, and so they were progressively rounded up and destroyed, or effectively eliminated, in detail.

In the south-east General Erichsen, in command of the 1st Division, though isolated by his geographical position from the rest of Norway, kept up the fight for a week around the forts of Mysen, Askim, and Fossum, originally constructed as frontier defences against Sweden. He had managed to mobilise a number of troops and he prevented any arsenals or stores from falling into German hands. But he was forced back to the frontier and compelled to choose between crossing the border and being interned with his force of 3,000 men, laying down his arms and surrendering to the Germans, or fighting to the

[1] C. J. Hambro, *I saw it Happen in Norway.*

last man. General Erichsen chose the first of these alternatives. It should be remembered that it was at that time very generally supposed that circumstances would rapidly force Sweden into the war and therefore any troops interned in that country would soon be in a position to become operative once more.

The main body of the 3rd Division surrendered in Setesdal. They were presented with an ultimatum: either surrender immediately or Kristiansand and neighbouring towns would be bombed out of existence. Placed in this cruel dilemma and unable to get in touch with Headquarters, the commanding officer had little option but to surrender. Seven hundred of his men, however, withdrew to a strong position at Vinjesvingen in Telemark. In this mountain fastness they continued to defy the Germans for more than two months. When all their munitions were exhausted the troops were given orders to disperse, and were successful in making their way back to their homes in civilian clothes.

The troops mobilised in the Stavanger area, reinforced by a battalion from Oslo, tried to establish contact with those in Setesdal to the east. Finding that the latter had capitulated, they fought their way back to their own valley, capturing a number of prisoners and arms in the process. Against the intensified German air attacks, however, they were helpless. After Major Brandt, commander of the Oslo battalion, and three of his officers had been killed on April 23rd the remainder of the troops were either captured or made their way north to join up with those still fighting in Telemark.

At Bergen the mobilisation, despite the early occupation of the town by the Germans, was carried through fairly smoothly, and General Steffens, commander of the division based on the town, soon had about 5,000 men at his disposal, a very useful force if it could be held together and adequately munitioned. But General Ruge very properly ordered the greater part to be sent east to block the German advance north of Oslo. This was undoubtedly a sound and necessary decision. The Hamar–Elverum sector had become the main front for the Norwegian forces. It was the natural route for German exploitation towards Trondheim and central Norway. It was also the area where the first British troops could be, and in fact were, contacted. The troops despatched helped to block the Valdres and Hallingdal valleys to the west of the Oslo–Hamar axis, thereby forming a further extension of the ring which General Ruge was striving to throw around Oslo to contain the German forces until such time as the British, who were daily expected in large numbers and with great strength of armament, could arrive.

The remainder of General Steffens's force—those who had not been detached to strengthen the main front—fought their way back from Bergen along the railway to Voss. But they were subject during the retreat to heavy fire from the German warships in Hardanger fjord; and Voss, completely destroyed by bombing and machine-gunning from the air, was stormed by a German force 3,000 strong on April 27th. General Steffens, with the 1,000 men who remained to him, crossed the mountains northwards into Sognefjord. His force remained in being until the news of the Allied evacuation of southern Norway. General Steffens then demobilised his troops and himself flew to re-establish contact with the patriot forces in northern Norway. He was evacuated with the Allied troops in Narvik in June and travelled subsequently to Canada where he was appointed commander of the Norwegian liberation army training there.

At Trondheim and Narvik the Norwegian forces were able to establish contact with the Anglo-French troops soon after the landing of the latter and their subsequent activities will be described in the chapters dealing with those sectors.

Immediately west of Oslo an early engagement was fought at Solihogda, where a scratch force of volunteers ambushed and annihilated 200 Germans on April 12th.

To some extent it was the counterpart of the action at Midtskogen in front of Elverum on the night of April 9th–10th. Each little action was mainly the work of volunteers; in each the attacking German force was taken by surprise and suffered heavily, and each helped to provide a breathing space which prevented immediate German exploitation northwards and gave some opportunity for the mobilisation of further Norwegian forces which might, it was hoped, bar the way permanently and ring the Germans round in the Oslo area. The action at Solihogda prevented an exploitation into the western valleys and made possible the subsequent campaign which the Norwegian 4th Division fought back through the Valdres valley throughout the month of April. The fighting of the 4th Division during this period was of the utmost importance. The Valdres valley runs roughly parallel and to the south of the Gudbrandsdal where the British were operating. By their resistance, particularly by their heroic stand at Tonsaasen from April 23rd–26th the Norwegian division prevented a turning action against our right flank which might have eliminated the whole of General Paget's force.

Little actions of this sort were going on all over Norway during these first days. But almost everywhere it was much the same tale. The first mood of bewilderment was succeeded by one of courage and determination to improvise resistance. We knew, surely, something of the same mood in England after Dunkirk. But in England we were granted a respite and a breathing space. In Norway there was no such opportunity, for the barbarian was already within the gates. Here and there improvisation met with remarkable success. The Germans were feeling out with comparatively small—and at this stage, lightly-equipped—forces, and they never quite knew when they might bump into opposition. Consequently the first encounters, once the Norwegians had recovered from the preliminary shock of invasion, not uncommonly resulted in the local repulse of the invaders, since in the smaller local actions it was often the Norwegians who were on the alert and the Germans who were taken by surprise.

But such successes, though they helped to stiffen morale, were misleading and brought no permanent amelioration of the situation. They merely served to indicate to the Germans the points of crystallisation of the defence forces. And once crystallisation had begun their own task proved correspondingly easier. Thereafter the Norwegians had little to depend upon but their own courage and a pathetic belief in the imminent arrival in strength of their British and French Allies. Individual acts of great heroism were wrought. No deed of self-sacrifice in the whole course of the war had more of the classical quality of heroism than the action of the bus drivers of Oslo who were conscripted to drive German troops to the front in the Hönefoss sector north-west of the capital. The drivers had protested but their protests were ignored. Some of them therefore agreed amongst themselves that they would put an effective end to this practice.

The road to Hönefoss runs past a steep precipice on one side. There were four buses each carrying sixty fully armed Germans. As the first bus passed this danger spot the driver suddenly accelerated and without warning plunged his vehicle with its entire load into the ravine below. The second bus, following just behind, crashed down the slope following the first, so did the third. The German soldiers in the fourth just managed to stop their vehicle in time. But 180 of them had gone to their death, as had the three Norwegian drivers.

That little incident at Hönefoss was symbolic of so much of the resistance in Europe before a technique of 'smouldering opposition' and sabotage had been effectively developed. It could not postpone or seriously affect the conquest of the country, but it did something conceivably more important—it provided an imaginative basis for resistance of the spirit. The Germans might seize the towns, their armoured columns might sweep up the mountain valleys, their trained ski-troopers might comb the hillsides and compel the physical surrender of the last regular forces in the field. But the story of the three men of Hönefoss would live in Norwegian hearts, would inspire the patient courage of the resistance until the day of reckoning should arrive.

# CHAPTER II

# Aandalsnes

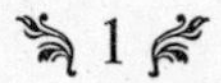

## *The Landing*

THE operation from Aandalsnes, conceived as the southern prong of the assault against Trondheim, was almost from the start diverted from its original purpose and developed first into an attempt to make contact with the Norwegian holding force north of Oslo in the Lake Mjosa-Hamar-Elverum area, then into a stubborn and on the whole well-conducted rearguard operation back up the Gudbrandsdal valley, punctuated by frequent sharp engagements with the oncoming Germans.

At the beginning of April the slowly maturing plans of the Western Allies had seemed to be ripening in the spring sunshine towards a modest degree of relative semi-finality. The decision to lay minefields in Norwegian territorial waters had at last been taken, and in the event of a German invasion resulting from this step Mackesy's force was in readiness to sail for Narvik, while a further force, under Major-General Carton de Wiart, V.C., was designated for Stavanger, Trondheim, and Bergen.

But meanwhile Hitler 'no question made of ayes and noes', and on the early morning of April 9th had struck in greater strength, as we have seen, with a far more carefully knit plan and with more clearly envisaged objectives.

The swift success of the opening day necessitated a speedy riposte unless all Norway were to be abandoned to the invader. The first reaction was naturally in the direction of Narvik, where a force of German destroyers still lay in the fjord. But Narvik, though its recapture would be of great economic value, was far away to the north.

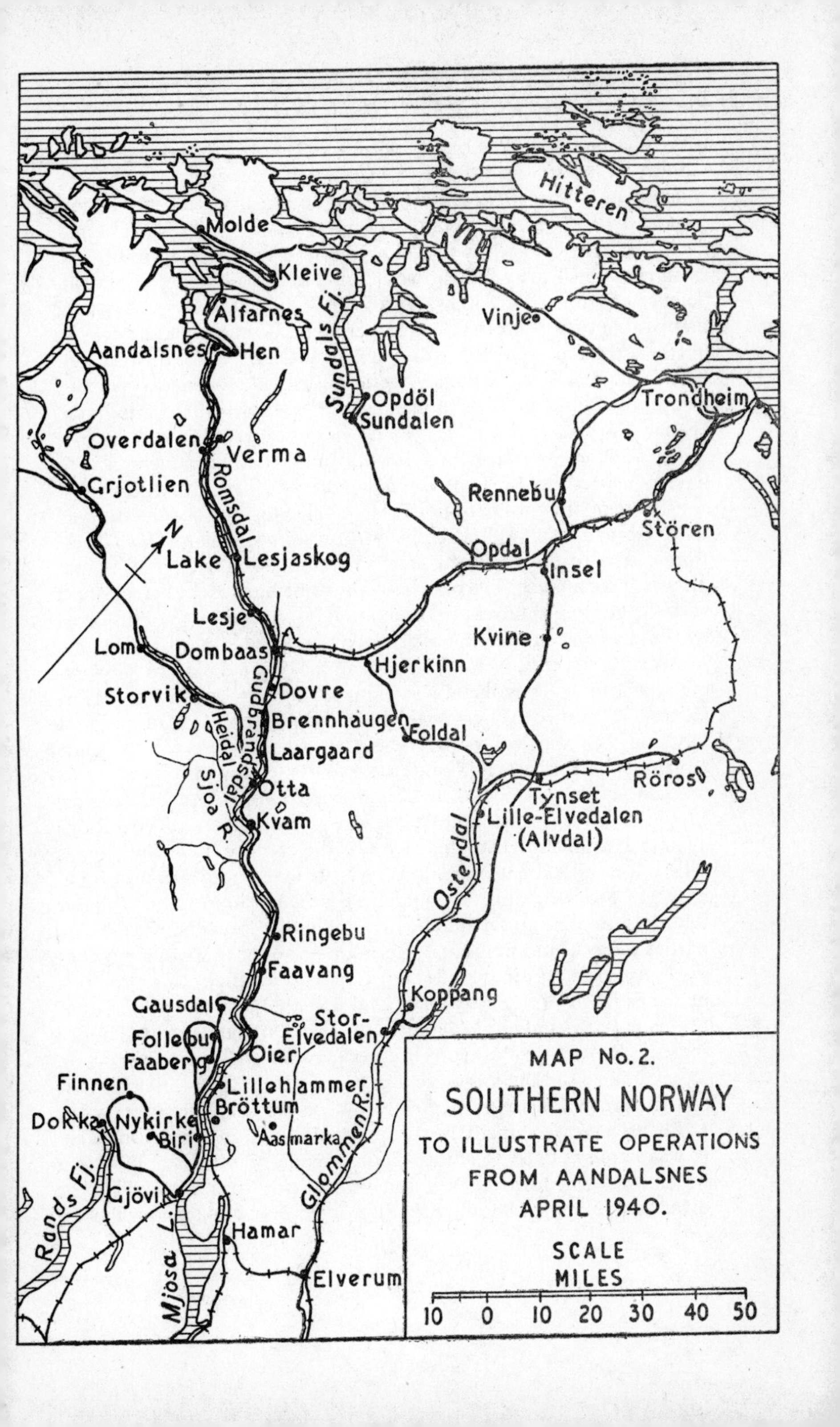

Hitteren
Molde
Kleive
Alfarnes
Sundals Fj.
Vinje
Aandalsnes
Hen
Opdöl
Sundalen
Trondheim
Overdalen
Verma
Romsdal
Grjotlien
Rennebu
Stören
N
Lake
Lesjaskog
Opdal
Insel
Lesje
Lom
Dombaas
Kvine
Hjerkinn
Gudbrandsdal
Dovre
Storvik
Heidal
Brennhaugen
Foldal
Laargaard
Sjoa R.
Otta
Röros
Tynset
Kvam
Lille-Elvedalen
(Alvdal)
Osterdal
Ringebu
Faavang
Koppang
Gausdal
Stor-
Elvedalen
Follebu
Oier
Faaberg
Lillehammer
Finnen
Bröttum
Dokka
Nykirke
Biri
Aasmarka
Glommen R.
Rands Fj.
Gjövik
Mjosa L.
Hamar
Elverum
MAP No. 2.
SOUTHERN NORWAY
TO ILLUSTRATE OPERATIONS
FROM AANDALSNES
APRIL 1940.
SCALE
MILES
10 0 10 20 30 40 50

If the Germans could be barred in central Norway, Narvik could be reduced at leisure. And the key to central Norway was Trondheim, situated at the narrowest part of the country, having direct rail contact with Sweden (a matter of importance if Sweden should decide to enter the war or should herself be attacked). Moreover, the existence of a nearby airfield would enable us to operate fighters in defence of our ground forces. With Trondheim in our hands it should be possible to seal off the further German advance and preserve the northern half of Norway from the invader. Both the British and French Cabinets agreed that operations should be undertaken to recapture Trondheim simultaneously with those already initiated against Narvik.

The advanced striking force for Stavanger and Trondheim was to have consisted of the 148th Brigade (Brigadier H. de R. Morgan), consisting of only two battalions: 1/5th Leicestershire (Lieut.-Colonel G. J. German) and 1/8th Sherwood Foresters (Lieut.-Colonel T. A. Ford). It is to be presumed that a battalion would have been employed at each place. The plan had now to be hurriedly altered, since, with the Germans already in occupation of our objectives, our forces were not strong enough to undertake an opposed landing which had, in any case, never been contemplated in the original plan. A converging attack upon Trondheim was planned, and on April 12th, Major-General Carton de Wiart with the Headquarters staff of the 61st Division was warned for overseas. His force was given the code name of 'Mauriceforce', and the same pleasing historical sense was to re-christen General Mackesy's Narvik force 'Rupertforce'.

On April 13th, Carton de Wiart was given the plan of operations against Trondheim. The objective was the capture of Trondheim as a base for subsequent operations in Norway and also, in all probability, in Sweden, since at this date it seemed more than probable that the latter country would be involved in the spreading war. Naval parties were to land that same afternoon or on the following morning at Namsos (about ninety miles north of Trondheim as the crow flies, but considerably further by road), and seize the town and port and the bridge of Bangsund immediately to the east. On that day it was hoped that the R.A.F. would neutralise German air striking power by an attack upon Trondheim's airfield at Vaernes. On April 18th a brigade of the French Chasseurs Alpins would be landed; alternatively the 147th Brigade with ancillary troops would land on April 20th–21st. It was contemplated that the 126th Brigade of the 42nd Division, which was scheduled to sail for France on April 17th might be diverted to Norway. Should Scandinavia develop into a major theatre of war, then further units might progressively be fed in from France, but the time involved between the decision and the arrival of the troops in Norway was estimated at about three weeks.

Brigadier Morgan's two battalions with the personnel of the 168th Light Anti-Aircraft Battery had embarked at Rosyth on H.M.S. *Arethusa*, H.M.S. *Galatea*, and S.S. *Orion*, on April 14th, but Morgan's instructions were more than once changed and it was not until 7 a.m. on the morning of April 17th that they finally sailed. The decision had been taken that the large liner *Orion* could not be risked in the narrow waters of the Norwegian fjords and would in any case probably be unable to get alongside the Norwegian jetties. Accordingly, some hasty re-loading had to be undertaken and the brigade eventually sailed in H.M. ships *Arethusa*, *Galatea*, *Carlisle*, *Curaçoa*, *Acheron*, and *Arrow*. While the convoy was actually at sea, Morgan received orders changing his destination to Aandalsnes. Carton de Wiart would take charge at Namsos with the 146th Brigade (Brigadier C. G. Phillips) under his immediate command. This brigade had been destined for Narvik and had actually set sail when, upon the receipt of the news of the British naval victory in the Second Battle of Narvik on April 13th, its destination had been changed. It was now assumed that all serious opposition at the northern port could be quickly eliminated and with fewer troops than had been anticipated. While this was to some extent true, it implied the speedy exploitation of the advantage that had been gained by the Navy. The longer we delayed and waited for favourable conditions of weather and a comfortable superiority of force the more likely it was that the opportunity would slip away.

While Phillips's brigade would now land at Namsos and operate against Trondheim from the north, Morgan, having landed at Aandalsnes would secure the important railway junction of Dombaas, thereby blocking the route from Oslo to Trondheim, and thereafter demonstrate northwards in the direction of Trondheim. The third force, under Lieut.-General F. E. Hotblack, consisting of the 147th Brigade, was to enter Trondheim fjord, escorted by the Navy, and strike straight at Trondheim itself. The date for this operation was fixed at April 22nd. The Germans at this time were estimated to have not more than 1,800 men in the Trondheim area, some of whom were dispersed along the railway to the Swedish frontier, masking the Norwegian-held fort of Hegra, and in outposts northwards along the fjords towards Levanger. They did not therefore appear to present an excessively formidable opposition. They were, however, receiving constant reinforcements by air, and by April 20th a War Office estimate had increased their number to something between 3,000 and 5,000.

And now a further and unexpected development occurred. General Hotblack, after having been briefed on the forthcoming operation at the War Office on April 17th, met with a most unfortunate mishap. He was found early on the following morning unconscious and suffering from severe concussion at the foot of the Duke of York's steps on the northern fringe of St. James's Park. General Hotblack knew nothing of the circumstances of his accident, which was found to be the result of a seizure and not, as might have been expected, of foul play.

A new commander for the force had rapidly to be found, and the choice fell upon Brigadier Berney-Ficklin. He was briefed that day for the Trondheim operation and took off on the following morning in a plane bound for the Orkneys. At 11 a.m. his aircraft crashed at Haston near Kirkwall, and the General, together with almost all those travelling in the machine, was incapacitated for further service for some time.

Two commanders thus having become casualties in two days, Major-General B. C. T. Paget, then commanding the 18th Division in East Anglia, was selected. He was contacted by telephone at 5 p.m. on April 18th and instructed to catch a train for Scotland at 8 p.m. the same evening. He was told that he would find a Staff Officer on the train who would give him further instructions. The only other information vouchsafed was that he should take warm clothing with him.

Only an hour later the instruction was cancelled, and General Paget was told to report instead to the War Office on the following day. Arriving there (afternoon of April 20th) he learned that he was to have proceeded to Scapa to take charge, in succession to Berney-Ficklin, of the force which had been planned to sail on April 22nd for the assault on Trondheim. But this plan had now been cancelled, and Paget would now proceed to Norway to take command of what was to be known as 'Sickleforce' with the task of co-operating with the Norwegian army in preventing an advance northward of the German troops based on Oslo, while protecting his left flank and rear from the German troops in and around Trondheim and possibly also from parachutists landed to attack his line of communication.

'Sickleforce' was to have consisted of a complete division, well found in A.A. and field artillery, transport, signals, etc., but in fact all that materialised was an incomplete divisional headquarters, two infantry brigades, one field company of engineers, and a few Bofors

A.A. guns. Paget received no artillery, tanks, aircraft, or medical organisation, and no proper signals.

The advance party of this force had already been committed by the time General Paget received his appointment. Morgan's revised instructions had placed his force directly under the War Office until such time as it came under the general commander of the Trondheim area (General Carton de Wiart). His landing would be preceded by that of a naval party about 600 strong on the night of April 17th–18th and it was not intended that his force should disembark in face of opposition. Having landed, it would immediately initiate offensive operations towards Dombaas, as part of the general operation against Trondheim. It would be without transport during the early stages and would have to depend upon what could be impressed locally.

The first party ashore at Aandalsnes was composed of 600 Royal Marines (Lieut.-Colonel Simpson) who were landed on April 17th and promptly disposed in platoon groups along the railway inland for a distance of about eighty miles. They had with them eight two-pounder naval guns and two 3.7-inch howitzers with crews taken from H.M. ships *Hood* and *Nelson*. They were the first to make contact with the Germans in this sector for they encountered a body of forty-five paratroops concealed in wooden shacks close to the railway line, having presumably been landed with a view to demolition operations. They formed part of a force of about 200 dropped around Dombaas and northwards. All, or nearly all, were rounded up in the course of the next few days. Many, both here and in the Narvik area, became casualties through being dropped from an insufficient height, and there were cases where the parachutes opened either partially or not at all. Some of the paratroops in the Dombaas area were so shaken and injured that they speedily surrendered. It is possible that this little action represents the furthest penetration inland ever made by a naval party.

On the night of April 18th–19th most of the two battalions of the 148th Brigade[1] and their anti-aircraft battery disembarked at Aandalsnes and at the adjacent port of Molde, which lies on the northern side of the fjord and much nearer the open sea. Their disembarkation which began at 10 p.m. had to be completed by 3 a.m., by which hour it was almost completely light at that time of year, and in view of the prospect of enemy air action it was important that the quays and neighbourhood of the port should be cleared as rapidly as possible.

[1] Two companies of the Leicestershire and some A.A. personnel and base details had sailed later and did not arrive until the evening of April 21st.

Having disembarked, the British forces dispersed rapidly throughout the town and the neighbouring woods as day brightened.

Aandalsnes itself was a mere village of some 1,500 inhabitants, and the port was of the most rudimentary nature. It consisted of a concrete jetty 150 yards long, only one side of which could be used for berthing ships, and a simple wooden quay. Under peacetime conditions it had a capacity of perhaps 700 tons daily, assuming the employment of ships' derricks for unloading and adequate supply of skilled labour. Under the conditions of total German air superiority which prevailed throughout the campaign unloading could not be carried out in safety for more than four or five out of the twenty-four hours, and the skilled labour soon melted away after the German bombing attacks began in earnest. It would be a good day, therefore, on which 100 tons were unloaded.

The port of Molde possessed slightly larger facilities for docking and unloading, but as it had no communication with Aandalsnes save by steamer, it did not prove a very effective supplementary base.

In the light of these facts it soon became apparent that no considerable force could be maintained through Aandalsnes, given the overwhelming German air superiority which was soon to manifest itself, and therefore the piling in of fresh troops to turn the scale was not a practical proposition—even if we had possessed the available troops. Under these circumstances, for Paget's forces to extend southwards and link up with General Ruge's Norwegian troops in the area of Lake Mjosa, at the same time advancing northward towards Trondheim was hardly a feasible operation. The move towards Trondheim, however, remained, in theory, a part of the rôle of 'Sickleforce' for about thirty-six hours after the landing of Morgan's brigade.

The immediate task, however, was to push inland as rapidly as possible in order to reach the road and rail junction of Dombaas. The route to be followed was the long narrow valley known as the Romsdal and, further inland, as the Gudbrandsdal. Down this valley flows the river Rauma, its course closely followed by a road and railway. The valley itself is seldom more than a thousand yards wide, often as little as five hundred, and the pine-covered hills which rise on either side, at first gently but then more steeply, were still covered with deep snow and only accessible to ski-troops.

The ski-troops whom the British and French had gathered for the contemplated campaign in Finland had been disbanded.

What was the military situation on this sector at the moment of disembarkation of the British force?

The Germans had now a corps organisation based on Oslo, but the advanced guard thrusting north was not more than a division strong, with support from armoured fighting vehicles. By April 17th two regiments[1] were moving towards the Gudbrandsdal and Osterdal. Armoured cars patrolling up the roads on either side of Lake Mjosa had reached Gjövik and Hamar on the west and east sides of the lake respectively, while other forces were in the neighbourhood of Elverum. Considering that the original German raid from Oslo on the night following the invasion had penetrated practically to Hamar and Elverum, the Germans had certainly shown no undue enterprise in this sector, and the temporary stabilisation of the front in this neighbourhood reflects great credit upon General Ruge and the troops who formed his hastily improvised defence ring.

In addition to these German forces about sixty parachutists were at large in the neighbourhood of Dombaas, a most important junction on the railway from Aandalsnes, and an unknown number near Kvikne, fifty miles south of Trondheim. These forces, small as they were, might be used to cut communications in the Gudbrandsdal and Osterdal valleys and hamper the British advance southward. The Gudbrandsdal was the natural line of advance from Aandalsnes to Oslo, and at this early stage it was optimistically hoped that subsidiary forces might penetrate by the two cross-routes eastwards into the Osterdal. Had we been powerful enough to do so in strength this would not only have blocked all possibility of the German Oslo force linking up with that at Trondheim but also would have provided us with a second line of advance upon the capital.

The Norwegian forces which could be effectively contacted by 'Sickleforce' were rather widely dispersed, partly through the accidents of a necessarily improvised mobilisation, partly because of the necessity of blocking as many routes as possible to the German advance. In addition to the heroic defenders of Hegra there was a force of about 500 men holding the vital point of Stören south of Trondheim. So long as Stören could be denied to the Germans the Trondheim force remained isolated and there was still some prospect that the Allied offensive from the south against the port might be developed.

Further south, about 1,600 men, forming part of the 2nd Norwegian Division were strung out along the Aandalsnes–Dombaas railway and were engaging the German paratroops dropped at the latter place. There was an indefinite number of troops forming up for the defence of the Osterdal and Glommen valleys to the east, where mobilisation

[1] A German regiment corresponds in size to a British brigade.

was still in progress, and ski-troops were operating in the mountains west of Lake Mjosa and on the flanks of the hard-pressed Norwegian infantry in the valley, where Ruge's strongest force, the 2nd Division of General Hvinden-Haug was fighting on either side of Lake Mjosa and towards Hamar and Elverum. And there was a scratch force, at one time a full 1,400 strong, officered in part by returned volunteers from the Finnish war, which after fighting two successful defensive actions against the invaders at Solihogda and Roa (respectively fifteen and thirty miles north-west and north of Oslo) had gradually retired to a strong position at Hornskleida on the Randsfjord protecting the southern and western flank of the main body.

Brigadier Morgan's first concern was to secure the railway junction at Dombaas in accordance with his instructions. Fortunately Colonel Simpson and his Marines had made good use of their day ashore and they had a train in readiness to cover the eighty-mile journey to Dombaas. Morgan decided to seize the opportunity and to push forward immediately with a company of Sherwood Foresters, under the command of Major J. K. L. Roberts. The train pulled out of Aandalsnes about 1 a.m. and reached Dombaas without mishap at first light on April 19th.

The German paratroopers, who were still theoretically in a position to interrupt road and rail communication with Lillehammer and the south, were now reduced very much to the defensive. Encircled by Norwegian troops, they had fortified themselves in a farm about five miles south of Dombaas. A gun crew from H.M.S. *Hood*, who had landed with the Marine detachment on the previous day, was engaging the position with a 3.7-inch howitzer, but at the request of the Norwegians was refraining from directly bombarding the farmhouse since it was believed that the parachutists held a number of hostages inside. However, at about ten o'clock that morning the Germans surrendered. The road and railway were now clear and the King of Norway and his Cabinet, who had been kept continually on the move by air bombing in the eastern part of the country, were able to pass through that day to the extremely relative security of Aandalsnes.

The news of the landing of the British force at Aandalsnes seemed to General Ruge to mark the end of his worst difficulties. His men had been gallantly holding the Germans north of Oslo and had prevented them from making any significant progress in this sector for more than a week. But they were inevitably lacking in training and short of equipment and, by this time, very tired. Ruge accordingly appealed, through Lieut.-Colonel E. J. King-Salter, the British military attaché, now at his headquarters, for Morgan's brigade to be moved south as soon as possible to support the Norwegian troops south of Lillehammer.

Following a telephone call to this effect, King-Salter arrived at Dombaas by car in the late afternoon. He found that Morgan had been given instructions not to proceed southward beyond Dombaas without specific authorisation from the War Office. This was because the plan for the converging attack upon Trondheim had not yet been abandoned. Dombaas was the point where the road and railway north from Oslo fork into two branches, one continuing north-west to Aandalsnes, the other north to Stören and Trondheim. It was therefore a natural point of concentration and a pivot of manœuvre if the plan of assault upon Trondheim were to be carried out.

King-Salter, however, was in a position to produce three powerful arguments in favour of the move southward.

The first was that no firm date had yet been fixed for the Trondheim operation[1] and therefore that the troops earmarked for it would merely be marking time around Dombaas for the present and missing the opportunity for a valuable exploitation inland.

Secondly, if the Norwegian troops were defeated in detail nothing could stop the Germans based on Oslo from pushing straight through to Trondheim from the south. The southward movement of the British brigade therefore became an indispensable preliminary to any attack upon Trondheim from whatever direction.

Thirdly, King-Salter claimed that the War Office instructions gave General Ruge the right to call upon the services of the 148th Brigade.

The British military attaché argued cogently and well, stressing the exhaustion of the Norwegian troops and the importance of our rallying to General Ruge, who was the driving force behind the resistance. In view of the urgency of the situation Brigadier Morgan decided to comply with the Norwegian commander's request for assistance, at the same time signalling the War Office for further instructions.

The man on the spot had thus been placed in the position of taking a decision of far more than local significance. It was clear that if Morgan's brigade were to be diverted south to help the Norwegians and not north to form the right-hand pincer for the assault upon Trondheim, the whole project necessarily took on a different and much less promising shape.

Yet Morgan's decision was endorsed by the War Office. For on the previous day a decision of the utmost importance to the course of the entire campaign in Norway had been taken by the War Cabinet in

[1] In fact April 22nd had been fixed as a provisional date.

London. The sea-borne assault upon Trondheim was called off, and the sailing of the 147th Brigade cancelled.

No more fateful decision was made on the Allied side in the course of this brief and ill-starred Norwegian campaign, and it is worth while looking into the cause for this abrupt *volte-face*.

It had only been with reluctance that the Naval Staff had concurred in the possibility of the Home Fleet forcing the passage of Trondheim fjord so as to permit the entry of the transports and the landing of the troops. The danger lay less in the shore batteries than in the threat of air attack in the narrow waters of the approach to Trondheim. Indeed, as late as April 15th it appeared that the threat to our naval forces from the air arm would prevent the project being put into operation. However, after further consideration, Admiral Forbes, the Commander-in-Chief, considered that the project might prove practicable, given a heavy bombardment of Stavanger aerodrome and of the airfield at Vaernes, near Trondheim, in order to compel the Luftwaffe to keep its head down. The R.A.F. and the cruiser *Suffolk* would be entrusted with the task of bombarding Stavanger, while the bombers of the Fleet Air Arm dealt with Vaernes. The presence of the capital ships *Warspite*, *Renown*, and *Valiant*, the aircraft-carrier *Glorious*, four A.A. cruisers, and some twenty destroyers, was judged to be necessary to cover the assault.

So far, so good. Mr. Churchill, though regarding Narvik as the major and more urgent objective, had been convinced of the importance of early action in force against Trondheim and used his authority to push forward the plan. It was formally accepted by the War Cabinet on April 17th.

But meanwhile second thoughts had occurred both at the Admiralty and at the War Office. Reviewing the situation the Chiefs of Staff became convinced that 'Operation Hammer' (the sea-borne assault on Trondheim with flanking operations from north and south) involved undue risks. The heads of their arguments may be summarised as follows:

1. The plan involved the concentration of almost all the Home Fleet in an area where it was liable to heavy attack from the air.

2. The lack of time for detailed preparation of the operation.

3. The danger to the land forces involved in undertaking an opposed landing in the face of enemy air superiority.

4. The success achieved by the two unopposed landings at Namsos and Aandalsnes respectively, which might enable a successful movement to be made against Trondheim by land simultaneously from the

north and the south. (General Carton de Wiart's entire brigade was by this time ashore at Namsos, and Aandalsnes had been secured by Colonel Simpson's force of Royal Marines. Neither force had met with any ground opposition.)

5. The prevalence of press speculation regarding the impending attack upon Trondheim.

There seems little doubt that Anglo-French strategic decisions at this time were influenced by the attitude of Italy. The dangerous consequences of adventuring so large a portion of our fleet in these northern waters were apparent, for soon these very units might be desperately needed for action in the Mediterranean.

The Cabinet therefore decided to rely exclusively upon the land forces for the capture of Trondheim. But the troops moving southward from Namsos would now necessarily be exposed to attack and the possibility of landings on their flank and rear from German naval units in Trondheim fjord which lay on the flank of their advance; while, at the same time, any prospect that the southern prong from Aandalsnes might be diverted northwards to carry out the attack via Dombaas and Stören was frustrated by the imminent collapse of Norwegian resistance around Lillehammer and the necessity for Morgan's brigade to go south to block the Gudbrandsdal valley against a rapid German advance.

So, once the decision to abandon the sea-borne operation had been taken, the chance of capturing Trondheim really disappeared and the British forces in central Norway largely lost their *raison d'être*. For without Trondheim they would possess no port adequate for the unloading of supplies and no airfield capable of ensuring them land-based fighter protection. And without either port facilities or air protection our troops could not be maintained in the field.

The British War Cabinet, faced with a choice of evils on that fateful afternoon of April 18th, took what appeared to be the lesser. But, having made their choice, there might well have been a corresponding and far-reaching change in the over-all plan. There was no such change. In fact, while the southern arm of the attack was diverted to help the Norwegians, and the central (sea-borne) assault was called off, General Carton de Wiart, who was in charge of the northern prong, was given no instructions to modify his strategy and was allowed to plunge his brigade south from Namsos in an endeavour to achieve an objective which had been rendered well-nigh unobtainable.

However, the consequences of this decision were not immediately apparent. What was known was that the road and railway were now clear from Aandalsnes to Lillehammer after the elimination of the parachutists at Dombaas. It seemed reasonable to suppose that Paget and the Norwegians might hold the German main force around Lillehammer while Carton de Wiart advanced upon and took Trondheim from the north.

Half the battalion of Foresters accordingly moved south by rail that same afternoon. The journey was interrupted by enemy aircraft, but by midnight the troops had completed their move. Detraining at Faaberg, north of Lillehammer, they continued by road down the west side of Lake Mjosa and established themselves at Biri eleven miles south of Lillehammer. Here they contacted Colonel Dahl, the local Norwegian commander, who was in charge of a body of ski-troops. The remainder of the battalion followed through by train and established themselves at Lillehammer in the early hours of April 20th. Here brigade headquarters was set up, and the rest of the brigade, consisting of about half a battalion of the 1/5th Leicestershire, followed on through Dombaas to Lillehammer and moved in trucks to Aasmarka, on the left flank, about eight miles south-east of Lillehammer.

During the night the Chief of the Imperial General Staff signalled his congratulations to the force for having pushed ahead so far and so fast, and in fact the advance looked very good indeed—on the map. Our forward troops on Lake Mjosa had raced ahead well over 150 miles from their base at Aandalsnes, but the advance had been made without opposition and the difficulties of the situation were only now about to be revealed. The troops were dependent upon a single line of communications down the narrow valley of Gudbrandsdal. The road and railway which followed this route were vulnerable to parachutists and *saboteurs*, and columns of troops or stores moving along it were at the mercy of air attack. There were no alternative routes and no satisfactory means of dispersal for vehicles among the mountains on either side. The troops had landed without transport and were dependent upon what they could obtain locally. The Norwegians provided some Chevrolet and Ford one-ton trucks, but these were in poor condition; moreover, the locally recruited drivers could not be trusted. They had a habit of disappearing, often with their vehicles, as the campaign progressed, and during the last few days trucks began to disappear in large numbers, for the drivers seemed always to keep spare ignition keys for their own purposes.

Our service 3-ton trucks, when they arrived, proved quite unsuited to the roads. They were too wide to permit convoys to pass one another easily, they proved difficult to turn in the narrow roads and they were all too easily bogged. When the banked snow began to melt unsuspected chasms appeared along the edges of the roads into which many an incautious driver plunged. No R.E. workshops ever arrived forward, and there were no local workshops to improvise repairs. Owing to the chronic vehicle shortage and the lack of despatch-riders and of signals equipment far too many messages had to be taken on foot, since the civil telephone line could not be used, for security reasons. As a result, orders, in forward areas, again and again arrived hopelessly late—or did not arrive at all. This led, on more than one occasion in the course of the retreat back to the coast, to units failing to receive instructions to withdraw and finding themselves cut off and having to get back as best they could, sometimes suffering considerable losses in the process.

And so Morgan's small force, thrust so far forward, was hopelessly hamstrung by administrative deficiencies, and was soon to find itself further jeopardised by the complete control of the air which the enemy exercised. The effects of this were to be repeatedly and bitterly driven home, but for the moment the situation appeared superficially satisfactory—viewed from the angle of Whitehall.

Such was not the opinion of General Ruge. At noon on April 20th he called a conference at his headquarters at Oier (a few miles north of Lillehammer) which was attended by Colonel Nilson, his chief Operations Officer, Colonel Berg, his Quartermaster-General, Brigadier Morgan, Lieut.-Colonel King-Salter, Major Bertrand-Vigne, the French military attaché, and two officers attached to Brigadier Morgan.

The Norwegian Commander-in-Chief did not mince his words, for he felt that we had not been sufficiently frank with him. He had not even been told of our landings nor of our proposed plans. He desired a unified control of all the forces south of Trondheim, since there would be chaos if two independent military authorities existed in the area. He realised that Norway needed the co-operation of the Allied forces to maintain her independence, but he himself had a responsibility for the defence of the whole country and if the Allies intended to make a private war for themselves on Norwegian territory and give direct orders to Norwegian authorities without his consent he would resign. He had no intention, he said, of being 'made to look a fool' by the Allies, and he reminded them that he alone had been responsible for persuading the Government to continue the war and that if he now resigned the army and the nation would give up the struggle.

The British commander found himself in an embarrassing position and was compelled to explain that he was no less in the dark himself about the over-all strategy on the Allied side. This is not surprising, for it is difficult, in following the repeated changes of the Allied plan, not to be left with the impression that there was scarcely anyone who visualised the whole picture or possessed a clear conception of practicable objectives.

The Norwegian commander readily accepted the explanation given him by Brigadier Morgan. He stressed the importance of stabilising the front in the south; after that it would be time to think of Trondheim. He would like, he said, Norwegian troops to co-operate in the attack and was prepared immediately, so it appears, to move one battalion north from Dombaas by way of demonstration. He described himself as 'not in the least apprehensive about the position at Trondheim'—which is the measure of his ignorance both of our strategic planning and of our tactical weakness. He added that he was short of light tanks, anti-tank rifles, and ammunition for his troops. To this request he had as yet received no reply. Nevertheless, he would try to hold the Lillehammer front, despite the risks involved, until Trondheim fell. He ended by expressing a desire to meet General Carton de Wiart, now at Namsos, in order to achieve a further co-ordination of plans.

This last request, like most of the others, proved to be an impracticable one: for the next day both the commanders were too deeply involved with operations in the sectors for which they were respectively responsible to have any opportunity for Staff talks.

That same afternoon, while Ruge was putting his plans and his requirements to the local British commander on the assumption that the sea-borne operation against Trondheim was imminent, General Paget was receiving his instructions at the War Office regarding the functions of the force which he was to command. In view of the latest change of plan, its object was now to co-operate with the Norwegian Army in preventing the advance northward of the German forces based on Oslo, while protecting his left flank and rear.

This meant that of the intended three prongs of the Trondheim operation the southern was diverted elsewhere by the local situation, the centre would not now operate; only the northern one was to be left to continue to do the best it could without land or sea co-operation from the other two.

General Paget's force was, in theory, to consist of a complete and adequately equipped division. In fact, it consisted only of two infantry brigades, one of which (148th Brigade) comprised only two battalions of Territorials, one field company of Royal Engineers, and a few Bofors. The force had no artillery, aircraft, tanks, or medical organisation. S.S. *Cedarbank*, bringing motor transport, guns, spare parts, predictors, ammunition and rations, was sunk while on its way to Norway on the following day. In following the subsequent operations what stands out as most remarkable is not that the force failed to achieve more but that it achieved as much as it did.

Morgan's brigade would now be supported by the 15th Brigade (Brigadier H. E. F. Smyth) composed of the 1st K.O.Y.L.I. (Major E. E. E. Cass), 1st York and Lancaster (Lieut.-Colonel A. L. Kent-Lemon), and 1st Green Howards (Lieut.-Colonel A. E. Robinson). It was the intention at this stage that the 15th Brigade should move down the valley of the Osterdal upon Elverum, while the 148th Brigade continued its advance from Gudbrandsdal down Lake Mjosa upon Hamar. Each brigade would thus be moving down ultimately converging valleys towards the Norwegian capital.

But what Whitehall proposed was only of academic interest, for already the German forces north of Oslo were about to launch their offensive, and every man of Smyth's brigade would soon be needed in the Gudbrandsdal in support of Morgan's sorely pressed force.

By the evening of April 20th the British order of battle was as follows:

At Biri (midway between Lillehammer and Gjövik) on the west side of Lake Mjosa: two and a half companies of the 1/8th Foresters (under command of Colonel Dahl).

At Bröttum (seven and a half miles south of Lillehammer) on the east side of Lake Mjosa: the other two and a half companies of 1/8th Foresters (under command of General Hvinden-Haug).

At Aasmarka (in the hills three or four miles to the east) half the 1/5th Leicestershire, covering a flank road through the hills. These were under the command of Colonel Jensen of the Norwegian Dragoons.

It will be seen that, as a result of General Ruge's insistence, all the British troops in this forward area were under the immediate command of Norwegian officers.

## 2

### *First Contact*

Sunday, April 21st saw the first clash of British and German troops in the Aandalsnes sector. That same day was notable for the first and only important encounter in the Namsos sector—the action at Vist.

It is not too much to say that up to the morning of April 21st our operations were still going forward towards a presumed, though not the original, goal, but that by the evening the tide had swung against us in both areas and the retreat that was to take our forces back to the ports had begun.

The action at Lake Mjosa started untidily at a time when British troops were in process of taking over from Norwegians who were to be progressively relieved as more of our units arrived in forward positions. Enemy air attacks had been made on the British forces on both sides of the lake in the course of the morning, but the infantry attack did not develop until two o'clock in the afternoon, when the Germans broke through Colonel Jensen's Norwegian Dragoons at Aasmarka on the eastern flank and forced them back on the Leicestershire, who had not yet completed the relief. It was decided that Lillehammer had become untenable and that a new position should be taken up at Faaberg five miles north of the town and at the head of the lake. A confused action continued throughout the afternoon, but the weather had clouded over and the Germans were unable to employ their airpower in low-flying attacks upon the troops. The withdrawal of the Leicestershire did not start until midnight, and they met with mishap on the way. The road was crowded with Norwegian troops and civilians pouring back in disorder, the transport which was to have picked our troops up on the main road failed to materialise and the men had to continue back on foot. Soon after daybreak German armoured cars began to catch up with the rearguard and a number of our men were rounded up in the outskirts of Lillehammer. What remained of the battalion was picked up in motor transport which had been locally requisitioned and sent back to Faaberg. Some delay was caused to the pursuit by our demolitions in Lillehammer itself; but throughout the retreat that followed it seems that demolitions were not always carried out very effectively. This was due both to the lack of mines and dynamite in sufficient quantities and to the inexperience of our troops in this type of warfare.

By 4.30 in the morning of Monday, April 22nd a composite force of about 650 men of Leicestershire and Foresters had arrived back at Faaberg. The last stage of the retreat had been made under conditions of considerable confusion, with Brigadier Morgan finally directing the troops in person. There was no particular likelihood that the new position would be any easier to hold than the one which had been abandoned. No previous reconnaissance of the ground had been made, and the troops had left their entrenching tools and all their wireless equipment behind when they began the withdrawal from

Aasmarka and Bröttum. Their ability to hold the Germans at Faaberg depended upon the degree of assistance they could expect from fresh infantry detachments with supporting arms and, above all, from aircraft.

Little could now be expected from the Norwegian troops. General Ruge, when visited at his headquarters (which had withdrawn twenty miles from Oier to Ringebu) in the course of the morning, emphasised that his men, now entering on their thirteenth day of continuous fighting in some cases, were worn out. The strong position at Hornskleiva on the Randsfjord in the parallel valley to the south had been forced by the Germans two days earlier, and the 400 men who were all that remained of the Norwegian force in this district were withdrawing north in confusion. At this point however there had arrived an unexpected reinforcement of about 3,000 well-equipped men of General Steffens's division, who had come across the mountains from Voss and who now proceeded to take up position at Tonsaasen protecting the Valdres valley. The courageous four-day battle (April 23rd–26th) which they fought at this position was to a great extent responsible for the fact that the British force fighting its way back through the Gudbrandsdal during this week was free from all danger of a wide outflanking movement from the south.

However, it was clear to Norwegians and British alike that the campaign in southern Norway would now be increasingly a British commitment. Two small bodies of troops were likely to be almost immediately available to support the mixed force at Faaberg. There was, in the first case, two companies of the Leicestershire which had not been accommodated in the ships which sailed from Rosyth for Aandalsnes on April 17th. They had left two days later and reaching Aandalsnes at six o'clock on the evening of April 21st had been sent straight up by train to the rail-head at Tretten, fifteen miles north of Faaberg. They arrived at noon on Monday. By that time the British troops at Faaberg were already engaged with the enemy.

Meanwhile there was the half-battalion of Foresters on the west side of the lake.

They had held their ground throughout the night, but in view of the retreat that had taken place on the further side of the lake it was necessary for them to withdraw in order to avoid being outflanked and possibly cut off. Soon after first light on Monday morning Major Roberts began to lead his force back. They came under mortar fire from across the lake but avoided serious loss, while the good work of Norwegian engineers in blowing bridges and felling trees in their rear prevented close pursuit. To avoid air attack, however, they lay up in a side valley throughout most of Monday and did not resume their retreat until 10.30 p.m. By this time the Faaberg position had already been forced and, hearing that the Germans were now pushing up the river valley to the north of Faaberg, they were compelled to make a long detour through the deep snow of the mountain valleys to the west. The retreat began again in the half-light at 3 a.m. on Tuesday morning, and they were fortunate in acquiring a number of open trucks in the process of withdrawal. Numb with cold after a long drive through the freezing night, without even greatcoats, they began to trickle in to the Tretten position (now no longer rail-head, but the front line) as the morning brightened. It was a highly creditable achievement on the part of Major Roberts to have so successfully extricated his men under such unfavourable conditions.

Major Roberts's force had been pushed forward into an advanced position. It was never seriously attacked, but to avoid isolation it had been compelled to make a two-day retreat through snowbound valleys, with the result that the men on their arrival were utterly exhausted. Yet, because the Germans had pursued their offensive elsewhere with vigour, these men had to be committed almost immediately to battle under conditions in which they could not possibly do themselves justice.

Apart from these two half-battalions of Leicestershire and Foresters there was, however, the prospect of support from the 15th Brigade, two battalions of which, with some light A.A. guns and a field ambulance detachment had sailed from Rosyth at 6 a.m. on Tuesday morning. Intended originally to exploit down the Osterdal to the east they would now have to be thrown in to hold the main German advance up the Gudbrandsdal.

Meanwhile steps were being taken to provide air support for 'Sickleforce', and on the previous day work had been begun in preparing the frozen surface of Lake Lesjaskogen (in the Romsdal, between thirty and forty miles forward from Aandalsnes) as a landing-ground for Gladiators, while another and smaller landing-ground was to be developed much closer to the port. With the use of the large surface provided by the lake it was optimistically hoped that we might achieve something approaching air parity.

The significance of the situation was not lost on Lieut.-General H. R. S. Massy, commander of the V Corps, who that day took formal command of what was now entitled the North-West Expeditionary Force,[1] although he was unable to proceed to Norway and had to exercise his command from the War Office throughout the

[1] The appointment was actually made on April 19th.

brief campaign. In the instructions which he issued to General Paget he made it clear that a force of Gladiators would have arrived by April 25th and that meanwhile an aircraft-carrier would be available off Aandalsnes to give some protection to the base. In view of the meagre capacity of Aandalsnes as a port and the probability of serious destruction as the result of air attack, he suggested the reconnoitring of the Sundal and Geiranger fjords, respectively to the north and south of Aandalsnes fjord, to provide subsidiary bases and lines of communication with the front. An administrative corps H.Q. was to be set up at Aandalsnes, with Brigadier Hogg as D.A. and Q.M.G.

Unfortunately, owing to the administrative difficulties of the forward troops and the delay consequent upon signals, the information at the disposal of the new Force Commander was seriously out of date. The main Norwegian force was still believed to be fighting a delaying action on the Hamar–Elverum line when it was in fact in a process of disintegration a full thirty miles to the north.

The Faaberg position, where the next stand was made, was not a good one. While the right flank rested on the river there was no secure bastion for the left, since the hills did not rise with sufficient steepness to preclude a turning movement by the enemy. At noon on Monday the Germans using incendiaries began to attack the mixed force of Foresters and Leicestershire, whose strength on paper was about a battalion, considerably reduced by losses on the previous day's retreat. The air attack was followed up by a bombardment with 3.7-inch howitzers and 4-inch mortars.

Under cover of this bombardment the German infantry on skis began to work stealthily round our open flank on the left. A scratch platoon hastily switched to this wing caused only a temporary check, and by the early afternoon the Germans were enfilading our position from the high ground overlooking the river. Brigadier Morgan therefore ordered the remaining half of the Leicestershire forward from the position which they had just taken up at Tretten, following their arrival by train from Aandalsnes, and appealed unsuccessfully to the Norwegian command for reinforcements. By this stage of the campaign the regular Norwegian forces in the south were exhausted and the only resistance they could provide in and around the Gudbrandsdal came from small bodies of trained ski-troopers and one or two isolated detachments on the flanks. It was learned also that the Norwegians had made no arrangements to organise a reserve position.

Soon after four o'clock the situation had become critical and in order to save his force from being surrounded and destroyed the British commander decided to disengage with the utmost speed and withdraw in the only transport that was at his disposal—twelve lorries loaded with stores. The stores had to be jettisoned and as many troops as possible were crowded into the lorries. Though attacked from the air on the way they succeeded in reaching Oier, six or seven miles back along the valley.

Unfortunately, our losses in this action were disproportionately heavy for the length of time that we succeeded in delaying the German advance. The two companies of Foresters who were involved appear not to have received their orders to disengage. Only remnants of them ever got back to Oier. Many seem to have been rounded up while attempting to make their way back on foot. The Leicestershire, who had been rushed up from Tretten to stem the tide, were raked with fire from the mortars and the guns of the German armoured fighting vehicles. Before dusk they were compelled to withdraw back through the scratch force composed of survivors of the Faaberg action under Lieut.-Colonel German. The latter held out through the night and then retired on Tretten.

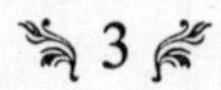

## *Action at Tretten*

Saint George's Day dawned under gloomy circumstances for the British forces in Norway. 'Rupertforce' at Narvik, had accomplished little as yet. 'Mauriceforce' having been beaten at Vist two days earlier was now retiring upon Namsos, and its commander on that day signalled the C.I.G.S. suggesting that evacuation might have to be contemplated; and finally, the troops preparing for action at Tretten had small cause for satisfaction, as the strength of the German forces contrasted with the paucity of their own equipment and means of resistance was becoming all too apparent.

At 2 a.m. Brigadier Morgan, who had little opportunity of sleep during these critical nights, had met General Ruge and had undertaken to hold the Tretten position throughout the day, retiring during the night through a fresh Norwegian battalion which would meanwhile have taken up its position at Faavang, nine miles north. It was hoped that during this period the force under Colonel Dahl, which as far as was known had not yet been engaged, would arrive back along the western bank of the Gudbrandsdal. Hitherto the fighting had been entirely confined to the eastern side.

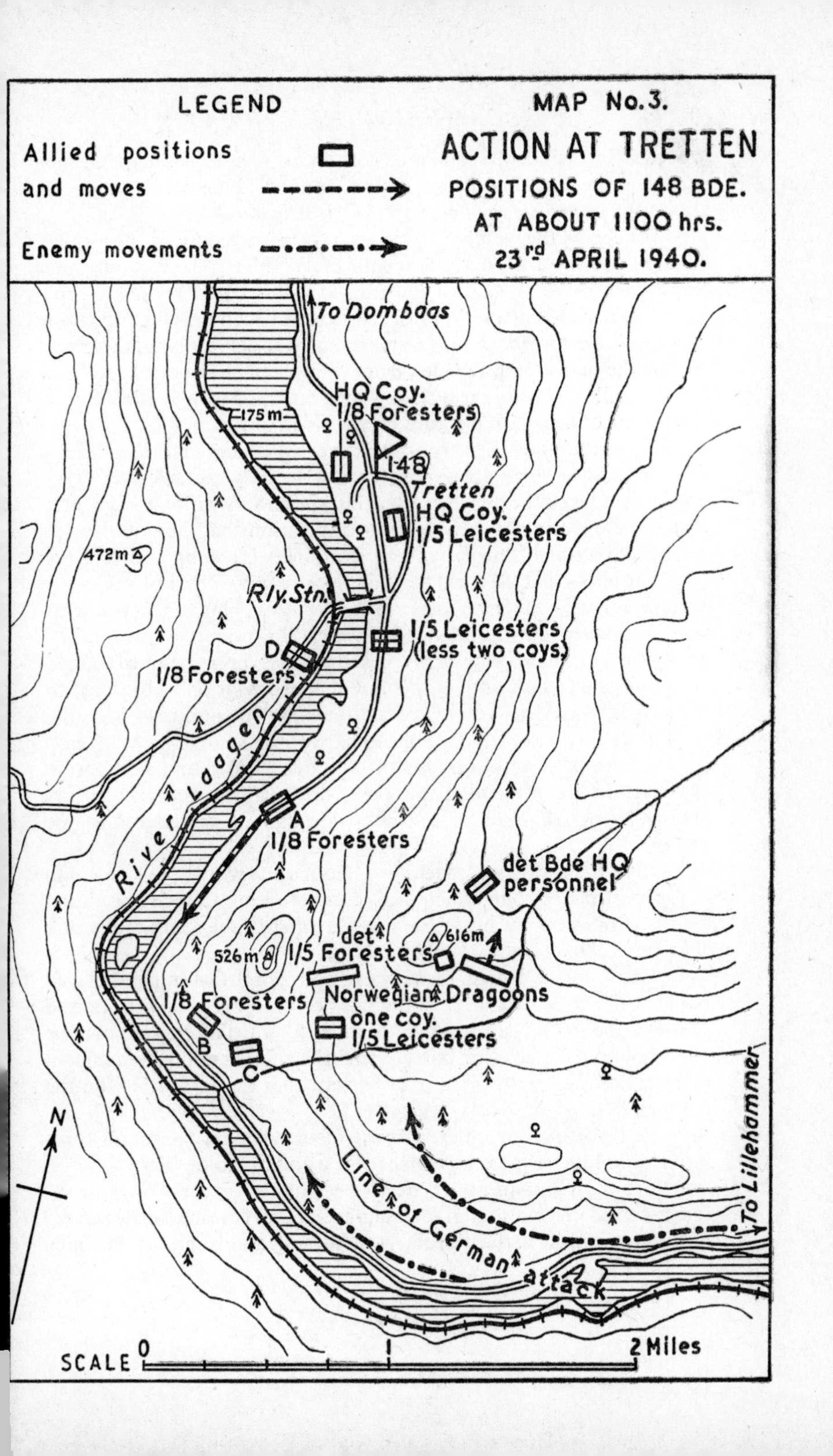
LEGEND
Allied positions
and moves
Enemy movements
MAP No.3.
ACTION AT TRETTEN
POSITIONS OF 148 BDE.
AT ABOUT 1100 hrs.
23rd APRIL 1940.
To Dombaas
HQ Coy.
1/8 Foresters
175m
148
Tretten
HQ Coy.
1/5 Leicesters
472m
Rly. Stn.
1/5 Leicesters
(less two coys.)
D
1/8 Foresters
River Laagen
A
1/8 Foresters
det Bde HQ
personnel
det
1/5 Foresters
616m
526m
Norwegian Dragoons
1/8 Foresters
one coy.
1/5 Leicesters
B
C
N
Line of German attack
To Lillehammer
SCALE
0
1
2 Miles

Meanwhile, since the left or eastern flank was, as at Faaberg, the danger spot, General Ruge placed Colonel Jensen's Norwegian Dragoons under command of the 148th Brigade.

Approach by the west bank was severely restricted, since the mountains rose almost abruptly from the river valley, leaving only the narrow ledge which carried the railway. This could be easily protected by a small force. It was the east bank which provided the best opportunities for the attacker. One narrow defile along the river carried the main road. Divided from it by a thickly wooded saddle a second defile carried a farm track which emerged by a gentle descent in the rear of the main position by the river.

There were not enough troops to cover adequately all three tracks and the saddle, where deep snow formed the only obstacle.

Our men faced the new day after thirty-six hours without sleep, and very short of food, for most of their own rations had been jettisoned during the evacuation of Faaberg. Rations were supposed to have been supplied that day by the 2nd Norwegian Division but were never received. Our men were without entrenching tools (such as they had were mostly abandoned when the retreat began). They were without supporting arms. As they had been neither trained nor equipped for movement in snow they were virtually confined to the roads. Lacking means of entrenching themselves—and the ground, in any case, was frozen too hard to make digging at all easy—they were without cover, for the wooden houses and farms were easily set on fire by shelling and, being obvious targets for the enemy gunners, proved more of a death-trap than a protection to the troops.

Against them was approaching a German force whose size could not be estimated but which was composed of trained mountain troops supported by heavy mortars, artillery and some tanks and armoured cars.

The bulk of the British force was disposed on the vulnerable east bank of the river. B and C Companies of the Foresters were posted to block the main road a couple of miles forward from Tretten; one company of the Leicestershire covered the centre; and a detachment of brigade headquarters troops was watching the farm track on the extreme left.

Some three or four miles forward Lieut.-Colonel German's force was still holding out in the fringes of a wood north of Oier.

Before the German attack developed, however, the troops in the line received certain material encouragement. A trainload of rations and ammunition arrived from Aandalsnes, and some of the men were able to receive a hot meal. At about this time Major Roberts's force, half a battalion strong, who had been retreating up the west bank through the night, began to trickle in to brigade headquarters. They were cold, hungry, and tired, but numerically almost intact, for they had not been involved in any fighting and, despite the length of their retreat and the détours imposed upon them, there had been few stragglers. The force, which consisted of A Company, D Company, and half the headquarters company of Foresters, was immediately put into line. D Company was held on the western bank covering Tretten bridge. A Company was posted in general reserve on the eastern bank, and the half-company of headquarters troops sent to the vulnerable eastern flank.

About 10.30 a.m. Lieut.-Colonel German's force arrived back from its outpost position and was stationed in general support just south of the village. The Norwegian troops who had been promised by General Ruge also arrived at this time and were posted on the saddle.

There had, therefore, been time for the Tretten position to be somewhat strengthened before the German advanced troops began to make contact with our outposts. Nevertheless it was clear from the first that this could be no more than a single day's holding action and a further withdrawal northwards was timed to start about sundown. The Germans, fortunately, on this as on succeeding occasions, had made no attempt to follow up through the short northern night. Had they done so they might have annihilated Colonel German's small holding force at Oier and fallen upon our troops in the Tretten position before the latter were in any position to fight even a temporary holding action. The deliberation which characterised the enemy pursuit during these days was always a factor in our favour.

It was about one o'clock in the afternoon before the forward detachments of the German infantry began to contact our position both along the main road and the farm track to the east. The enemy had only two tanks, for the country did not lend itself to their use, but as our troops had no anti-tank rifles or guns capable of stopping them the value of these two armoured vehicles was incalculable. They soon penetrated the position held by the Foresters on the main road. One of the tanks broke down inside our lines, but a platoon that was switched across from the east bank to deal with it was practically annihilated. On this, as on so many subsequent occasions, the Germans showed their skill in employing broken-down tanks in static positions as pill-boxes.

The forward infantry, now isolated by the break-through of the German tanks, were beginning to run short of ammunition. The

Germans kept up a continuous fire on Tretten village with their field-guns and heavy mortars, and all the time they were infiltrating troops around our open eastern flank and attacking not our forward but our support troops with a view to cutting off those further south. Colonel German gathered a small body of men together near Tretten bridge, hoping to keep the road open for the forward troops to withdraw, but few seem to have received any orders to this effect.

That was the situation on the east bank late in the afternoon, but west of the river things had gone much better. The position had proved as strong as was anticipated and the British commander had been justified in leaving so small a force on that bank. When the enemy advance began on the further side of the river the defenders had moved forward a couple of miles to prevent the enemy working along the ledge and opening enfilade fire, and a little later they succeeded in repulsing a German platoon with considerable losses to the attackers and little to themselves.

By seven o'clock in the evening Tretten had clearly become untenable. The orders to withdraw do not seem to have got through to the forward troops and the hard decision had to be taken to abandon them and evacuate those who could be withdrawn in the available transport. The retreat by daylight was of short duration. German aircraft swooped overhead continually attacking the lorries, and casualties were suffered from low raking machine-gun fire. There was still plenty of light for the planes to continue their attack, and the commander of the force judged it the lesser of two evils to call a halt and dispose the troops in a defensive position a mile north of Tretten. German armoured vehicles (they seem mostly to have been armoured cars) were close on their heels and kept up a fire which caused further casualties. It was clear, however, that the advance of the enemy infantry was being hampered by the forward troops whose fire could still be heard from their isolated positions beyond Tretten. This resistance prevented a complete *débâcle*, and the main body was able to hold out until nightfall and then begin a retreat on foot, the majority of their trucks having been put out of action by enemy fire.

Considerable loss was suffered in this action, and the two battalions were now reduced to nine officers and 300 men. Lieut.-Colonel German, commander of the Leicestershire, and Lieut.-Colonel Ford, of the Foresters, were both among the missing, and command of what remained of the two battalions was now taken over by Major R. J. German and Major Dowson respectively. Some miles back the troops reached the Norwegian support position at Faavang where they were able to pick up a few vehicles which were used to carry some of the more exhausted men. The remainder continued on foot a further twenty-five miles until they reached the sheltered valley of Heidal which runs off at an angle from the Gudbrandsdal. Here they were dispersed in houses and huts during the following day. Those that assembled here—some thirty per cent of the total—were utterly exhausted, and it was clear that the 148th Brigade was finished as a fighting unit. This was the outcome of the costly holding action at Tretten.

That same Tuesday evening, while the retreat from Tretten was in progress, the greater part of the 15th Brigade disembarked at Molde and Aandalsnes. It consisted of the 1st K.O.Y.L.I. and 1st York and Lancaster, both under the command of Brigadier Smyth. The 1st Green Howards was to follow by the next convoy with Major-General Paget, the divisional commander, and in fact embarked and sailed from Rosyth early on the following morning.

Brigadier Smyth had now a very different, and much more depressing, situation to face from that which had been envisaged when his troops embarked forty-eight hours earlier. Then it had been hoped that they could be fed into the Osterdal for offensive operations southward in conjunction with the 148th Brigade on their right; now it was clear that they would have to be speedily plugged into the Gudbrandsdal, since the 148th Brigade had practically ceased to exist. There was no longer any question of offensive action, and it was evident that the confidence of the Norwegians in their allies was waning and that they were likely to throw their hand in unless immediate and effective help on an adequate scale could be provided.

Since all the wireless equipment of the 148th Brigade had been either sunk on the way to Norway, captured by the enemy, or abandoned during the retreat from Lillehammer because there was no means of moving it, there was no opportunity for speedy communication between Brigadier Smyth and the troops in the advance positions. He had to assume, as indeed was the case, that his own brigade was the sole force in a position to operate in the Gudbrandsdal and to block the German advance upon Aandalsnes.

It was fortunate that the new arrivals were given time to get into position without interference from the Germans save by air. This was in keeping with the tactics adopted by the enemy throughout the campaign both in the Aandalsnes and Namsos sectors. In neither sector did the enemy make any very serious attempt at a close follow-up of the retreating forces. A little more boldness on the part of the German command and there might have been no evacuation from either port—for there might have been no troops to evacuate.

## 4

### *Action at Kvam*

Brigadier Smyth, in conference with Brigadier Morgan and General Hvinden-Haug of the 2nd Norwegian Division, decided on the morning of April 24th that the 15th Brigade should make its stand at Kvam, a strong position more than thirty miles back up the valley from Tretten and covering the Heidal, where the exhausted remnants of the 148th Brigade were now resting and re-forming.

Meanwhile the Norwegian forces would hold the positions at Faavang and Ringebu, further south, until the night of April 25th–26th.

Events, however, were moving too fast for the Allied plan. During the afternoon it was learned that the Norwegian troops were already falling back from their positions and it became clear that the K.O.Y.L.I., who arrived in the Kvam position that night, would have to face an attack on the following day.

The battalion had been railed up to Otta in the course of the morning, but found difficulty in getting further, since the Norwegian lorry drivers refused to proceed beyond that point. The road was regarded as unsafe, not only on account of the German planes, strafing backwards and forwards at will, but also because it was choked with the transport vehicles of the retreating Norwegian troops to such an extent that the ten miles from Otta to Kvam took on an average three hours to cover throughout the day.

As supporting arms the 15th Brigade had a company of nine anti-tank guns on portées. Five of these were got into position at Kvam with some difficulty, three were held in reserve while one was irretrievably ditched during the move forward. A field ambulance had also arrived and opened a forward dressing-station at Dombaas and another at Aandalsnes. Owing to lack of transport, however, it never proved possible to evacuate many of the badly wounded from their battle positions, and these casualties therefore generally fell into enemy hands.

Throughout the day German air activity was widespread—a softening up process before the attack developed on the following day. Their planes swept at will up and down the valley from Faavang to Aandalsnes, paying particular attention to the anti-aircraft sites around Aandalsnes and to the new rail-head of Otta, where the three Bofors guns available were all put out of action for the time being.

More significant, however, than these attacks was an enemy reconnaissance flight over Lake Lesjaskogen in the course of the day, for it was here that we were in the process of establishing a base for fighters to give air cover to the forward troops. In the absence of broad, grassy plains in central Norway, the surface of frozen lakes would serve as provisional landing-grounds. Of the lakes available to our forces in the Gudbrandsdal, Lesjaskogen was much the largest and most convenient. Local opinion estimated that it could have been used for as much as three weeks longer before the spring thaw made the ice too thin for safety.

No one had better cause to be aware of the critical nature of the situation than the Norwegian Commander-in-Chief, General Ruge. Following an interview with the Allied attachés at his headquarters he despatched a signal couched in the most urgent terms to the Chief of the British Naval Staff, the C.I.G.S., the Chief of the Air Staff and to the Ministry of National Defence and the Admiralty in Paris.

In this he stated that the Norwegian troops were utterly exhausted after fourteen days of fighting. They had been continually bombed and machine-gunned from the air and on the previous day long-range artillery had made its appearance for the first time. All important points and railway junctions from Aandalsnes to the front were being systematically destroyed and communications were daily interrupted.

The Norwegian commander stated that a definite promise of relief had been given to him personally and had not been fulfilled. This had been the promise of the attack on Trondheim, which he had been led to believe would have taken place some days earlier.

It was quite impossible, he stated, to make his dispositions unless he were given prompt and precise information of the Allied intentions. The situation was critical and the front might now at any time be irretrievably broken. The need for artillery and aircraft to support the troops was of the utmost urgency. Unless immediate help were forthcoming a *débâcle* would occur.

General Ruge requested an immediate reply to this signal.

On the morning of April 25th the K.O.Y.L.I. stood at Kvam, where the river Laagen runs from west to east, split in the middle by an island, something less than three-quarters of a mile long, bare, flat but fringed with willows along its banks. The position was somewhat stronger than at Tretten, for on either side the slopes rose more sharply and were thickly wooded, rendering a flank attack in strength, such as had proved so fatal at Tretten, a matter of considerable difficulty, though ski-troops might be successful in infiltration. The river at this point was broad and shallow. The right (south) bank, however, was even less suitable for an advance in any strength than had been the case at Tretten. The hills rose sharply from the riverbank and neither road nor railway followed the bank on this side.

Brigadier Smyth, who was directing the action, disposed two companies of K.O.Y.L.I. on the island, one forward and one in support, with a detached platoon on the south bank—all that was needed there, under the circumstances. Two more companies were disposed on the hillside above Kvam, one forward and one in support near the village of Veikle, both about 300 feet up from the river. A fifth company and the headquarters company were posted in the centre at Kvam itself. Five 25-mm. anti-tank guns were available; one was sited on the island, the others on the north bank. There were a further three in support.

As in previous actions the Germans were slow to develop their attack, and although a small battle patrol, sent forward from Kvam soon after first light, ran into a German tank and was annihilated, it was not until eleven o'clock in the morning that the head of the advancing German force began to approach Kvam. First, three armoured vehicles (two tanks and an armoured car) nosed their way forward. They were followed by artillery, lorried infantry, and marching infantry, a very pretty picture of an army on the move, but one that suggested that the German command did not expect to encounter resistance at this point.

On came the German tanks, the British holding their fire until the enemy were well within range of their anti-tank gun on Kvam island —a distance of not more than a quarter of a mile. Then the gun spoke. With its first shots it hit and stopped both tanks, and the armoured car withdrew hastily into dead ground round a bend of the road. First blood to the British; and had the enemy depended only upon their tanks and infantry the Kvam position would have taken a lot of forcing. But the German artillery now came into play. The heavy 5.9's began to rake our positions, and soon the small houses of Kvam were blazing in the morning air. Our troops, with little opportunity for taking cover were suffering casualties without the means of effective reply. One by one, our forward positions were being literally blown away by the German guns. Brigadier Smyth was wounded, and Lieut.-Colonel Kent-Lemon took over his command, Major Tennant succeeding him in charge of the battalion. The troops stationed on the island were suffering particularly severely. It was as flat as a

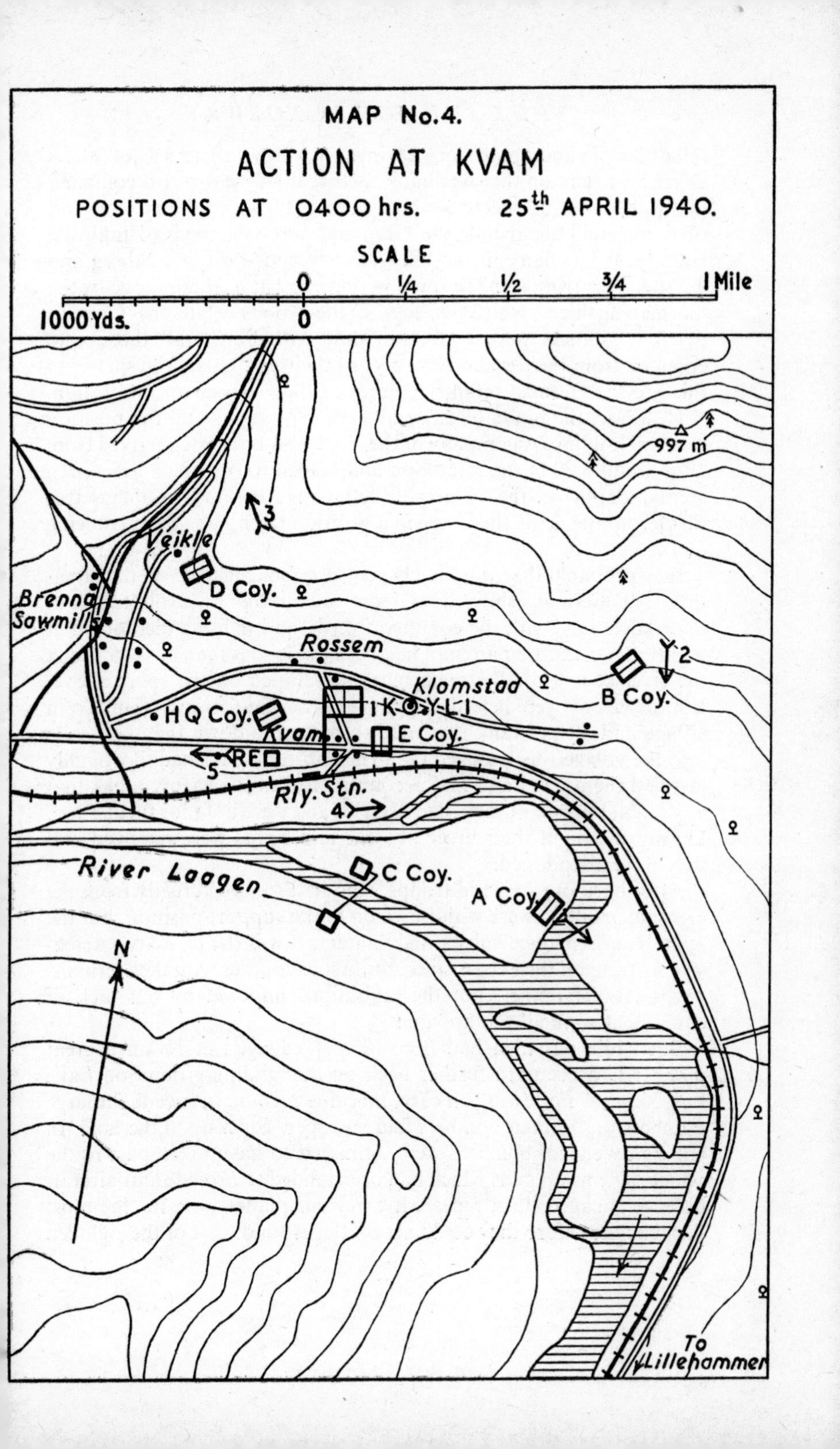
MAP No.4.
ACTION AT KVAM
POSITIONS AT 0400 hrs. 25th APRIL 1940.
SCALE
0
1/4
1/2
3/4
1 Mile
1000 Yds.
0
997 m
3
Veikle
D Coy.
Brenna
Sawmills
Rossem
2
Klomstad
B Coy.
1 K.O.Y.L.I.
HQ Coy.
Kvam
E Coy.
RE
5
Rly. Stn.
4
River Laagen
C Coy.
A Coy.
N
To
Lillehammer

billiard-table and apart from a fringe of willows there was even less cover here than on the river bank. Before long the forward company had lost half of its effectives and was forced back to the extreme end of the island. Meanwhile the Germans were beginning to infiltrate round our left flank in the hills, as they had done at Faaberg and Tretten. Our troops on the spurs were shelled at medium range by the German artillery which set fire to the woods while the German machine-gunners were ready to riddle with bullets all those who emerged from the treacherous cover of the trees. Under the shelter of this fire the German infantry continued their process of infiltration.

However, the hours of daylight were slipping by and the position was still holding. A company of the York and Lancaster arrived from Otta about 5.30 in the afternoon and helped to provide a defence in greater depth on the vulnerable left flank. By posting themselves further up the slope they were in a position to enfilade the advancing Germans.

It is probable that this timely reinforcement just saved the situation. The Germans showed no desire to continue the exploitation of their advantage with the coming of dusk, and fighting died down at nightfall. One further attempt had been made to force a passage along the river-bed, while the main battle developed on the spurs above. But the enemy were held there by troops moved forward from Kvam village and a third tank that tried to penetrate down the main road into the village was knocked out. The anti-tank guns had thoroughly justified themselves and had accounted for all the enemy tanks that appeared, but two of them had been hit and were unfit for further use. During the night their breech-blocks and sights were removed and they were abandoned.

After dark our forward troops, who had suffered cruelly from the German artillery, were withdrawn on to the support position, but the main front remained substantially intact. It was the best day's defensive fighting on this sector since our first encounter with the Germans beyond Lillehammer, but the limitations imposed by our lack of equipment were all too apparent.

But while our men had been heavily engaged at Kvam a great disaster had occurred further back on the landing-ground on Lake Lesjaskogen. Following an early morning reconnaissance flight large numbers of German bombers had swooped down upon the lake. In all, eighty enemy bombers were estimated to have taken part in the attack. The naval guns which had been landed to provide anti-aircraft defence engaged them repeatedly, but our planes were for the most part caught before they could get off the ground. Out of the eighteen

Gladiators which were to have been employed as fighter protection to the forward troops, thirteen were destroyed on the ground, and only three of those which were got away subsequently proved serviceable. With more experienced ground crews, accustomed to refuelling aircraft under fire, it is likely that several more planes might have succeeded in taking the air and getting clear of the bombing.

Our planes did in fact make forty-nine operational flights during the day and shot down at least six enemy machines, but by evening all prospect that the hard-pressed troops might receive adequate air protection was at an end. Moreover the German air victory left the enemy free to concentrate upon our shipping off Aandalsnes and Molde. They raided the port and fjord at will throughout the day, sinking several ferry steamers.[1]

That evening the convoy carrying General Paget and the rest of the 15th Brigade (1st Green Howards and headquarters troops) reached Molde and Aandalsnes. Paget now assumed direct command of 'Sickleforce' and went immediately into conference with Brigadier Morgan and other senior military and naval officers in the tiny wardroom of the Norwegian destroyer to which the British commander transferred after arriving at Molde. The commander ironically described it as a 'Strength through Joy' conference, for there were few cheerful factors in the situation, and all present agreed that the expedition was ill-equipped at almost every point and that the lack of air support, A.A. defence, base facilities, means of communication and transport was already gravely jeopardising its success.

In a report despatched to the War Office that same night, General Paget stressed the many unfavourable factors of the situation. Above all, and conditioning everything, was the German air superiority. The German air force was being used, as in Poland, in a role closely coordinated with the army. They bombed and machine-gunned exactly as they chose, attacking not only the forward troops and the base (taking a long-term view the latter constituted the more dangerous threat) but also the road and railway from Aandalsnes to the front. The railway from Aandalsnes to Dombaas had been cut five times in the course of the previous day. The vital junction of Dombaas had been destroyed by bombing, and Aandalsnes had been attacked by relays of planes throughout the hours of daylight. Our own air strength was, for the time being, non-existent. The Gladiators had been eliminated by the German raid on Lesjaskogen, and though Blenheims had been promised for April 27th, it now seemed doubtful

[1] We should have needed to rely on these a good deal in the event of Molde being developed, as was intended, into a subsidiary base.

whether there would be any suitable landing-ground from which they could operate.

The situation on the ground was certainly no more encouraging. The 148th Brigade had to be written off so far as front-line service was concerned. Only five officers were left in the whole brigade and the men were excessively tired and shaken after their gruelling experience of the past few days. For the present they could be employed only on lines of communication. The Norwegian troops were, by this time, also in a bad way after more than a fortnight of fighting against heavy odds. Their strength in the Gudbrandsdal and Romsdal probably added up to as much as two brigades, and those who possessed skis were useful for protecting our flanks on the hills, but of late they had been tending to thin out and disappear. Moreover, the road all the way back from Lillehammer to Aandalsnes was cluttered with transport and refugees. It was pretty clear that when the thaw, which had already begun, took effect on the roads in about a fortnight's time, the surface would go to pieces under pressure of traffic, thus adding yet further to our troubles.

Since the troops at Kvam could not be expected to hold out for more than another day, Paget proposed to make the next stand at Otta, a good ten miles back and almost the last position from which the Dombaas junction could be defended. For the expedition to have any meaning at all it was vital to hold Dombaas. Once that fell, the Germans would have free access to Trondheim from the south and all chance of our operating offensively against the port would be at an end.

It was clear also that the Norwegian Government had now largely lost control of the situation (which was not to be wondered at in view of the fact that every single large town in Norway was in German hands) and was in danger of throwing in its hand. General Ruge alone was keeping the army together and he remained the effective head of the resistance in the country.

No action by the ground troops could ensure more than a temporary delay of the advancing German forces, unless it were backed by a strong air striking force. Paget emphasised that we needed air parity at least. Continuous daylight attacks must be made upon the advancing German troops and upon their communications back to Lillehammer, while fighter patrols, which might be provided from aircraft-carriers, should operate over both front line and base. Owing to the damage done to both railway and road it would be desirable, as well, to have Whitleys available for dropping supplies in forward positions by air. More anti-aircraft artillery was needed, heavy as well as light; one or two field regiments of 25 pounders would be necessary to reply effectively to the German 5.9's. Finally, the immediate despatch of the 147th Brigade,[1] to be followed by more Regular troops, was desirable as soon as Aandalsnes base could be developed. At present, however, it was out of the question for further troops to be maintained through Aandalsnes, not only owing to the extremely meagre capacities of the shattered port for berthing and unloading but because transport facilities were totally inadequate. The local transport vehicles which had been impressed at the start were now a vanishing asset and the 3-ton lorries which had been sent proved much too wide for the narrow road that threads the Gudbrandsdal.

General Paget indicated, as General Carton de Wiart had indicated from the Namsos front two days earlier, that the possibility of an evacuation must be considered and that arrangements should be made before the German troops arrived in the outskirts of Aandalsnes.

General Paget then drove forward to meet the Norwegian Commander-in-Chief at his headquarters in a farmhouse about ten miles south of Dombaas. It was clear that even General Ruge was beginning to lose heart. He was gravely concerned by the numerical smallness of the British force (though without considerable air support and greater base facilities it could not have been increased at that time) and was very conscious that his men in the Gudbrandsdal were at the end of their tether. To the south, in the Valdres valley, the detachment of General Steffens's Bergen Division was fighting a magnificent defensive action at Tonsaasen, but in the north the Germans, racing up the Osterdal, were reported to have reached Tynset and even Röros. This meant that they were not only near to opening up communications with Trondheim, but also that their advanced forces might swing across by the two practicable routes that were now available to them and descend upon Dombaas from the flank. In that case, any troops south of Dombaas were liable to be cut off and annihilated.

That Whitehall, though it might appreciate, seemed in little position to cope with the difficulties of the situation, was apparent from the replies received by Ruge and Paget to their signals in the course of the night. Promises of field artillery and anti-tank guns were made, and it was stated that two carriers would lie off Namsos and Aandalsnes respectively to provide fighter cover for the next three days at least. The importance of demolitions was urged upon General Ruge as a means of delaying the German advance. It was cold comfort.

[1] Originally to have made the sea-borne attack upon Trondheim.

With the morning light on April 26th, the Germans renewed their attack upon the Kvam position. Scarcely had dawn come than their guns opened all along the line with such a weight of fire that there was good reason for supposing that they had received artillery reinforcement during the night. At seven o'clock their infantry began to move forward against our left flank on the hillside where, on the previous day, the arrival of a company of the York and Lancaster had just sufficed to save the situation. The frontal assault was held, but with increased fire-power the Germans were able to keep our men pinned down, while their troops carried out the new familiar tactics of infiltrating around the flank, which probably could only have been effected successfully on these steep slopes by men trained in mountain warfare. They pushed further and further round, and our troops, who had at first formed front to flank to deal with them, now began to form round facing their own rear.

By eleven o'clock the enemy detachment had worked its way round to a point overlooking our support troops at Veikle, and all was ready for the final attack to go in. German planes began a series of low-level attacks on our troops, machine-gunning up and down the valley. More German guns opened up, and under this double barrage the German infantry crept in nearer establishing machine-gun positions close to our lines and commanding all movement from them. At one time the York and Lancaster company on the hillside was completely isolated, but Second-Lieutenant French, with a single platoon, rushed the new positions which the German infantry had taken up and drove them out with severe losses. It was a desperate action, but one which temporarily restored the situation on the hills.

By five o'clock it was clear that the position could be held no longer, and General Paget ordered the K.O.Y.L.I. to withdraw at nightfall. No more could be hoped than a series of forty-eight-hour stands at the best, until such time as artillery and air support arrived. With adequate support from these arms General Paget remained confident that he could hold up the German advance.

He was the more encouraged in that, when the withdrawal began at dusk, there was little interference from the enemy, who throughout the campaign showed the utmost reluctance to commit himself to any night operations—presumably the result of a general directive. The Royal Engineers were able to carry out demolitions in the rear of the retreating troops, and three of the six anti-tank guns which had been engaged were successfully withdrawn. Unfortunately the York and Lancaster company in the hills failed to receive orders to withdraw, but the majority were successful in making their way through.

Among those reported missing was Second-Lieutenant French, the young subaltern who had led the counter-attack during the afternoon. The German communiqué claimed less than forty prisoners as the result of the two-day battle, and the disengaging of our troops after so harassing an action may therefore be regarded as a highly satisfactory achievement.

Three depressing developments elsewhere in the course of the day must have deprived the British commander of any satisfaction he may have felt for having extricated his force from Kvam in the very teeth of the enemy.

German troops were now definitely reported at Alvdal in the Osterdal, whence a cross-road runs to Dombaas. Only weak Norwegian detachments were strung out along this route through Foldal and Hjerkinn. Since there seemed little to prevent a rapid German flank descent upon Dombaas, General Paget ordered Brigadier Morgan to organise the defence of the junction with the remnants of his brigade (about 400 strong) and a company of Green Howards with Bren-carrier and mortar platoons. The anticipated attack never came, for the Germans in the Osterdal, instead of swinging left to cut off the British, were under orders to continue north to effect the junction with the Trondheim forces, and in attempting to do so they ran into some very determined Norwegian resistance at Röros which kept their hands full until the end of the month.

Secondly, the heroic defence of Tonsaasen, which had blocked the way into the Valdres valley to the south, had broken down that day. The Norwegians had repeatedly repulsed the Germans and taken a number of prisoners during the three preceding days, and the final collapse was due to the penetration of the position by a German tank.

Thirdly, Aandalsnes had received its heaviest raid in the course of the afternoon. Between three o'clock and 4.30, waves of Heinkels had swept over the town. Fire had spread from house to house and the wooden jetty had been burned out. Among the stores that were destroyed on the quayside were 300,000 rounds of ·303 ammunition, 3,000 rounds of 40-mm. Bofors ammunition, and 800 3-inch mortar bombs. The damage was far greater than any that had yet been done, and there was little interference with the raiders after the anti-aircraft ship in the harbour had run out of ammunition. The Skuas sent off from the *Ark Royal* did not arrive on the scene of action until after the departure of the raiders. They patrolled over the smoking ruins until dusk.

It was now clear to the representatives of all three services that it was only a question of time before activity at the port diminished to such an extent that it would no longer be possible to maintain a force in the Gudbrandsdal. General Paget's signal of the previous night could not have received a grimmer postscript.

It was on that day that the French radio transmission in the Norwegian language announced that the Allies had control of the air over the battlefields of Norway.

## 5

### *Action at Kjörem*

After the evacuation of Kvam the K.O.Y.L.I. had moved back through the new position which the York and Lancaster had taken up at Kjörem about two miles back and through the further position which the Green Howards were preparing at Otta and had arrived in the valley south of Dombaas where they joined the remnant under Brigadier Morgan's command. At this stage, on April 27th, the retreat had begun to assume an almost rythmic nature. The front would be held by one battalion as long as possible, while the reserve battalions prepared alternative positions in the rear. When the position became untenable the forward battalion would be withdrawn back through the support positions. Careful timing was required, for if the forward troops withdrew too soon the troops in the rear risked being overrun; if, on the other hand, they held on too long they risked annihilation themselves or, at the best, they might receive such punishment that they could not again be put into the line.

The Kvam battle had been fought by the K.O.Y.L.I. with the support of one company of the York and Lancaster. The defence of Kjörem was entrusted to the last-named battalion with one company and one carrier platoon of the Green Howards. The valley was narrower than at Kvam and more of its floor was taken up by the river-bed, but the position was accessible from both sides of the river and the defending force had therefore to be divided. There were also two islands in midstream to be held.

The fighting at Kjörem was in many respects a repetition of what had gone before. The German attackers were earlier off the mark than on the preceding day and, following an air reconnaissance, their infantry began to appear along the road from Kvam not long after eight o'clock. They were checked by enfilading fire from our positions in the woods and hills and quickly dispersed and deployed to either flank. Then it was the old story. German tanks moved forward along the road to give protection to the infantry, and their artillery and mortars began to fire the woods which gave cover to our men and which came close down to the road. The smoke from the burning woods provided a screen behind which German tanks and infantry could advance.

It was the technique with which our troops were becoming painfully familiar. The tanks well forward along the road (it was seldom possible to deploy more than two or three effectively at the same time); the artillery and infantry employing their great superiority of fire-power in accordance with a well-synchronised plan, so that our men had the grim alternative of being destroyed in their fixed positions by shell-fire or forced out into the open and riddled by machine-gun bullets. For the first time our troops had mortar support, but the range-finding was inaccurate (probably owing to lack of experience), and many of the shells fell among our own men.

By seven o'clock in the evening the enemy had worked round our northern flank and established a road-block covered by machine-gun fire to the rear of the battalion. Once again we were faced by a critical situation, but Major Tennant, who was now commanding the battalion, promptly detached a battle patrol which succeeded in driving the Germans out. In another half-hour the German position would have been firmly established, it would probably have proved impossible to dislodge them and the whole battalion would have been in danger of capture or annihilation. Nothing is more remarkable in these successive rearguard actions than the heroism shown by scratch parties usually commanded by quite junior officers, called upon to dislodge the enemy by frontal attack in the face of heavy fire.

Quite early in the afternoon the two companies south of the river had been withdrawn in the direction of Sjoa, a few miles further back, with a view to taking up a position covering a general withdrawal during the night. They did not reach Sjoa until after dark and, missing their way, turned off into the cul-de-sac of the Heidal valley which had served the remnants of the 148th Brigade as a resting place three days earlier. Entering this valley late on the Saturday night it was some time before they discovered their mistake, and as the Germans, following up the retreat, were soon in occupation of Sjoa at the entrance to the valley they had to make their way across trackless snowfields and did not reach Dombaas until midday on the Monday afternoon, April 29th. Both in the battle and in the subsequent retreat they had suffered considerable losses, one of the companies being reduced by half.

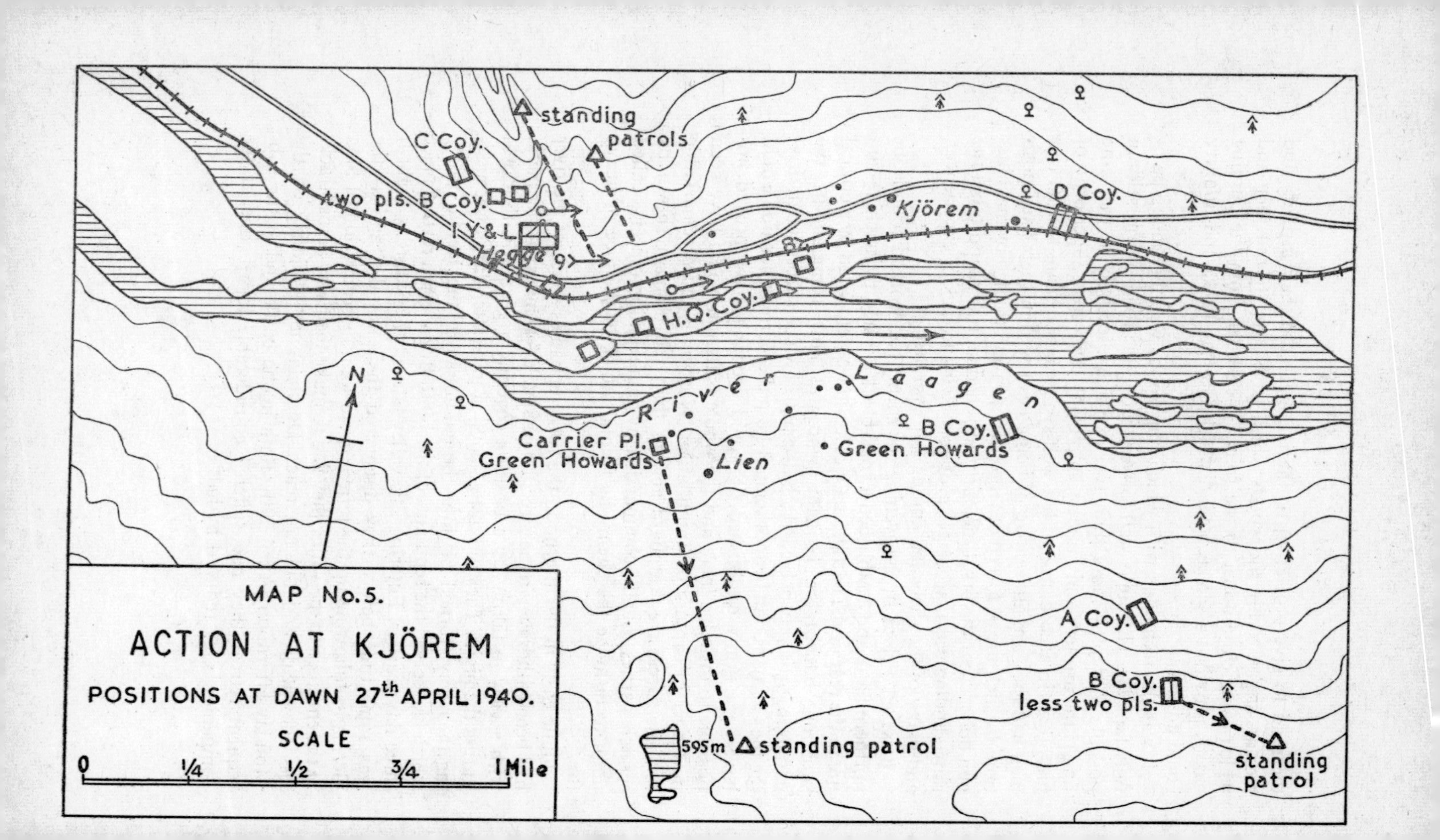
standing
patrols
C Coy.
two pls. B Coy.
1 Y & L
Hegge
Kjörem
D Coy.
H.Q. Coy.
N
River Laagen
B Coy.
Carrier Pl.
Green Howards
Lien
Green Howards
A Coy.
B Coy.
less two pls.
595m
standing patrol
standing
patrol
MAP No. 5.
ACTION AT KJÖREM
POSITIONS AT DAWN 27th APRIL 1940.
SCALE
0
1/4
1/2
3/4
1 Mile

The main body on the north side of the river hung on until after dark and began their retreat between 10 and 11 o'clock at night. The withdrawal was not so successful as on the previous night, for parties of the enemy had succeeded in infiltrating deeply into our main position and attempted to carry out an ambush. It was reported that these German troops were dressed in Norwegian uniforms. This may have been the case, but it should be remembered that the German and Norwegian uniforms bore a close resemblance. Some of the forward troops were cut off, though many succeeded in rejoining the battalion later. The force that arrived back at Otta had been reduced in strength to thirteen officers and 300 men. They brought with them, however, most of their transport and all their gun trucks. Among those missing was Major Tennant, who had succeeded two days earlier to the temporary command of the battalion. His place was taken by Major F. H. Jordan.

One result of the losses suffered in the action and in the subsequent withdrawal was that the remains of the York and Lancaster were in no fit condition to assist in the defence of Otta as had originally been planned. This task would now have to be left solely to the Green Howards, and it was again doubtful whether the defending force disposed of sufficient numbers, quite apart from the enemy superiority in air-power and supporting arms, to make sure of holding the position.

## 6

## *The Decision to Re-Embark*

While the north-countrymen were fighting their battle at Kjörem vital decisions affecting the operations in Norway had been taken at very high levels.

The decision to re-embark had been taken by the Cabinet as early as the morning of Friday, April 26th, following receipt of General Paget's despatch indicating that this course might have to be considered. General Carton de Wiart had already reported from Namsos in the same sense. The reasons for the decision were fourfold:

1. The overwhelming German air superiority to which we had been quite incapable of making any adequate reply.

We could establish no fighter fields in Norway and, lacking adequate anti-aircraft protection, the airfield which we had established on Lake Lesjaskogen had been shot up and almost all the aircraft on it destroyed. Our only means of replying in kind was by raids upon the German-held airfields of Stavanger, Fornebu (Oslo) and Aalborg (in Denmark). From the last-named of these places the German transport planes were being constantly flown to Norway with troops and supplies. Such attacks as we had made had not been without success, but they had had no influence in altering the balance of air-power. The real danger was caused by the attacks on our bases at Namsos and Aandalsnes which were making it difficult for us to maintain even the small forces (13,000 in all) which had hitherto been landed at these ports and were rendering virtually impossible the landing of the heavy equipment without which the troops could not maintain their position in the field.

2. The reversal of the military situation on land in the course of the week.

Up to Sunday, April 21st, things had looked quite promising. The troops had been landed at both ports without loss. Carton de Wiart's force, advancing from Namsos had passed through Steinkjer; Morgan's Brigade had pushed inland nearly 150 miles, beyond Lillehammer, and made contact with the Norwegians. No enemy resistance had then developed. On that day, however, the enemy struck back and defeated our northern force at Vist, south of Steinkjer and began to drive our southern detachment back from Lillehammer in a counter-stroke that was developing with increasing force.

3. The administrative difficulty, itself an outcome to a large extent of the German air superiority.

Adequate forces and adequate material to stem the German advance could not be landed because the ports through which they must be landed were in ruins and unloading must necessarily be a very slow business With the decreasing hours of darkness this handicap would be intensified in the coming days and weeks.

4. The intention to attack Trondheim, an operation which was pivotal to the whole campaign in Scandinavia, had been abandoned on April 19th.

In view of the probability, as it then seemed, of the extension of the war to the Mediterranean in the immediate future and the vital necessity to the Alliance of Britain maintaining her naval preponderance in that quarter, our commitments in northern Europe took on an entirely different character.

That same Saturday, Lieut.-General Massy submitted an appreciation of the military situation to the Cabinet. He had had no opportunity of exercising his command on the spot, but the reports from

Carton de Wiart and Paget provided an adequate basis for deduction. In recommending evacuation he was further influenced by the rapid progress which the Germans were now reported to be making up the Osterdal. According to information supplied by the French military attaché at Norwegian Headquarters a force of infantry and A.F.V.s having pushed up the valley as far as Alvdal had swung left at the road fork at that point and had reached Foldal[1] on the way to Hjerkinn near which place a small Norwegian force was stationed. From Foldal to Hjerkinn was no more than twenty miles, and from Hjerkinn to Dombaas was scarcely as much. The threat to the rear of the 15th Brigade, already envisaged by General Paget, was becoming very much a reality, particularly as there was news of a mountain regiment in the area equipped with skis for operating across country where the British troops would be helpless.

This was not the end of the discouraging information from the Osterdal, for the German progress northward was very rapid. They were now in the neighbourhood of Röros and it was therefore becoming extremely doubtful whether 'Sickleforce' could hold even the Dombaas–Opdal line, which was regarded as a minimum for the security of the troops and their base.

Reviewing the known facts of German superiority in the air and in support weapons and our own administrative difficulties General Massy considered that the best that could now be hoped from 'Sickleforce' was that it might be strengthened sufficiently to enable it to hold on long enough to ensure an organised evacuation beginning about May 10th. However, German air and land superiority might produce a situation which would compel a much earlier evacuation. In that case, the earliest date on which ships could be ready to take off the troops would be the night of May 1st–2nd and under those circumstances much or all the material might have to be abandoned.

As this latter alternative appeared to be the more probable General Massy recommended that the two ships carrying guns and M.T. which were due to unload at Aandalsnes that night should not put into the harbour, nor should any further troops be landed there; secondly, that the personnel of 'Sickleforce' should be re-embarked

[1] This force was either very much smaller than was supposed or else it suffered from a strange paralysis. It made no further attempt to develop this threat to our flank and rear. It seems likely that the force sent west from Alvdal was pursuing a purely reconnaissance role. The Norwegian commander in the Dombaas-Hjerkinn area reported next day that no contact had been made with German troops anywhere in his sector. As his forward posts were at Hjerkinn it would seem that the Germans did not actually penetrate as far as the village.

at the earliest date and orders given for empty ships to be in readiness to receive them.

General Massy went on to point out that no further resistance could in any case be expected from the Norwegian troops and that it was unlikely that they would co-operate in the withdrawal of the British towards their bases. As soon as they became aware of the retrograde movement of our troops they would in all probability either take to the hills and disperse or surrender wholesale.

Finally, he emphasised the importance of Namsos being evacuated at the same time as Aandalsnes, since once the latter port had been evacuated Carton de Wiart's force would be left quite needlessly to bear the brunt of the German attack with no strategic objective of its own to pursue. If immediate evacuation were decided, he considered that there would be enough shipping to carry all the troops in southern and central Norway on the night of May 1st–2nd. But if the build-up were to be developed in accordance with the provisional plan of operations then there would be a total of 28,000 men in 'Sickleforce' and 6,400 in 'Mauriceforce' and evacuation would take at least thirty-five days.

Events in Norway were soon to implement the points made in Massy's memorandum. Aandalsnes was raided four times in less than six hours during April 27th. All the demolition stores and explosives lying on the quays or in the neighbourhood of the port were destroyed and a large quantity of ration boxes as well. In addition, telephone communications with the forward troops finally broke down in the course of the day. Brigadier Hogg, who was in charge of the base area, was so impressed with the gravity of the position that, on his own responsibility, he cabled the War Office that he was planning evacuation on the basis of a total of 6,500 to be evacuated. Owing to the difficulties of communication, General Paget only learned for the first time of Brigadier Hogg's initiative when he received a signal late that night from General Massy informing him that evacuation had been decided in principle though there were alternative plans to be considered of evacuating the whole force on the night of May 1st–2nd or spreading the embarkation over two or even three nights. In the event of the former plan being adopted, troops were to be given priority regardless of the loss of equipment involved. If any equipment could be salvaged anti-aircraft and anti-tank guns were to receive priority, but it was realised that the former would have to be kept in action until the end.

General Paget, while he had shown a high sense of realism in his earlier reports on the situation, was reluctant to throw in his hand if any chance of saving the situation remained. Of the British commanders he was the most closely in touch with General Ruge and therefore the one most competent to estimate Norwegian reactions to the news of a British withdrawal.

He signalled Whitehall in emphatic terms that in his opinion the situation at the front did not necessitate evacuation, provided that effective action could be taken to deal with enemy aircraft which continued to operate with little hindrance and were systematically and thoroughly destroying his base and communications. The troops, he pointed out, were in good heart, but urgently in need of artillery support, of which as yet he had none.

## 7

### *Action at Otta*

Early on April 28th Paget visited Ruge to break the news of the proposed evacuation to him. The Norwegian Commander-in-Chief had not been unprepared for this development, but he spoke strongly of the betrayal of his country. This he followed up with a signal to the C.I.G.S. strongly protesting against the withdrawal. He felt that he had been wasting his troops by maintaining the costly and wearing struggle north of Oslo on the assumption that British reinforcement would arrive in adequate numbers to stem the tide. For the British to give up within a few days and without landing any serious force would constitute a most damaging blow to the confidence of the Norwegian army and people. His whole plan of operations had been based on the retention of Dombaas as an essential pivot of manœuvre either against Oslo or Trondheim, or against the German communications in the Osterdal. (Even now, it seems, Ruge did not grasp the full scale of the proposed evacuation and did not think in terms of the total abandonment of the Trondheim project and the evacuation of all central Norway.)

Paget was sufficiently influenced by Ruge's arguments and by his own confidence in the staying power of his troops, given a modicum of support weapons and air cover, to signal the C.I.G.S. emphasising the hazardous nature of evacuation under the present conditions and pointing out that it was only possible with Ruge's co-operation. Dombaas could be held, he wrote, 'for a time' if further landings were carried out and air and artillery support provided. All three conditioning factors were, as we see, most unlikely to be fulfilled, in view of Massy's recommendations to the War Office.

That afternoon Paget received the final decision of the Cabinet, through his corps commander. The decision to evacuate must remain irrevocable. His Majesty's Government had expressed themselves as deeply moved by General Ruge's appeal, but their inability to provide air support and the strength of the German advance from the south left them with no option. General Ruge was to be told that we were continuing to help and would aim at embarking his army so that it might fight elsewhere in Norway properly equipped and supported. In a further signal that evening he added that the possibility of adequate air support had been fully investigated and that it would not be possible to provide this on a scale that would enable Paget to keep his forces fighting or even to maintain them.

The events of the day around the base provided sufficient commentary on the decision which had been reached. The Germans had evidently decided to have done with Aandalsnes, and air attacks continued to be launched against the port almost without intermission throughout the day. By evening there was little left of the place. A British sloop in the fjord kept up fire against the raiders and succeeded in downing one of them but presently ran out of ammunition. After that the bombers had things all their own way. As the result of the destruction of supplies in this and previous raids Brigadier Hogg was compelled to put all troops on half rations from that day onwards, and it seems clear enough that, had the decision to evacuate forthwith not been taken, we might have been faced with the danger of wholesale surrenders by our troops owing to acute shortage of food and ammunition. Paget had been right to urge a reconsideration of the decision to withdraw, for viewed from the purely tactical point of view the situation was by no means desperate. But modern warfare depends increasingly upon supply, and the quartermaster is the final arbiter of battles. In this case there was no possible ambiguity about his verdict.

The final decision to abandon southern Norway was taken, ironically enough, at the very time when the British troops in the field, though lacking the support weapons which their commander quite rightly adjudged the pre-requisite of success, had administered the sharpest check upon the oncoming Germans which they received in the course of the campaign. The defence of the Otta position by the Green Howards was perhaps the most satisfactory action fought by British land forces in Norway.

The village of Otta stands on a tongue of land where the river of the same name enters the Laagen river at an acute angle. Approach to this position is covered by two spurs, each about 1,200 feet high,

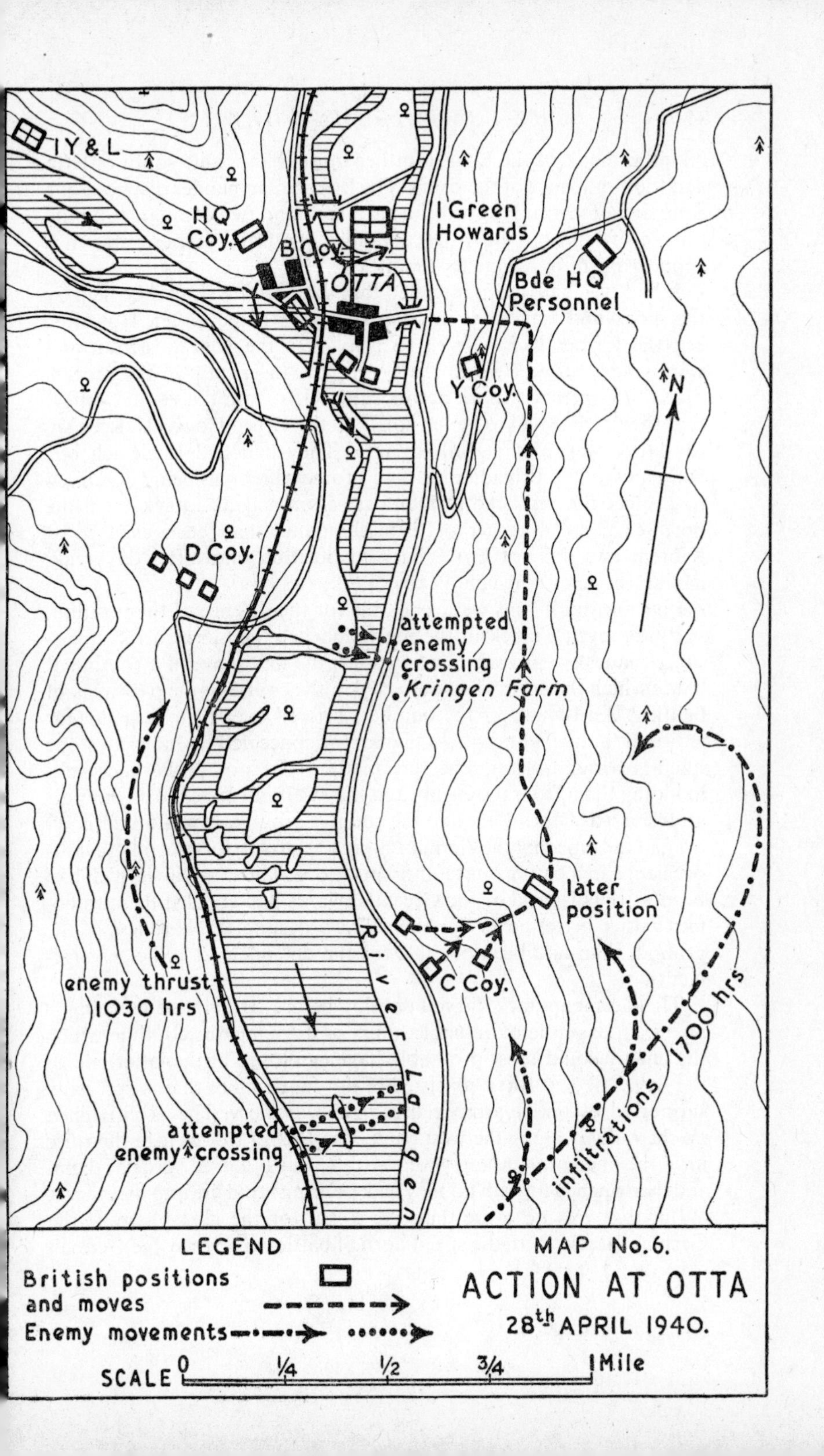


MAP No. 6.
ACTION AT OTTA
28th APRIL 1940.

on either bank of the Laagen rather more than a mile south of Otta and the confluence of the rivers. The British commander disposed one company of Green Howards on each spur and two companies on the tongue of land on which Otta stands. The fifth company was in a support position on the east bank.

It had originally been intended that the position should be held by the York and Lancaster in conjunction with the Green Howards, but the former had suffered so heavily in the Kjörem action and were so exhausted (two of their companies were still in the process of making their way back across snowdrifts from the Heidal valley) that the defence had to be left solely to the Green Howards. Even so, the latter were not at full strength. They had had to detach one company to join Brigadier Morgan's force which was being organised to protect the rail-head at Dombaas from a flank attack from the north-east, and another of their companies had been engaged at Kjörem and did not arrive back in position until after daybreak, having retreated throughout the night.

Five anti-tank guns were available for the defence of the position.

It was seven o'clock in the morning when the German reconnaissance planes swept over our positions, the first move in a routine of battle which the enemy had perfected in the course of the past week of fighting. An hour later the bombers arrived over their targets. Our anti-tank guns had been to some extent concealed by building stone sangars around them, but this method did not prove successful in hiding them from the enemy and they were subjected to a heavy air attack as was Otta village and the country around. It was noted, however, at the time that the Germans were less successful than on previous occasions in locating our infantry positions. The extra time which had been at the disposal of the Green Howards had enabled them to obtain rather better cover for themselves, despite the hardness of the ground, than had been possible for the defenders in earlier engagements.

The German attack did not develop before 10.30 in the morning—again, an example of valuable hours of daylight wasted, time which the enemy could most profitably have employed at the latter end of the day. The first wave consisted of not much more than a company supported by tanks, armoured cars, and artillery. They approached up the railway along the west bank. The British troops held their fire until the oncoming infantry were within four hundred yards of them, and then opened up with all they had, pouring rapid fire into the enemy.

But that was no more than the signal for the next phase of the German attack. With the speed born of battle experience, the German infantry promptly deployed to either flank, and the artillery and air began to batter away at our positions as they had done at Kjörem and Kvam. With nothing more than small arms and 3-inch mortars at their disposal the British counter-fire was nevertheless so controlled and accurate that it caused the enemy many casualties. The German tanks, never very effective in this type of action where the front was narrow and numbers of no avail, failed conspicuously in their attempt to exploit along the road close to the river. A single British anti-tank gun knocked out two medium and one light tank. Nor was an attempt of German troops to cross the river from west bank to east in rubber boats, in order to take our forces to the east of the stream in the flank, any more successful. They made the attempt too close to our lines, and the party was practically annihilated. An effort to erect a pontoon bridge to span the river was also frustrated and about twenty-five Germans were killed in the process.

All through the afternoon it was a tale of frontal attacks on the west bank, repeatedly repulsed with loss, and infiltration up the wooded slopes to the east, combined with further unsuccessful efforts to pass troops across from the west side of the river, where they were firmly held, to the east, where there seemed more possibility of exploitation.

Already General Paget had decided that a withdrawal would be necessary that night, and it was once more a case of holding off the Germans until darkness, and preventing such an infiltration as had almost proved disastrous at Kjörem. One British platoon, sent to deal with the German enveloping movement on our left, was caught by cross-fire and practically wiped out while getting into position. At about five o'clock Captain Armitage, commanding C Company of the Green Howards who held the spur east of the river, withdrew his men further up the slopes and to the rear to a position where a precipice behind them prevented any possibility of a close-range attack from that side. Here they successfully pinned down German forces about double their size and frustrated the further progress of the enveloping movement.

Before nightfall the German effort was temporarily spent, and fighting had died down to desultory exchanges of artillery and machine-gun fire. The forward troops were to have begun their withdrawal at 10 p.m. that night, the support troops an hour later. But once again, as so often during this long retreat, the orders failed to get through to all the troops and C Company in their outpost position on the ridge above the river never received information about the withdrawal. This turned out to be in some ways a fortunate accident, for the Germans launched a final desperate attack about 10.30 p.m. which was repulsed with heavy losses. Had C Company received their orders they would by this time have been on the move, counting on the reluctance of the Germans to engage in night operations, though it was as yet scarcely dark.

After repulsing the German attack Captain Armitage broke off the engagement and dividing his men into four detachments instructed them to move off in absolute silence, keeping as near the crest of the ridge as possible, with a rendezvous at Otta. Most of that night journey had to be done on hands and knees over icy rocks, but the troops were undetected and seven hours later they reached Otta only to find that the remainder of the battalion had already evacuated the position. They then started off on the thirty-mile march back to Dombaas, which was reached the same day. Captain Armitage had throughout shown the greatest skill and determination as a commander in the field and considerable resolution and resource in bringing his command safely back without loss.

The rest of the battalion withdrew without interference from the enemy, who showed little desire or ability to press home the attack after taking heavy casualties throughout the day. As much ammunition as possible was shot away immediately before the withdrawal; the rest had to be abandoned, as had the five anti-tank guns, all of which were rendered unfit for further use.

It had been a model defensive action by troops who had to contend against every superiority of arms and equipment. The Green Howards had fought splendidly, and the classic British tradition of accurate and controlled infantry fire had vindicated itself; but against the enemy superiority in air and artillery the accurate marksmanship of our infantry could no more play a decisive role than could the longbow after the coming of cannon. The engagement at Otta does credit to the troops who fought there; but it could not affect the issue in Norway or give reason to modify the decision to evacuate.

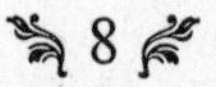

## 8

## *The Evacuation*

The evacuation from Aandalsnes would now be conditioned by the moral need to cover the Norwegian troops in the neighbourhood, by the logistics of the shipping available and by the capacity of the single road and railway from Dombaas to the sea. The remnants of Morgan's

148th Brigade were now taking over from the Norwegians along the line of communications between Dombaas and the sea, where the danger of interception or sabotage by enemy parachutists was very real. Paget, in conference with Ruge at 9 a.m. on April 29th, undertook to hold Dombaas throughout the day. Ruge would order his troops to carry out the necessary demolitions along the road and railway north-east of Dombaas and hoped to have them clear of the Romsdal (the Dombaas-Aandalsnes valley) by May 1st. In the Osterdal the Norwegian troops were fighting magnificently and they twice re-took Röros from the Germans during the course of these days, but no successes here could prevent a link-up between the German forces based on Oslo and those in Trondheim, once the former reached Dombaas; nor could they affect the general strategy of the campaign in any other respect. The men of Röros were fighting for honour, but there would soon be nothing else left that they could fight for.

The action of Otta gave the hard-pressed British troops in the Gudbrandsdal a welcome day of comparative quiet. The Green Howards having leap-frogged back through the supporting troops, the K.O.Y.L.I. now held the forward position, just in front of Dombaas, while both Green Howards and York and Lancaster re-organised in and around the village. They were little troubled from the air, for the German planes spent the day systematically polishing off what remained of Aandalsnes, machine-gunning everything moving along the road up the Romsdal from the port, and dealing with our landing-ground at Setnesmoen, in the immediate vicinity, whither the remnants of the Gladiator squadron had been evacuated.

There was still considerable doubt about the date and manner of our evacuation, and the difficulty of communication between the base and the forward areas led to further misunderstandings. Paget was hoping that, since the decision to evacuate was final, the withdrawal might begin that night. Brigadier Hogg, however, at the base still knew nothing of Paget's views, and in the small hours of the Monday morning he again signalled the War Office on his own responsibility. He stated that no decision regarding evacuation had yet come from Paget, that the Staff officer sent to obtain it reported that the General was about to engage in battle against very heavy odds from which only a portion of the troops might emerge. The road was breaking up under the combined effect of the enemy bombing, the heavy transport that it was compelled to carry and the thaw. Hogg suggested the establishment of a defensive perimeter to facilitate the evacuation of non-fighting troops and such troops from the forward areas as might return to the base. He requested ships and aircraft to cover the evacuation on the nights of April 29th–30th, and April 30th–May 1st.

Paget saw Ruge again in the course of the afternoon and found that the latter, while personally friendly, resented the decision having been taken without consulting the commanders in the field and without giving them full reasons for it. Ruge stated that he was himself prepared to advise his Government in favour of continuation of the war if any hope could be held out of further Allied intervention in Norway. Otherwise, he would advise peace negotiations.

The two Generals parted on friendly terms, and the C.I.G.S. subsequently signalled Ruge to assure him that it was our intention to continue to fight for Norway. The Aandalsnes evacuation in no way weakened this resolve, and the Allied forces operating in the northern part of the country were being rapidly reinforced.

Paget had hoped to begin evacuation that night, but the shipping situation did not render it practicable, though the York and Lancaster (now reduced to 16 officers and 280 other ranks) were moved by rail and on foot (the line was cut at Lesjaskog) back to Aandalsnes with a view to being embarked at once. The Germans seem to have suspected that evacuation was imminent, for early that night, contrary to their practice, their bombers raided Aandalsnes, their targets being brightly illuminated by the blazing houses and woods. In the end, only a few hundred, including wounded, were embarked and sailed in the course of the night. Those evacuated included the King of Norway and his personal attendants and the French and British Legations, all of whom sailed from Molde for Tromsö in the far north.

Tuesday, April 30th, saw the last action between 'Sickleforce' and the enemy. The K.O.Y.L.I. were now holding the most advanced position, in front of Dombaas, with three companies forward and two in reserve. They had the support of a battery of four Norwegian field guns and in this respect were more fortunate than any British force had been in the successive stands made in the Gudbrandsdal. All was peaceful until the afternoon when towards 4 p.m. a large body of German infantry came into sight along the road, without tanks or supporting artillery but dragging hand-carts with mortars. Our troops, who were extremely well concealed, the cover being abundant, opened fire, and the Germans, taken by surprise, suffered heavy losses in the first minutes. On this, as on some previous occasions, their ground reconnaissance was markedly inadequate, and the tendency to advance with infantry in close formation without a covering patrol to probe our position once again cost them unnecessary loss of life.

Following this clash, a single German plane swept low over our troops dive-bombing them until brought down by small-arms fire. The engagement did not continue long, for the Germans lacked their customary artillery and air support and showed little disposition to press the attack. By 6 p.m. Brigadier Kent-Lemon was able to report that the danger to his position from the frontal attack was at an end and there was no sign of a flank attack from the north-east. During the evening he withdrew his force, company by company, to Dombaas where a train was waiting in the shelter of a tunnel which also housed our rations and ammunition and stores. The bulk of the troops were to leave by this train, the rear parties by motor transport.

That night over 2,600 troops, chiefly from the 148th Brigade, 1st York and Lancaster, Royal Marines, and base detachments, were successfully evacuated from Aandalsnes, Molde, and two neighbouring ports.

The troops, journeying by train over the sixty-mile stretch from Dombaas, had a lengthy and adventurous journey. The train got away soon after 11.0 p.m. and, proceeding slowly through the mountain gorges, had reached Lesjaskog, thirty-six miles from Aandalsnes by 1 a.m. on the morning of May 1st. German aircraft had been raiding up and down the valley throughout the previous day, but the line was believed clear. Suddenly the weary soldiers, huddled together in carriage and truck, were awakened by a violent shock. The train had crashed in a newly blown bomb crater.

Both engines were overturned, and the front trucks were telescoped. Many casualties resulted, and it was clear that there would be no possibility of restarting the train. No other train could be got further forward than the tunnel at Verma, seventeen miles distant. So the exhausted and shaken troops had to set out on a long march, without even the protection of darkness after the first hour or two.

At Verma there was a long tunnel, which proved invaluable as a hide-out throughout the whole of that dismal May Day. In view of the dominance which the enemy enjoyed in the air there could be no question of any train leaving Verma by daylight. Some M.T. was collected, which went up the road and managed to bring in stragglers, and by 9 a.m. the last of the column had arrived. They had suffered nothing worse on the march than a little machine-gunning from early morning reconnaissance planes—another example of an opportunity missed by the enemy. The troops had brought their equipment back with them, and their morale, despite the depressing conditions, was remarkably good. Throughout the day they lay hid up in the Verma tunnel, where already an ammunition train was waiting and also the train which was to carry them back to Aandalsnes. The men dropped down on the rails and slept in their full equipment just where they lay, packed close like sardines so that, as General Paget has remarked, 'it was scarcely possible to move without walking on prostrate men'.

There was, of course, the danger that the enemy, whose morning reconnaissance had noted the wrecked train and the men on the march, might follow up in haste and scupper the entire force, about 1,700 strong, in the tunnel. They had certainly observed the troops enter the tunnel and their airmen continually bombed and machine-gunned its entrances during the course of the day, though without inflicting any casualties. A greater danger than that of spasmodic air attacks came from the possibility of a quick follow-up by the ground troops. The demolitions carried out when Dombaas was evacuated helped to delay the pursuit, but about 5 p.m. the standing patrol which the Royal Marines had placed over the gorge was engaged by a German advance guard. In the face of superior numbers it was compelled to withdraw upon Verma, whereupon the Green Howards and K.O.Y.L.I. promptly deployed and the enemy did not press the attack. They followed up so closely, however, that their forward troops under General Pellengahr arrived in Aandalsnes by 10 a.m. on May 2nd.

It had been planned that the train should start on its journey at 10.30 p.m., by which time darkness would have fallen. General Paget, who had come forward the previous night and who spent the day in the tunnel with his troops, felt, however, that no further delay could be risked. He therefore ordered the train to be got ready for an immediate departure by daylight, a decision that seems justified by the circumstances and was in fact justified by the event. It did not prove possible to get the train started, however, before 8.30 in the evening. Then both the troops in the tunnel and the rearguard in the gorge were successfully withdrawn, arriving without further mishap at Aandalsnes at 11 o'clock at night and promptly going on board H.M. ships, *Manchester*, *Birmingham*, and *Calcutta*, which were lying in the harbour. The rear party of Royal Engineers, after having destroyed all the remaining guns and prepared demolitions in the port area, went on board H.M.S. *Auckland* and all were at sea by half an hour after midnight.

The number of troops evacuated from Aandalsnes and the adjacent embarkation points was 340 on the night of April 29th–30th; 2,627 on the night of April 30th–May 1st; 2,117 on the night of May 1st–2nd. A total of 5,084.

The following casualties were reported after the completion of the evacuation. The figures are somewhat misleading, unless it is realised that when a force is involved in almost constant retreat there is a little means of identifying the killed and many of those actually killed will appear among the missing.

| | *Officers* | *Other Ranks* |
|---|---|---|
| Killed . . . . | 4 | 17 |
| Wounded . . . | 21 | 128 |
| Missing . . . | 76 | 1,156 |
| Total . | 101 | 1,301 |

The heaviest losses were those sustained by the 148th Brigade as a result of its fighting at Faaberg and Tretten. From its two battalions it reported 52 officers and 654 other ranks lost. Thirteen officers and about 400 men were ultimately brought back to Aandalsnes and re-embarked. The 15th Brigade, out of its three battalions, lost 32 officers and 552 other ranks, a considerably smaller proportion.

Forward units lost almost all their equipment, and it would seem that insufficient attention was paid to the importance of troops bringing their small arms with them. The York and Lancaster reported a deficiency of 576 rifles; the K.O.Y.L.I. 211; the Green Howards, who fought the very creditable action at Otta, only 26.

# CHAPTER III

# Namsos

## 1

### *The Landing*

THE landing at Namsos was planned as complementary to that at Aandalsnes with the object of forming the northern prong of the attack against Trondheim. The task in this case, though it proved formidable enough and, in fact, impracticable in execution, had not the complexity of the Aandalsnes operations.

At Namsos the force which was landed in mid-April had a definite and single objective—to get to Trondheim as quickly as possible. Their line of advance was to be southward, and pressure to divert any part of their force elsewhere did not occur until the Trondheim attack had been abandoned and evacuation was already imminent. At no time, also, did their advance take them as much as half the distance from their base that the vanguard of 'Sickleforce' covered in the first two or three days of the deceptively swift gallop to Lillehammer and beyond. They therefore escaped some, though not all, of the administrative problems that beset the latter force, and, apart from isolated units, no part of the force was threatened with outflanking and envelopment.

The story of 'Mauriceforce', which landed at Namsos on the night of April 16th–17th and was evacuated on the night of May 2nd–3rd, can therefore be told more briefly than that of 'Sickleforce'. But, though the period in which our troops were involved in close combat was very much shorter, the major causes of failure were identical—enemy air predominance, enemy superiority of armaments (particularly of those suitable for campaigning in a country of the nature of Norway) and our own administrative limitations.

Major-General Carton de Wiart, V.C., an officer with a fine record for personal gallantry, had been entrusted with the general plan of operations on April 13th. 'Mauriceforce', was to be landed at Namsos, a small port nearly a hundred miles north of Trondheim. Namsos was larger and more pretentious than Aandalsnes. Its population was nearly double the size and its docking facilities somewhat greater. There was safe anchorage in the bay, with a depth of 20–25 fathoms, and the navigation was free from ice all the year round, unlike the inner waters of the Trondheim fjord further south.

The original landing-party here as at Aandalsnes, was a naval one, and it was expected to go ashore on the afternoon of April 13th or the morning of April 14th and secure Namsos and the important Bangsund bridge across the fjord east of the town. The main body consisting of Brigadier Morgan's two-battalion brigade, would follow. It was originally to have been landed on April 17th, before the news of the naval victory in the second battle of Narvik caused a re-disposition of the forces, Morgan's 148th Brigade being directed south to the Aandalsnes landing and the 146th Brigade (Brigadier C. G. Phillips) in turn diverted in transit from Narvik to Namsos. The Brigadier, who had sailed in a separate ship from the rest of his command, was also instructed to proceed to Namsos where he arrived on the day after the disembarkation of the vanguard of the 146th Brigade.

This brigade consisted of the 1/4th Lincolnshire (Lieut.-Colonel H. W. Newton), the 1/4th K.O.Y.L.I. (Lieut.-Colonel W. S. Hibbert) and the Hallamshire Battalion (1/4th York and Lancaster) (Lieut.-Colonel C. G. Robins).

Their disembarkation was to be followed either by that of the French Chasseurs Alpins or by the 147th Brigade, with its ancillary troops on April 20th–21st. The 126th Brigade, due to sail for France, might also be diverted to Norway. The first troops were to land with the bare minimum of stores and medical supplies.

The small advance party duly landed on April 14th, made contact with the Norwegians, and established their headquarters at the Grand Hotel. General Carton de Wiart himself arrived in Namsos fjord in a Sunderland with two staff officers in the course of the following afternoon, but, owing to the delays caused by an air raid and the necessity of transferring to a ship, did not actually get ashore until 11 p.m. He promptly called a conference on board that night and the important decision was taken that the heavily laden, slow and vulnerable troopships should not be brought up Namsos fjord but should be re-directed to Lillesjona, a hundred miles north of Namsos, and there trans-shipped to destroyers for the final stage of the journey. There was much to be said for this argument on the grounds of affording greater security to the troops, but it led to serious administrative difficulties owing to the fact that units which should have travelled together were broken up, drivers being landed without their vehicles, and so on.

The diversion of the 146th Brigade had been determined on the previous day as soon as the news of the naval victory at Narvik was received. It was a wise decision. Although administrative difficulties made the maintenance of large forces at Namsos or Aandalsnes impracticable without air superiority, and very difficult even with it, it was certainly right to shift the centre of gravity of our attack southwards from Narvik, where success would bring us only very limited strategic though important economic results, to the Trondheim area where success might save half Norway for the Allies.

Turning south, the two large converted luxury liners, *Chrobry* (carrying the Hallamshire, 55th Field Company R.E., and 146th Brigade Headquarters) and *Empress of Australia* (carrying the Lincolnshire and K.O.Y.L.I.) reached Lillesjona early on the morning of April 16th, where General Carton de Wiart arrived a little later. The latter had already had time to note one or two ominous factors that were likely to prejudice the chances of the expedition.

The first of these was the air activity of the enemy. Their planes had been active on both April 14th and April 15th and as yet we had no means of replying to them. It was for this reason the General had decided in favour of the slower and administratively vexatious method of trans-shipment of troops from transports to destroyers one hundred miles to the north. As early as April 15th he expressed himself as 'most concerned about the air situation'. Subsequent developments were to increase this concern.

In view of this, the absence of cover around Namsos was a matter of some importance. There were no large woods or other natural forms of concealment, and the snow, which still lay fully two feet deep in most places, formed the very reverse of camouflage.

Nor did the British commander anticipate very much help from the Norwegians. Cut off as they were in this sector from the main body of troops far to the south under General Ruge, the Norwegian troops, apart from the heroic garrison defending Hegra fort, had fallen right back from the Trondheim region and were now some distance to the north-east around the town of Grong and the shores of Lake Snaasa. They were no longer in touch with the Germans. Their commander, Colonel Getz, stressed, then and subsequently, their lack of equipment and training, and they could not, in Carton de Wiart's opinion be relied upon for any real assistance. The civil population of Namsos gave the impression of being bewildered and somewhat apathetic.

General Carton de Wiart had received instructions that the object of the force landing in central Norway was to provide encouragement to the Norwegian Government, form a rallying-point for the Norwegian armed forces, and secure a base for subsequent operations in Scandinavia. The particular rôle assigned to him was to secure the Trondheim area and, subsequently, the road and rail communications of the town, more especially towards the east.

Carton de Wiart came to the conclusion that, despite the lack of supporting arms and the unchallenged predominance of the enemy in the air, the earlier and the speedier that the advance upon Trondheim could be developed, the greater the chances of success. He had hoped to get his two battalions of the 146th Brigade ashore on the night of April 16th–17th and to be in a position to attack by April 21st. He learned for the first time during the night of April 15th–16th that 600 Royal Marines were being landed at Aandalsnes on April 17th and that, as it was necessary to exploit this landing to the full with any troops that were available, the 148th Brigade might be used to reinforce them. General Carton de Wiart was asked in a signal by the C.I.G.S. how he would view the subtraction of this force from his command.

The General replied, very reasonably, that he would need an approximately equivalent body in its place, and suggested the Chasseurs Alpins. These, it was decided, were to follow the 146th Brigade, which would now be placed at his disposal.

After the arrival of the General at Lillesjona on the morning of April 16th the trans-shipment of the troops of this brigade began to take place. German early morning air reconnaissance had spotted the concentration of shipping at Lillesjona and, less than an hour after the trans-shipment to the destroyers had begun, a number of aircraft swooped up from the south and proceeded to bomb the ships. Though we suffered no losses at this time, the British commander decided that the destroyers should sail forthwith, carrying such troops as they already had on board, rather than remain stationary—a perilous target for the enemy attackers. *Afridi*, *Nubian*, *Matabele*, *Mashona*, and *Sikh*, therefore got under way for Namsos, carrying Carton de Wiart, Lieut.-Colonel Newton, acting commander of the Brigade since Brigadier Phillips had not yet arrived, with 36 officers and 1,208 other ranks.

The convoy was repeatedly attacked in the course of its voyage but succeeded in getting through unscathed and reached Namsos at 9 p.m. on the evening of Tuesday, April 16th, with about five hours of the short northern night available for disembarkation.

From Namsos there are two roads south towards Trondheim. The more direct route, which is also the better road, runs roughly south by west crossing the Namsos fjord by the Bangsund bridge a mile east of the port. The alternative road runs due east to Grong, crosses to the south bank of the Namsen river there, then continues south and finally south-west along the northern shore of Lake Snaasa. Both roads join two or three miles north of the little town of Steinkjer, which stands on an isthmus between Lake Snaasa to the north-east and the head of the Trondheim fjord to the south-west. From Steinkjer onwards the road to Trondheim runs along or close to the shore of the fjord.

Three points of importance stand out from this description of the topography.

The first is that the supply lines of the Allied force would necessarily be dependent upon the bridges at Bangsund and Grong respectively. The route through Bangsund would be the natural line of advance. But, in view of the extreme vulnerability of the Bangsund bridge to bombing from the air—it was about half a mile long—it would be essential to treat the longer route through Grong as a supplementary line that might have to be developed into the main channel of supply and reinforcement.

Secondly, the position of Steinkjer covering the most important, though not the only isthmus along the route, made it vital that our troops should reach there before the enemy. It was the first position upon which a defence of the Namsos bridge-head could be organised.

Thirdly, from Steinkjer onwards the line of our advance would intermittently follow the fjord, always within easy range of ships' guns on its right, or seaward, flank. It was therefore vital for offensive purposes that the British fleet should have obtained control of the inner waters of the fjord by the time the land forces reached Steinkjer. Otherwise our troops would lay increasingly open to galling fire at close quarters from the flank and to the danger of a landing in their rear from the ships in the fjord, a danger that would increase with every mile that they advanced southward.

It was clear, therefore, that within a very few days Steinkjer would become of crucial importance. If we could reach and establish ourselves firmly at Steinkjer we should possess a satisfactory position for

*Photo: Imperial War Museum*

A ROAD-CONTROL POST: NAMSOS–STEINKJER

LOCAL TRANSPORT FOR AN A.-A. GUN

*Photo: Imperial War Museum*

STRETCHER BEARERS IN BOMBED NAMSOS

*Photo: Imperial War Museum*

CAMOUFLAGING A LORRY IN A NORWEGIAN VALLEY

*Photo: Imperial War Museum*

exploitation southwards. If we should fail to maintain ourselves there, Namsos could no longer be effectively defended.

The first wave of troops was disembarked with great speed. A great deal of stress was put upon the importance of concealment and of getting the men well dispersed and all stores cleared from the quay-side. In this way it was hoped that the enemy might be kept in ignorance of the scale of our landing and, to some extent, of the dispositions of our troops.

Headquarters was set up in Namsos. The long bridge where the river joins the fjord was guarded in strength by the Hallamshire, while others of the same battalion moved across preparatory to exploiting southward next day, and a detachment of the Lincolnshire, about 300 strong, moved east to Grong, thereby opening up the secondary route and also establishing contact with the local Norwegian troops of Colonel Getz, whose headquarters was now at Kvam, towards the southern end of Lake Snaasa.

By midnight General Carton de Wiart was able to inform the War Office that he had brought 1,000 men to Namsos that day and hoped to bring the remainder of Phillips's brigade on the morrow; he was occupying Grong, Bangsund, and probably positions astride Beitstadfjord, twenty-five miles south of Namsos. He added that enemy aircraft were still bombing at leisure.

Yet another change had been made with regard to the movement of the troops from their temporary anchorage at Lillesjona. Admiral Layton, the naval commander of the expedition, had decided that, in view of the absolute enemy air superiority, destroyers should not be used to convey the remainder of the troops to Namsos but that the men should, after all, sail in *Chrobry*. This involved further transshipment of troops, since most of those who remained were in the *Empress of Australia*. The task was achieved, and the troops sailed and reached Namsos just before dawn on April 17th; but in the violent hurry to get them disembarked, and the ship out of these narrow waters before the arrival of the German bombers, a good deal of kit and equipment was lost. *Chrobry*, and *Vanoc* which accompanied her, put out to sea before they had finished unloading the kit and only returned on the following night to complete the task.

However, all troops of the 146th Brigade had now been disembarked and dispersed before daylight and all stores were got under cover directly they were unloaded. When the German morning reconnaissance plane flew over—punctually on time, as always throughout the campaign—there was little for it to record. So far as swift unloading, dispersal, and concealment were concerned, we had conceded no points to the enemy.

General Carton de Wiart, however, was soon to be made sombrely aware of the hampering limitations within which he must endeavour to carry out his mission.

Changes of circumstances caused changes of plan but of these the local commander was not kept informed. This was the more unfortunate, in view of the fact that the operation against Trondheim, which was to have been a threefold offensive (Carton de Wiart from Namsos, Paget from Aandalsnes, Hotblack attacking directly into the Trondheim fjord), demanded the punctual and exact exchange of information among the three commanders and between them and the War Office. This was never achieved, and Carton de Wiart, who was committed to advancing southward under the impression that a synchronised attack would be made by Hotblack's force, was never informed that the decision to launch a direct attack upon Trondheim had been called off. Indeed, throughout its operations, 'Mauriceforce' was completely in the dark regarding the developments on the other fronts.

Not less unsatisfactory were the means at the disposal of the commander. The troops who composed the 146th Brigade were most imperfectly trained. Many had scarcely fired a rifle and they had practically no experience either with the Bren gun or with the 3-inch mortar, which was issued only a day or two before sailing. While they received an excessive quantity of clothing, no snowshoes or skis were provided, nor could the troops have used them if they had been. As a result the men were tied to operations along the roads, a fact which would have hampered their prospects of success in any serious advance and greatly increased the hazards of retreat.

The maps received were too few and out of date, difficult to read owing to indifferent printing, and only arrived in bulk when the campaign was almost over; signals equipment was quite inadequate and only four despatch riders were available for the whole brigade; practically no interpreters were supplied for working with the French troops which were to form an integral part of 'Mauriceforce'.

All these points became apparent at the outset of the campaign, and when the pulverising effect of the total German air predominance is taken into account it will be seen that from the first there were few grounds for optimism.

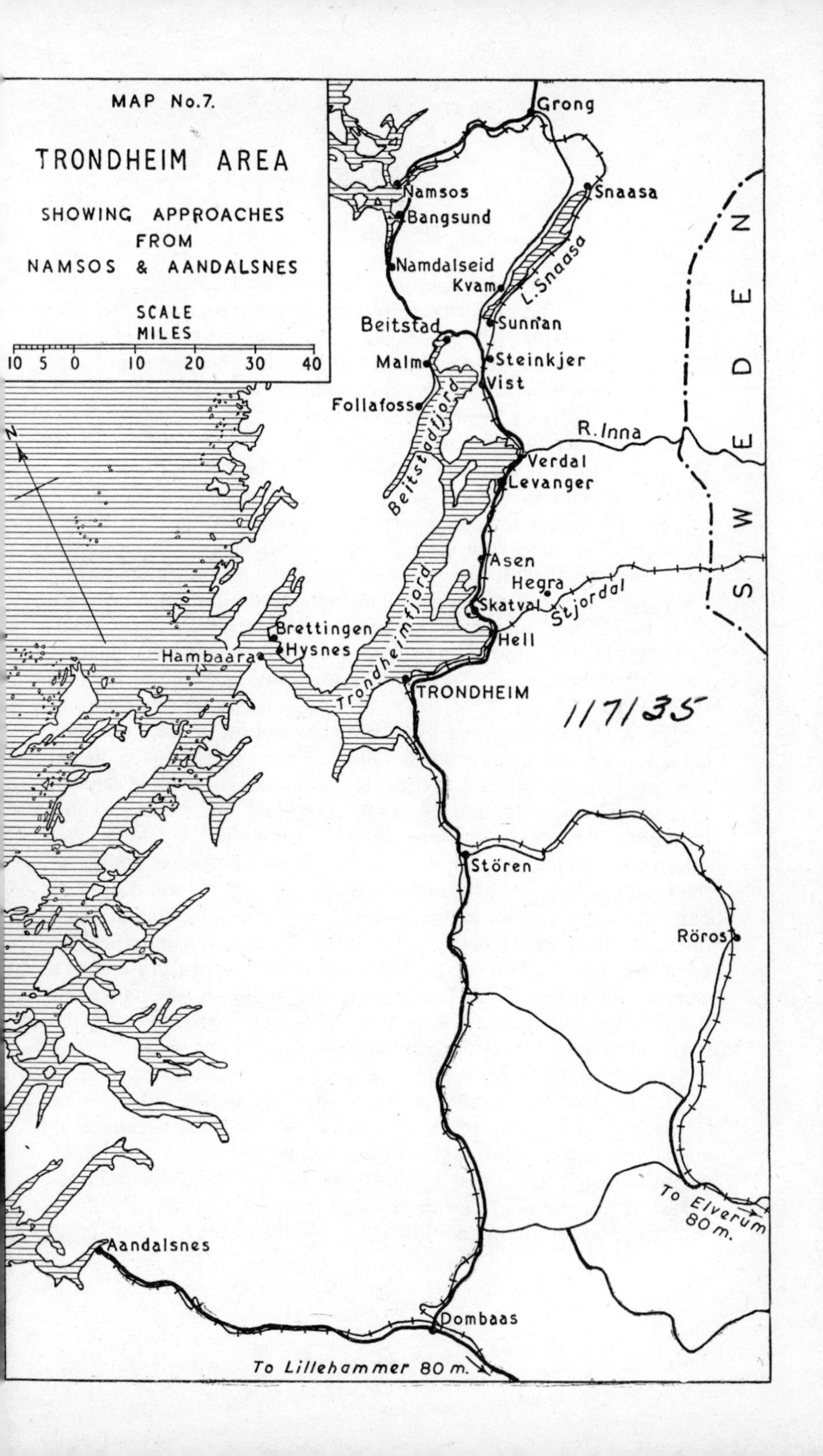

MAP No.7.
TRONDHEIM AREA
SHOWING APPROACHES
FROM
NAMSOS & AANDALSNES
SCALE
MILES
10 5 0 10 20 30 40
N
Grong
Namsos
Bangsund
Namdalseid
Snaasa
L. Snaasa
Kvam
Beitstad
Sunnan
Malm
Steinkjer
Vist
Follafoss
Beitstadfjord
R. Inna
Verdal
Levanger
Asen
Hegra
Stjordal
Skatval
Hell
Brettingen
Hysnes
Hambaara
Trondheimfjord
TRONDHEIM
SWEDEN
117135
Stören
Röros
To Elverum
80 m.
Aandalsnes
Dombaas
To Lillehammer 80 m.

## 2

### *The Advance*

With the Hallamshire, the only battalion that had yet arrived in full strength, General Carton de Wiart carried out a rapid exploitation southward on April 17th. One company was pushed on to Steinkjer and sent a platoon forward to Vist; another was established a little to the west at Malm, with a platoon holding the power-station at Follafoss, seven miles to the south-west.

All four places are situated on the innermost waters of Trondheim fjord. The ice here was now breaking up in the spring thaw.

At 9.30 p.m. General Carton de Wiart, who had visited the troops at Lillesjona in the course of the day, returned in H.M.S. *Afridi* to Namsos where he was joined by Brigadier Phillips, who had just arrived with his brigade-major from Narvik after having been twice attacked by enemy aircraft en route. In conference with these two officers and with Captain Vian of *Afridi* the G.O.C. outlined his plan for pushing on to Trondheim. The brigade would establish itself at Steinkjer next day, and forward troops would push on as far as Verdal, nearly twenty miles beyond, where another important bridge, at present guarded by Norwegian troops, crossed the Inna close to its entry into Trondheim fjord. Everything must be moved forward as fast as possible in order to leave room for the first echelon of French troops around Namsos, Bangsund and Grong. Three battalions of Norwegian troops under the command of Colonel Getz were available in the neighbourhood of Grong and Lake Snaasa to the east. All that was asked of this force was that it should provide parties of ski-troopers for protecting our flanks and for harassing operations towards Trondheim. This the Norwegians undertook to do. No mention was made of the existence of a strong pro-German element in Malm which had caused the senior Norwegian commander, General Laurantzon, to confiscate all wireless sets in the town. The dangers of espionage in this part of Norway were deemed considerable, and they explain to a great extent the extreme reserve of the British commander in conveying operational information to his Norwegian colleagues. In actual fact no case of leakage of any importance is known to have occurred and the enemy reaction to our movements was at first much slower than we had dared to hope.

Just before midnight Carton de Wiart received further instructions from the War Office. In addition to the 146th Brigade he would have under his command the first echelon of the French Chasseurs Alpins, three battalions strong, under the immediate direction of Général de Division Audet. Major-General Hotblack,[1] who would command all the forces involved in seaborne operations for the capture of Trondheim, would be withdrawn once his force had been effectively established ashore, and Carton de Wiart, who would be acting as a corps commander, would take control of them. The force based on Aandalsnes (still at this time under command of Brigadier Morgan, but to which General Paget was appointed two days later) would for the present remain an independent force under War Office control.

Estimates of German strength showed a rapid increase in the numbers of their troops believed to be operating from Trondheim. When Carton de Wiart landed at Namsos on April 15th the figure had been about 1,800 disposed from Trondheim along the railway eastwards to the Swedish frontier, masking the Norwegian-held fort of Hegra and covering the Vaernes airfield.[2] At that time they had pushed very few troops northward towards Namsos, their most advanced outpost being no further forward than a village called Asen, nearly forty miles short of Steinkjer.

By the morning of April 18th it was clear that the German reinforcement by air had been proceeding with considerable, indeed with unexpected, speed. They were now estimated to have some 3,500 men based on Trondheim, their control of the railway to Sweden appeared to be complete, and their forward patrols had reached Verdal. Assuming the accuracy of the earlier report, this would mean that air reinforcement had enabled them to double the size of their original force in barely three days, while their advanced troops had procured a further twenty miles depth for defensive manœuvre.

At Verdal a railway and a road bridge spanned the river. The former had been demolished by the local gendarmerie but the latter was still held by a weak company of Norwegian troops armed with rifles and machine-guns, and the German patrols having established this fact had withdrawn for the time being without attempting to force the position.

Through the day the newly arrived brigade commander wrestled

[1] This was the night of his accident.

[2] A good deal of confusion existed at this time, owing to ignorance of the calibre and carrying power of the guns in the Hegra fort, and for some little time it was believed that the Norwegian garrison in the fort was in a position to neutralise the German-held airfield. This was not the case, as our troops soon found to their cost, when the enemy began to launch short-range bombing attacks upon the base at Namsos.

with the intractable problems of establishing a solid administrative basis for our subsequent operations. He had been greeted with the information that, owing to the constant trans-shipment which had taken place between Lillesjona and Namsos, his men had just two days' instead of two weeks' supplies immediately available, and it was most unlikely that these could be increased on any important scale by local purchases. He found the local authorities, while helpful and friendly, quite lacking in any initiative. They appeared dazed and bewildered by the sudden turn of the wheel of war which had brought their own remote villages and salmon streams into the dazzling glare of imminent battle. They willingly agreed to the requisitioning of the town hospital for military purposes, but it soon became clear that a difficulty would arise over the use of local labour, which was urgently needed for clearing the quays. Little Norwegian currency was available for paying these men, and the fact called the whole credit position of the force in question.

Nor did Colonel Getz, the Norwegian commander at Grong, who was visited by Phillips in the course of the day, provide very much encouragement. He described his troops as 'inexperienced militia' whose rifles were obsolete and whose ammunition was in short supply and irreplaceable. However, the front being likely to be but a narrow one, the co-operation of Norwegian troops in regular formations in this sector did not appear essential to success.

After nightfall the next move forward was carried out. The Lincolnshire entrained for Steinkjer and were billeted in and around the town, their stores following them up in the course of the next day. The K.O.Y.L.I. were moved forward by train to positions further south among the villages between Steinkjer and the Verdal bridge which was about twenty miles to the south. The Hallamshire who had hitherto covered all the forward positions, could now be concentrated around Beitstad, on the northern side of the Beitstadfjord, the innermost of all the Trondheim inlets.

It was the objective of the British commander on April 19th, while pushing his troops forward in the direction of Trondheim as fast as possible, to make sure of the maximum concealment during the period while the Germans would continue to hold undisputed supremacy in the air. To this end all troop movements by day, except those absolutely indispensable to the maintenance of the force, were to be discouraged; no firing upon enemy aircraft was permitted, except as a means of defence against direct attack. This order was probably enjoined almost as much by the importance of conserving supplies of A.A. ammunition as by the need for concealment. Finally, wireless silence was to be maintained 'until such time as it was really necessary to break it'.

That these precautions did much to postpone the full impact of the German counterblow is quite certain. The enemy were still groping during these days and had little idea of the strength in which we had landed or precisely how far forward our troops had established themselves. The crew of a crashed German aircraft who were brought in during the day were found to have been engaged upon wireless interception and to have reported back that no wireless was operating anywhere in the Namsos area. The steps taken by General Carton de Wiart and Brigadier Phillips were therefore successful in reducing the information available to the enemy to the barest minimum.

That morning, however, an ominous shadow of the shape of things to come appeared in the Beitstadfjord. Two armed Norwegian trawlers and one or two motor-boats were sighted off Follafoss and other vessels off Tranes, just north of Verdal. It was clear that the enemy possessed, or would very soon possess, the capacity to operate against the flank of our troops from Steinkjer southward, unless and until a direct seaborne attack against Trondheim gave our ships control of the fjord.

At nine o'clock that night the first French convoy arrived off Namsos. It carried the 13th, 53rd, and 67th Battalions of Chasseurs Alpins with the headquarters staff of the demi-brigade under General Audet. Like the British convoy it had been attacked at sea, though unsuccessfully, during the last stages of its voyage.

By the morning of April 20th the troops were dispersed to bivouacs in the mountains with the exception of 200 men of the headquarters staffs, but unfortunately the unloading of the stores proved a considerably slower process than on the previous nights, when smaller numbers of troops had been landed. The German early morning reconnaissance flight at 5 a.m. spotted the kit and stores scattered all over the quayside, and the scale of the disembarkation immediately became apparent. Throughout the day wave after wave of German planes, appearing usually in flights of fifteen and at frequent intervals, swept over Namsos and before dusk the town had been almost wholly destroyed. The railway station had been demolished, rolling-stock shattered, the tracks torn to ribbons. The school, which contained most of the Hallamshire's stores, was destroyed. The hospital, which possessed a supply of medical stores estimated as good for two years at the normal rate of civilian consumption, was so badly damaged as to be unusable. The quays had suffered relatively little and the warehouses were almost intact. Force headquarters, which had moved out of the Grand Hotel three days before, also escaped, but it was clear that the whole situation as regards maintenance and supply had now taken on a new and most unfavourable aspect as the result of the day's air attack. The British command was faced with the same dilemma which was already becoming apparent at Aandalsnes. If only small forces, lightly equipped, were to be employed they might escape many of the destructive effects of heavy bombing, but they could not hope to achieve their military objective and must ultimately be destroyed on the ground; but if larger forces and their corollary of more equipment were landed, then they laid themselves open to the paralysis resulting from the deadly effects of destruction of their base facilities and supplies from the air. It was a vicious circle from which there was no escape unless we could achieve something approaching air parity. A small force could do nothing; a large one could not be maintained.

There was little development on land during the day. The K.O.Y.L.I. moved a company forward up to the village of Stiklestad, just short of the Verdal bridge, in daylight without any interference, and a section of the Royal Engineers moved forward to examine the possibility of repairing the Verdal railway bridge. The French troops, who were as yet in the rear positions, were bivouacked amid slushy snow around Namsos under conditions of extreme discomfort. It had been hoped that their ski-troops might have been employed as an offensive and harassing force against the enemy, but lack of motor transport prevented more than a small fraction of them ever being moved forward into contact positions.

A clash with the advanced forces of the Germans was now imminent. Reports reaching the War Office and retransmitted to Namsos suggested a steady increase of the numbers of the enemy at Trondheim. By April 19th they were believed to have some 5,000 men based on the port and it was not to be supposed that this represented a final figure. They were understood to be well-equipped in general, but lacking in field artillery.

The dispositions of the troops on either side suggested that the first action was likely to occur in the neighbourhood of the Verdal bridge, twenty miles south of Steinkjer, which had been reached both by our own forward elements and by a patrol of the enemy. But Brigadier Phillips in a signal to the War Office on the evening of April 20th, had called attention to a more dangerous possibility. The ice in the Trondheim fjord was already breaking up, as has been mentioned, and it was estimated that before the end of the month the fjord would be quite clear for navigation so that our line of advance from Steinkjer to Hell and thereafter to Trondheim would be open to any action by German naval craft in the upper reaches of Trondheim fjord—which, he pointed out, would be difficult to deal with, considering our lack of artillery.

The warning note had been sounded, and it is not clear why the authorities at home, who had decided on the previous day to abandon the sea-borne assault upon Trondheim, fixed for April 25th, did not inform Carton de Wiart of this fact. From now onwards his force would be advancing with its line of communications increasingly vulnerable to attack by naval craft and by the troops which might be landed from them.

## 3

### *Action at Vist*

Already the Brigadier had accurately appreciated the position, and before the action actually developed orders had been issued to pull back our advanced forces from their positions in the neighbourhood of Verdal. This decision is important, because when the news of the action at Steinkjer (more properly the action at Vist) reached England it was believed that 'Mauriceforce', pushing blindly ahead, had run slap into something in the nature of an ambush. This was very far from being the case. The commander on the spot was perfectly well aware of the situation before the action opened and was already taking steps to minimise the potential hazards to his force.

The orders issued at first light on Sunday, April 21st (that same day that saw the British troops in the Aandalsnes sector going forward to relieve the Norwegians south of Lillehammer only to be caught up in their retreat) instructed the K.O.Y.L.I. to pull back their advanced company and the detachment of R.E. from the neighbourhood of Verdal bridge and Stiklestad and to concentrate on a line from the Strommen causeway to Röra and to the north round Maere and Sparbu. The advantage of these dispositions was that they provided for practically the entire battalion the cover of the big Strommen lake on their west flank into which enemy warships could not penetrate. But the move implied the abandonment of any attempt to make good the Verdal crossing of the Inna and therefore necessarily the abandonment of the further advance upon Levanger and Trondheim.

The Lincolnshire were to hold their positions from Vist back through Steinkjer to Egge; the Hallamshire were to remain in reserve around Beitstad, Malm, Follafoss, Elden and Namdalseid, well to the north of the Steinkjer isthmus.

Soon after daybreak a small 300-ton German vessel, followed by a German destroyer, was seen passing through the Inderröy narrows into the Beitstadfjord, and a little later two armed trawlers were observed sailing through the straits in the opposite direction. These moves appeared to presage the possibility of an attack against the rear-most of our battalions, the Hallamshire, or—which was more probable—against the Steinkjer isthmus itself, with a view to cutting off the retreat of the troops echeloned from Steinkjer southwards—about two-thirds of the British force. The Lincolnshire accordingly detached a carrier platoon to cover the beach at Egge, one of the few points along that stretch of coast where there was really deep water close inshore and therefore where a landing was to be feared.

It was 6 a.m. when the action of Vist (though it was, in fact, a scattered operation covering a wide area) opened with the approach to the Verdal road bridge of a German force about 200 strong, the vanguard of the 1st Battalion of the 130th Regiment, veterans of the Polish campaign, who had been transported by air to Vaernes and who now received the specific task of seizing and holding the bridge.

One part of the battalion was to attack from the south, coming up by the main Trondheim road, while another would be landed on the Trones peninsula to take the position in the rear. The Norwegians had only about 80 men armed with heavy machine-guns to cover both the road and the railway bridge (for there was a possibility of the enemy repairing the latter sufficiently to effect a crossing there). They engaged the Germans, and the section of Royal Engineers which was on the spot deployed in defensive positions to support them. No explosives had been available for mining the bridge, which was merely defended by a wired barricade across it. The troops on the north bank kept up a brisk fire from the houses of Verdalsoren, from earthworks close to the river and from the railway trucks on which they had mounted their machine-guns. Several German attempts to rush the bridge, using hand-grenades to keep the defenders down, were beaten off; but after about an hour and a half news was received that a German force of unknown strength had landed on the Trones peninsula, about a couple of miles to the rear of the Verdal bridge. This was one of three or four landings made on the Anglo-Norwegian flank in the course of the morning.

The Norwegian commander accordingly decided to withdraw his men to prevent them being caught between two fires. He detached a machine-gun section to cover the debouchment from Trones and

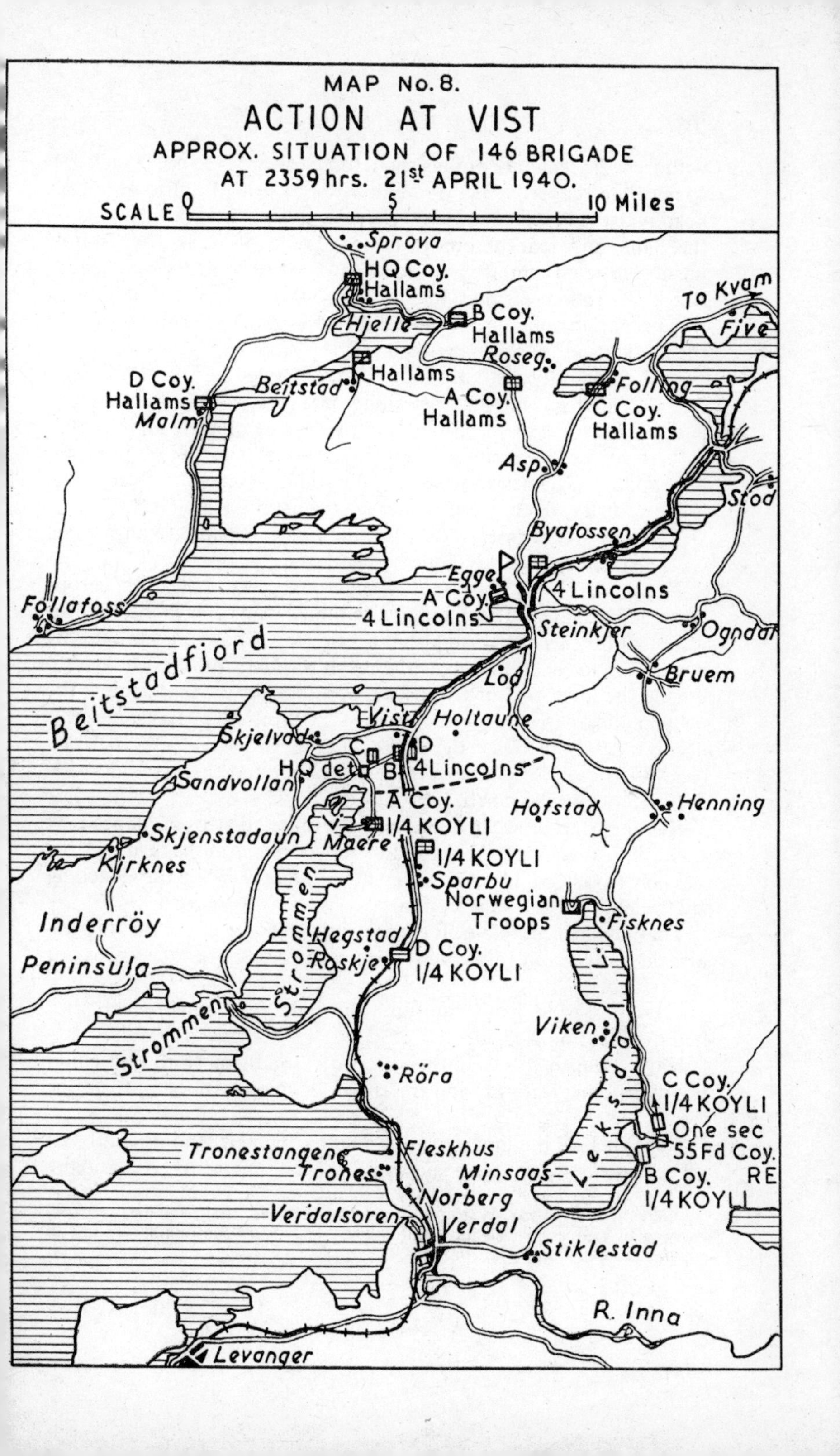
MAP No. 8.
ACTION AT VIST
APPROX. SITUATION OF 146 BRIGADE
AT 2359 hrs. 21st APRIL 1940.
SCALE 0 5 10 Miles
Sprova
HQ Coy. Hallams
Hjelle
B Coy. Hallams
To Kvam
Five
Roseg
Hallams
Beitstad
D Coy. Hallams
Malm
A Coy. Hallams
Folling
C Coy. Hallams
Asp
Stod
Byafossen
Egge
4 Lincolns
A Coy. 4 Lincolns
Follafoss
Steinkjer
Ogndal
Beitstadfjord
Lod
Bruem
Vist
Holtaune
Skjelvad
C
D
HQ det
B
4 Lincolns
Sandvollan
A Coy.
Hofstad
Henning
1/4 KOYLI
Skjenstadaun
Maere
1/4 KOYLI
Kirknes
Sparbu
Norwegian Troops
Fisknes
Inderröy
Peninsula
Strommen
Hegstad
Roskje
D Coy. 1/4 KOYLI
Strommen
Viken
Röra
C Coy. 1/4 KOYLI
One sec 55 Fd Coy. RE
Leksdal
Tronestangen
Fleskhus
Trones
Minsaas
B Coy. 1/4 KOYLI
Norberg
Verdalsoren
Verdal
Stiklestad
R. Inna
Levanger

withdrew the remainder of his small force towards the north and east. Meanwhile reports were beginning to pour into the British brigade headquarters of the landing of German troops at various points on the flank and rear of our positions. Some of these were simply unsubstantiated rumours, passed on by civilians on hearsay evidence.[1] But it was soon clear that, in addition to the force landed at Trones, three separate columns were established ashore and moving against the flank of our position between Steinkjer and Verdal.

1. A force estimated at about 400 had landed at Skjenstadaun at 5.30 a.m. and was moving east along the north coast of the Inderröy peninsula against the positions held by the Lincolnshire at Vist.

2. A force of unknown strength had landed in the same neighbourhood at Kirknes and was moving south to secure the Strommen isthmus, from which it could operate against the K.O.Y.L.I.

3. An hour or so later, yet another landing was made at Vangshyllen on the extreme tip of the Inderröy peninsula.

The position was not acutely dangerous, certainly less dangerous than a landing at the Steinkjer isthmus would have been. For, although the Germans had about a battalion ashore on our flank by about 8.30 in the morning, as the result of the dispositions taken up during the night by our troops we were largely covered against the new landings by the broad extent of Strommen Lake. It was necessary only to block the approaches at either end—the narrow, road-wide Strommen causeway in the south and the two-mile wide Vist isthmus in the north.

But these negative advantages were more than overbalanced by the technical advantages enjoyed by the Germans in the field.

Their troops could manœuvre across country, while ours, lacking snow-shoes or skis, were confined to movement by road.

They enjoyed complete air superiority and could utilise the Vaernes airfield, only about thirty miles distant, as a base for attacks on our troops.

They possessed heavy mortars and light field guns, which they had mounted on sledges.

Having armed vessels in the waters of Trondheim fjord they could bombard our positions, and the roads leading up to them, from the sea.

Nevertheless, the first moves to counter the new landings and seal off the enemy troops were successful for the time being. A company

[1] General Carton de Wiart subsequently reported that Intelligence from Norwegian sources proved most unreliable. 'They were continually sending in erroneous reports and wild rumours.'

of the Lincolnshire was moved forward from Steinkjer to strengthen the position at Vist. These new arrivals were posted in some cottages about a mile in advance of the village, with a fair field of fire, and began to loophole and sandbag them for defence. A further detachment was sent to the southern end of the Vist isthmus to cover a cross-roads near the Strommen lake, where the advancing German troops might be expected to appear. At the same time two companies of K.O.Y.L.I. were moved forward, one to block the Strommen causeway, the other to cover an advance northward from the Trones landing force.

These dispositions were skilfully made and appeared to check the advance. The German force moving upon Strommen, observing that it had lost its race for the causeway, swung away northward to support the advance against Vist.

This latter place was clearly becoming the focal point of the battle and the pivot of our defensive position. A German success against the K.O.Y.L.I. at the southern end of the line would merely result in thrusting them back upon the Lincolnshire, whereas, if the Lincolnshire could be dislodged from their positions and overrun, there was great risk that the K.O.Y.L.I. might be cut off. Accordingly, from about noon onwards the enemy began a series of intense attacks against Vist, mortaring and machine-gunning our troops, particularly in the sector nearest the coast, while infantry equipped with snow-shoes began to infiltrate through the gaps between our posts which were too widely spaced to block the whole isthmus. Major Black, commanding the two forward companies, who were bearing the brunt of the action, therefore withdrew them at about 6 p.m. to a position just west of Vist.

The same policy of infiltration was proving effective against the K.O.Y.L.I. further south. Under the pressure of this advance the battalion was driven back along divergent lines of retreat, the main body falling back north along the main road to Roskje and Maere, while two companies withdrew by the safer but much longer route up the east side of Lake Leksdal. All ranks of the battalion were ordered to jettison all but their battle equipment, for there was no transport available save the little that could be requisitioned locally.

The enemy concentration against Vist coincided with a furious air attack upon Steinkjer, the bottleneck of our supply line. The town was built entirely of wood, and in the absence of any effective anti-aircraft defence it was soon reduced to a blazing and then to a blackened shell. The civilian inhabitants, wise in their generation, had streamed out of the place in the course of the morning, two or three hours before the bombardment began. Bridges were destroyed, the telephone lines wrecked, the water supply ruined. It was clear that the place could no longer serve us as a unit headquarters, and this raid, following the equally destructive air attack upon Namsos on the previous day, gave cause for fear that the arrival of British troops in a town of any size was likely to become the signal for the almost immediate obliteration of the place.

A large quantity of stores was lost in Steinkjer, but, thanks to the initiative of Major A. S. T. Godfrey, R.E., a good proportion of rations was saved. With Captain A. G. Gill-Davies and Staff-Sergeant Simpson of the brigade headquarters staff he drove a train consisting of an engine and four trucks across the blazing railway bridge of Steinkjer. The rations, which were urgently needed by the force, were thereby saved and were eventually brought back to Grong.

By nightfall Brigadier Phillips had concluded that no good purpose could be served by maintaining his troops in position around the fjord since they were open to attack from sea and air and it was impossible to guard all the points where a landing might be made, since 'we had no weapons to fire at ships in open water'. The road and railway both ran far too close to the foreshore and were therefore peculiarly vulnerable. The ration situation might soon become acutely difficult, so much having been lost among the ruins of Steinkjer. He could not afford to wait until things got worse and then beat a rapid retreat, since he did not possess the transport to make this possible. He had only eighteen requisitioned lorries at his disposal for moving the best part of two thousand men. These lorries he decided to allot in the first instance to the K.O.Y.L.I., who had the farthest to retreat. To the Lincolnshire would be given the not very enviable role of maintaining a Horatius stand at the Vist isthmus throughout the following day. The route through Kvam and along Lake Snaasa in the direction of Grong had been considered as a possible line of retreat, but General Carton de Wiart decided against this in view of the fact that it would bring our troops into the main communications line of the Norwegian forces in the district. And so the two battalions of the 146th Brigade would fall back along the better Beitstad-Namdalseid-Bangsund road where the Hallamshire were already in position.

The regular German morning reconnaissance on April 22nd promptly spotted the K.O.Y.L.I. concentrations east of the Strommen lake, and, guided by flares, German infantry went in to attack at Roskje while ski-troops, dragging sledge-borne machine-guns with them worked their way well round both flanks. The reserve company at Maere, two or three miles back along the road, was rushed forward in the few lorries and buses available in the hope of stabilising the position at Rosjke, but before they had covered half the distance they almost ran into an ambush of ski-troopers. Reversing with the utmost speed, most of them succeeded in getting back to Vist and joining up with the Lincolnshire, but some were ambushed on the way. The K.O.Y.L.I. kept up the fight until midday and then received orders to break contact and to pull back to the north-east to Fisknes, at the northern end of Lake Leksdal, where a rendezvous had been arranged with the two companies which had been retiring from the Verdal area during the night.

On this second day, as on the first, the hardest fighting occurred on the sector held by the Lincolnshire at Vist. Though attacked by infantry advancing from the west, shelled by destroyers and machine-gunned from the air, the battalion held its position throughout the morning and succeeded in escaping serious casualties. The company of K.O.Y.L.I. which dropped back on to their position in the course of the morning after its encounter with the ski-troopers on the Verdal road brought reports of fighting in their sector which suggested that the enemy had made a larger number of prisoners than seems to have been the case. Major Black, who commanded the detachment of Lincolnshire defending the Vist isthmus, had already decided that it would be necessary to withdraw without waiting for darkness, as had been planned. Unfortunately, the instructions to break off the action and retire, which were issued at 11.20 did not reach some of his troops until 2.15 p.m., and the retreat, beginning late, lost coherence. Colonel Newton did his best to try and organise a line in front of Steinkjer, but he had to be content with setting up stragglers' posts in Steinkjer and Byafossen during the afternoon.

About 7 p.m. the Germans, after subjecting Steinkjer to a further shelling from the fjord, began to land troops from their ships on the waterfront of the town. By this time most of the Lincolnshire were safely through the bottleneck, but nothing was known of the fate of Major Stokes's detachment, nearly 200 strong, which had been holding the southern end of the line, and for the next two days they were given up as lost. That they were not lost was due to the enterprise of their leader.

Receiving the order to retreat very late, Major Stokes withdrew his party into a wood where they were re-grouped and where he learned at about 8 p.m. that the Germans were now in occupation of Vist in his rear. The main road back being thus blocked he ordered his men to make their way across country in an easterly direction, keeping well to the south of the road. The snow was lying as much as three or four feet deep and progress was appallingly slow. The men had been ordered to discard almost all their equipment, including their steel helmets, which rendered them too conspicuous from the air, but even so the struggle through the deep snow was such heavy going that after four and a half hours they had only managed to cover a distance of one and a half miles. At 3 a.m. on the following morning, when Major Stokes judged it essential to call a halt, the little force was less than two miles beyond Vist and therefore still in danger of immediate annihilation. Their retreat had been observed by several Norwegian civilians, but oddly enough not by the German troops at Vist.

Marching all next day and making a wide detour to avoid Steinkjer, they got safely through the isthmus and eventually reached the village of Five on Lake Snaasa about 1 a.m. where they contacted a Norwegian battalion. Here they passed the night, but it was necessary for them to start off again after dawn, for the Norwegian and British routes of retreat were proceeding along diverging lines. A full day's march brought them to a village in the Beitstad neighbourhood through which the line of retreat of the 146th Brigade had passed. Though there was news of British troops bivouacked not far away every man in the force was too spent with exhaustion to march further. However, a farm cart being produced by a friendly villager, one of the officers drove on until he contacted an advance party of the Hallamshire. He reported the plight of his 180 men and they were all provided with shelter for the night. During the succeeding days they were filtered through to their battalion further north along the road to Namsos.

They had covered forty-five miles in forty-seven hours, much of the journey being made through deep snow with no tracks to guide them. Snow had continued to fall during the greater part of their march.

The remainder of the brigade had succeeded in disengaging without any serious incident. The rest of the Lincolnshire, having got past the Steinkjer isthmus, bivouacked for the night of April 22nd–23rd about three miles north of Steinkjer. The K.O.Y.L.I., moving further east by difficult forest tracks, had a longer route and were still in danger of being cut off on the wrong side of the isthmus when they reached Henning on the morning of April 23rd. They had jettisoned some of their equipment, including their anti-tank rifles (which could be spared, since the enemy had no tanks in this sector) when they learned from Norwegian sources that the Germans were advancing from Steinkjer through Byafossen to cut the neck of the isthmus at Sunnan which lies on the further side.

It took them eight hours to get to Sunnan through blinding snowstorms which continued without intermission all day and throughout the following night. This was a disguised blessing, for it kept the enemy planes grounded. Had the sky been clear it was almost certain that the force would have been spotted on the march and that German troops would have been at Sunnan before them.

By 3 p.m. on the afternoon of April 24th the whole of the K.O.Y.L.I. was beyond the Sunnan bridge and in reasonable safety if the demolition squad, left behind for the purpose of destroying the bridge, had carried out their task. But they were persuaded by the Norwegians on the spot to spare the bridge—an error which might have led to serious disaster for both British and Norwegians. The battalion continued its march, jettisoning still more equipment in the last exhausting stages, and reached their concentration area around Beitstad after dawn on April 24th.

They had marched fifty-eight miles in forty-two hours.

The Lincolnshire bore the brunt of the fighting during both days. Their losses were two men killed and eighteen wounded. The K.O.Y.L.I. lost only four killed and one wounded. The Hallamshire were not engaged. Rather more losses were naturally suffered in the process of withdrawal, but as the total number of missing reported for the two battalions during the whole period between the landing and the evacuation only mounted to fifty-two for the Lincolnshire and forty-four for the K.O.Y.L.I., it will be seen that even here the losses were trifling. Many stragglers from both battalions, who had been at first written off as lost, rejoined their units during the following days. It is significant moreover that the Germans claimed no more than eighty prisoners as a result of the action.

The loss of equipment and stores was more important. Some of the troops abandoned their arms during the retreat and a large quantity of stores was left in the ruins of Steinkjer. But when all is said and done we were lucky to come off so lightly from Vist, particularly in view of our unfavourable position and our inferiority in every form of armament, to say nothing of battle training and experience.

Nevertheless, the situation by the evening of April 22nd was very different from what it had been on the morning of April 20th, and Carton de Wiart was constrained to point out to the War Office that he could no longer hope to make a dash for Trondheim and must be content with extricating his troops from Steinkjer; and that no adequate cover remained for troops or stores at Namsos as the result of the German bombing of the town. On the day on which he sent this depressing but realistic report (April 22nd) he received information that an A.A. cruiser had been despatched to Namsos to stand by until anti-aircraft guns, already on their way, could arrive. An aircraft carrier would arrive to provide fighter protection on April 24th, and it was hoped that shore-based fighters could begin to operate about April 25th.

But these tardy and purely defensive reinforcements confirmed the impression that we were sending much too little decidedly too late. In a signal to the C.I.G.S. despatched on the afternoon of April 23rd the British commander suggested for the first time the possibility that evacuation might have to be considered. The German air and artillery and their ships in the fjord, he said, had very roughly handled Phillips's brigade and it was doubtful now whether an additional two battalions would be of any effect in altering the situation. Only with air superiority could he hope to maintain himself very much longer at Namsos with a bridge-head south of the fjord in the Bangsund area. All hope of offensive operations, under the present conditions, had now vanished.

That the Germans did not immediately follow up their success at Vist with a swift pursuit and an annihilating blow at the shaken British force was due in part to the inability of their air force to give them any support during the three days that followed the battle, in part to the considered caution of their strategy. Heavy snow-storms kept the German planes grounded during April 23rd and the following day, while early on the morning of April 25th a determined attack upon Vaernes aerodrome by between thirty and forty British planes inflicted a good deal of damage upon the runways and kept the enemy planes out of the air all that day. But the German command was quite prepared to deal with a situation of that nature. They impressed 800 Norwegian labourers and the damage was quickly repaired.

It was no part of the German plan to pursue the advance beyond the Steinkjer bottleneck until they were reinforced in strength from the south. They had done what they wanted and sealed off Trondheim from any danger from the north. The forces that had been engaged in the action at Vist were not large. There is no evidence that numerically they greatly exceeded the British troops opposed to them, and they were almost certainly less numerous than the total British, French, and Norwegian forces in the Namsos district. Their superiority had been due to their better equipment and arms and the support which they had received both from naval and air units; to some extent also, it must be admitted, to their better training and battle experience. To advance against Namsos might render them liable to a dangerous counter-stroke, since they had little means of knowing during the next day or two of obscured air observation what additional forces had been landed to reinforce Carton de Wiart or what air strength he might have available whether from carriers or of shore-based fighters.

And so, somewhat to the surprise of the British command, and certainly to its manifest relief, the German troops proceeded to adopt defensive measures and to dig in around Steinkjer. They did not even carry out any active patrol work during this period, and such offensive patrolling as occurred in the next few days was the work of the British who now lay echeloned back along the road that crosses the water-shed between the Trondheim and the Namsos fjords, with the Hallamshire now in the forward position to the north of Beitstad.

One result of the enemy activity was that a patrol of the Hallamshire was able to push across country on the night of April 25th–26th to Kvam, where a depot of stores had been established during the course of the Vist action at a time when it seemed likely that our retreat would follow the easterly road through Kvam and along Lake Snaasa to Grong. The stores were successfully salvaged and brought back to Namsos. The following night a fighting patrol was pushed out south, slipped through the Steinkjer isthmus and in broad daylight actually got as far as Maere, more than six miles beyond Steinkjer, where they successfully raided a German post, inflicted casualties and returned without loss to their base.

But these tentative jabs on the part of our battle patrols could in no way affect the issue, any more than could the arrival on April 27th of the troopship *Chrobry*, carrying Divisional Headquarters with base and ambulance units, a Royal Marine 3·7-inch howitzer battery and rifles, ammunition and tobacco for the Norwegian troops. The Royal Marine gunners turned out to be totally untrained and had never fired a shot. No ammunition for the guns was ever got ashore and there was no means of transporting them. None of the arms destined for the Norwegians could be unloaded as, owing to the danger of air attack, the ship had to put out from Namsos on the approach of dawn without completing its unloading.

## 4

### *The Decision to Re-embark*

On April 21st, General Massy had taken command of the Force despatched to central Norway, and on April 27th he issued a balanced appreciation of the situation, to which reference has already been made. The decision to evacuate central and southern Norway had already been taken by the British Cabinet and Massy's report did little more than supply reasons to confirm this decision. There were not more than 6,000 troops ashore in 'Mauriceforce' (British 146th Brigade and three battalions of Chasseurs Alpins), and evacuation presented an easier problem at Namsos than at Aandalsnes, since the troops lay close to their base, were under no immediate threat from advancing German land forces and had recently received a certain amount of motor transport and guns. But this advantage would wither away once the German forces from Oslo achieved their now imminent junction with the Trondheim detachment. They would then be able to develop a great superiority on the ground supported by their pulverising strength in the air. In Massy's estimation their final offensive against Namsos could be staged within a week of the junction of the Oslo and Trondheim forces.

For this reason there could be no case for leaving 'Mauriceforce' at Namsos to bear the brunt of the German onslaught after the evacuation of 'Sickleforce'. It was desirable that the two evacuations should take place concurrently, preferably on the night of May 1st–2nd, guns and stores being abandoned on the quays since the delay imposed by endeavouring to transport them might jeopardise the safety of the whole expedition.

Carton de Wiart learned before the end of the day that evacuation had been decided in principle, with priority for personnel at the expense of equipment. A two-night evacuation (May 1st–2nd, May 2nd–3rd) had been decided by the Inter-Services planners, and the British commander had now to concentrate upon taking what opportunities he could of thinning out his force while keeping the remainder in being and as clear as possible from air attacks.

Namsos was twice heavily raided during the following day, a good deal of damage being done to the quays, the wooden jetty and what remained of the warehouses, though after the first of these raids Admiral Vivian deputed two sloops *Bittern* and *Janus* to remain in the harbour and provide A.A. defence.

The French had now got ashore all their three battalions of the Chasseurs Alpins, and this made possible the relief of the Hallamshire in the course of the night April 28th–29th by the 13th Battalion Chasseurs Alpins, who took over their position in the Elden-Namdalseid area near the crest of the watershed between the two fjords. That night, too, French ships unloaded further stores and re-embarked the 53rd Battalion Chasseurs Alpins.

It was at this point (April 29th), when 'Mauriceforce' was being progressively 'concentrated towards the rear' and was conveniently grouped for evacuation, with its extreme forward unit barely more than twenty-five miles from Namsos and most of its components much nearer, that a further complication developed.

General Gamelin, viewing the over-all strategy of the Norwegian campaign, expressed himself as highly concerned about the possibility of a threat to our dispositions at Narvik through a rapid advance of the Germans northward from Steinkjer. For this reason he judged it important to establish troops at the intervening coastal towns between the two places, as a means of blocking the German advance. Mackesy was requested to detach a force from the Narvik area for the occupation of Bodö, nearly 150 miles to the south, and at the same time a methodical retreat by road of some part of the forces based on Namsos was suggested. Otherwise it was feared that the operations proceeding—or at present failing to proceed—around Narvik might be 'fatally compromised'.

Carton de Wiart was accordingly instructed by Massy to supply a strong detachment proportionate to the transport available to take part in a land withdrawal to Mosjöen. One half of this detachment was to proceed forthwith by road to Mosjöen, the other to remain as a rearguard at Grong. Some troops were also to be sent by sea to Mosjöen as speedily as possible, as an enemy attempt to seize the place with parachutists was to be feared.

Carton de Wiart replied, strongly discouraging the adoption of the plan. He had neither vehicles nor drivers adequate to convey a strong force and he learned by a reconnaissance that owing to the thaw the road became impassable about thirty miles north of Grong. The withdrawal of these troops on foot and subject to continuous air attacks by the enemy seemed scarcely likely to provide a significant increase in the security of the Narvik force, it might even lead to the loss of the detachment.

Subsequent telegrams, stressing the importance of the operation, failed to persuade him to change his mind, and the Germans, as if to underline the justice of his argument, subjected the Grong–Mosjöen road to heavy bombing attacks on May 1st, just two days later.

Viewed in the light of subsequent developments, Carton de Wiart would seem to be justified in his reluctance to commit any portion of his troops to an operation which could be carried out only with difficulty, if at all, and with no reasonable prospect of strategic benefit.

## 5

### *The Evacuation*

The Germans continued to bomb Namsos during April 30th and May 1st. The R.A.F., operating from bases in distant England, were replying with raids upon Stavanger, Oslo and Vaernes (the last-named being attacked by carrier-based planes of the Fleet Air Arm), but these attacks, though pushed home with great gallantry, appeared to have little effect in diminishing the intensity of the enemy's striking power, and it was obvious that the sooner we could get clear from Namsos, as from Aandalsnes, the better. Elaborate orders were issued for evacuation which was to take place on the two successive nights of May 1st–2nd, 2nd–3rd, though not until nearly 9 p.m. on the evening of May 1st did Carton de Wiart win his struggle to avoid committing any portion of the troops under his command to the hazards of a withdrawal by road northwards to Mosjöen. That evening, however, he received a specific order authorising him to embark all British and French troops under his command, with the exception of a small French detachment to be left attached to the Norwegians at Grong in accordance with Gamelin's instructions to Audet. There was no question of any troops being left based on Namsos.

French troops, apart from two sections of *skieurs* who were to act as rearguard, were to be evacuated first and then, on the following night, the British. Officers would be allowed to take up to 40-lb. of kit, other ranks would carry their rifles, personal kits and packs with greatcoats and one blanket and thirty rounds of ammunition per man. Anti-tank rifles and ammunition would be evacuated; no equipment was to be burned in the open where the tell-tale evidence of large fires would give all too clear an indication of the proposed move. Secret papers were to be burned indoors.

All was in readiness and the two battalions of the Chasseurs Alpins were already embarked on the trawlers or waiting on the quays just before midnight, when news came that the evacuation would be postponed for twenty-four hours. The cause of this necessary but hazardous delay was the weather, which unexpectedly played false now, as it was to do on a much more historic occasion just over four years later. Off Namsos itself the night was fine and clear, but further down the fjord, where the transports and escort ships were assembling, a thick fog had begun to descend from about seven o'clock in the evening, blotting out all landmarks and rendering it impossible for any vessel to venture up the fjord.

'Mauriceforce' headquarters did not receive the information until 9.30 p.m. and the waiting troops not until some time later. It was clear that grave possibilities were now raised, since it would be impracticable to re-disperse the troops during the course of the next twenty-four hours to any great extent. Moreover, the aircraft carriers, *Ark Royal* and *Glorious*, whose planes were to cover the evacuation, had been forced to leave Norwegian waters earlier in the evening owing to the weight of air attack that was being directed against them.

Finally, to add the last particle of discomfort to the unfortunate troops at Namsos, the evacuation of 'Sickleforce' from Aandalsnes was announced that afternoon in the House of Commons. General Carton de Wiart anticipated that this announcement might well lead the enemy to assume that evacuation from Namsos was also imminent and to muster all the air forces available for the purpose of inflicting the maximum damage as the operation proceeded. His fears were only too well justified.

One result of the fog and the consequent postponement that resulted was a determination on the part of the Joint Planning Staff to complete the evacuation in a single night. One battalion of Chasseurs Alpins had already gone, but a total of about 5,000 remained to be lifted. Massy had signalled during the afternoon that an attempt would be made to shift the whole force that night, but it seemed to Carton de Wiart that the number was too large to be embarked and cleared through the narrow waters of the fjord in the five hours of only partial obscurity, which was all that there was of night at this season of the year. He added an urgent request for air cover on the following day, in view of the Prime Minister's announcement in the House of Commons and of the probable enemy reaction to it. Admiral Vivian, on the other hand expressed himself in favour of a single-night evacuation. The decision had been left to Carton de Wiart and Vivian to act as they thought best after consultation, and at 7.35 that evening Force headquarters despatched its last message: every endeavour would be made to complete the evacuation that night.

Fortunately the night proved reasonably fine and at 9.30 p.m., before it was yet quite dark, the French troops began to go on board. The actual embarkation of the 5,000 was accomplished with great speed, though at the cost of sacrificing a good deal more equipment than had been intended. The great Bangsund bridge across the fjord, which had withstood all the attempts of German bombers to destroy it, was blown at midnight and at 1 a.m. (May 2nd–3rd) the British contingent began to go on board.

By 4.30 a.m. *Afridi*, carrying the last of the rear guard, pushed off from the quay, its gunners having carried out the melancholy task of shelling our own massed M.T. on the dockside before departing. The light A.A. battery, which had provided air defence to the port during the last days, succeeded in destroying its ten guns prior to embarkation.

The British commander had been correct in his estimate of the German reaction to the prospect of our impending departure. It was already light when *Afridi* and the tail of the convoy moved out into the fjord. By good fortune the customary German early morning reconnaissance was rather later than usual, but from 8.45 onwards the ships were subject to repeated attacks from about fifty German planes operating apparently from Vaernes airfield, which it had been supposed was badly damaged by our raid two days earlier. The A.A. cruiser, *Carlisle*, did excellent work with its accurate fire in keeping the planes at a distance, but the French destroyer *Bison* and H.M.S. *Afridi* were sunk in the course of the morning, fourteen of the lives lost when the latter went down being the only British military casualties suffered in the course of the evacuation. Two German planes were brought down.

The casualties suffered by 'Mauriceforce' do not compare with those of 'Sickleforce', since only one clash occurred between British and German troops—the two-day action of Vist—as compared with the six actions (Faaberg, Tretten, Kvam, Kjörem, Otta, Dombaas) fought by the troops under General Paget's command. Losses were as follows:

| | *Officers* | *Other Ranks* |
|---|---|---|
| Killed . . . . | 1 | 18 |
| Wounded . . . | 2 | 40 |
| Missing . . . . | 1 | 95 |
| Total . | 4 | 153 |

We had certainly come off more lightly than we had any reason to expect in view of the German superiority and the manifest limitations of our own force.

It was inevitable that large quantities of arms and ammunition should be left behind at Namsos, as at Aandalsnes. Considerable stocks, landed but never utilised, could not be brought away; and these included war material for the Norwegians.

# CHAPTER IV

# Narvik

## 1

### *A Missed Opportunity?*

THE lightning German occupation of the Norwegian ports, including far-distant Narvik, on April 9th produced just that situation which 'Avonmouth', under Major-General Mackesy, had been formed to meet. The Germans had invaded Norway, not indeed as a counter-stroke to our decision to lay minefields in Norwegian waters but in pursuit of their own policy of anticipating the Western Allies by striking first in strategically important theatres. Mackesy had received his original instructions, based on the assumption of an unopposed landing, on April 6th. The German initiative had assuredly not robbed them of their significance or their timeliness; it had merely emphasised the necessity for a swift execution, making such modifications as the changing naval and military situation demanded.

Yet in the revised instructions issued to General Mackesy, Narvik was not specifically mentioned as the objective. The British commander was told to establish his base at Harstad on the island of Hinnoy, thirty-five miles N.W. of Narvik and separated from it by two channels, the Vaagsfjord and the Ofotfjord, with the barren Skaanland peninsula between them. The only naval anchorage on the mainland indicated to him as being known to the Admiralty was Salangen, at the head of the fjord of that name, a good thirty miles in a direct line from Narvik, and much further if one takes into account the need for making detours around the heads of the fjords and following the indifferent road through the mountains.

Finally, Mackesy's instructions, issued at a time when the German seizure of Narvik was already known, specifically restrained him from landing in face of opposition.

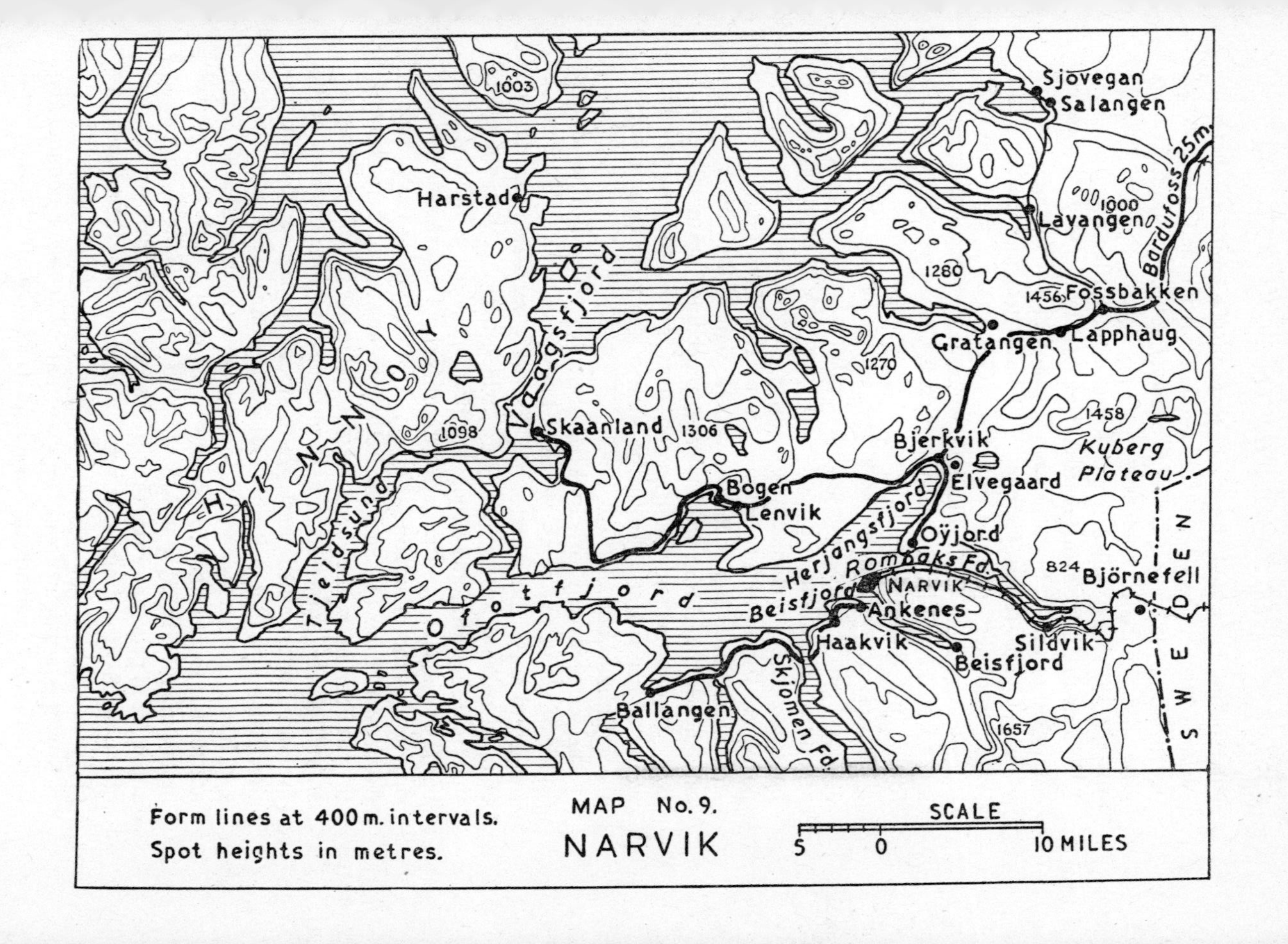


Form lines at 400 m. intervals.
Spot heights in metres.

MAP No. 9.
NARVIK

It should be added, however, that on the point of departure General Mackesy received a personal letter from the C.I.G.S. which instructed him to take advantage of naval action should the chance arise, and counselled boldness.

The force which sailed from Gourock, just after noon on April 12th, consisted of the 24th (Guards) Brigade (Brigadier Hon. W. Fraser), composed of the 1st Scots Guards (Lieut.-Colonel Trappes-Lomax), 1st Irish Guards (Lieut.-Colonel W. D. Faulkner), and the 2nd South Wales Borderers (Lieut.-Colonel P. Gottwaltz); also the 146th Brigade (Brigadier C. G. Phillips), which was diverted, before landing, to Namsos. Elements of the French Chasseurs Alpins were to follow subsequently.

The instructions given to Phillips, Fraser having sailed with the advance party, were to establish the force ashore in the Narvik area in co-operation with such Norwegian troops as might already be there, as a preliminary to further operations. An advance party, consisting of two companies of the Scots Guards and an Advanced Force Headquarters with a signals detachment, would sail ahead in H.M.S. *Southampton*, preceding the main body by twenty-four hours and would reconnoitre for the initial landing which would be dependent upon the position of the Norwegian troops in the neighbourhood.

The sea approach to Narvik is formed by a fjord of an average width of about ten miles, which is known as the Vestfjord and is fringed to north and south by rocky, barely populated islands. This channel narrows to the Ofotfjord, which averages something less than half its width, and which had been the scene of the first naval battle of Narvik. At its eastern extremity this fjord thrusts five long fingers into the mountainous coast. At points along the subsidiary fjords small fishing villages can be sighted, clusters of from twenty to fifty wooden huts; elsewhere the mountains rise harshly up from the shore. The Herjangsfjord thrusts north-east. It is the broadest of the five and it offers a little more room along its coast for disembarkation than do the others. Rombaksfjord is a long narrow inlet running east. It was here that the final phase of the second naval battle was fought and the last three of the German destroyers finally beached themselves in its extremity. Between this fjord and Beisfjord is the mountainous and wooded promontory on the tip of which stands the town and port of Narvik. Beisfjord runs south-east, and, divided by the promontory of Ankenes, the fifth finger, Skjomenfjord, runs almost due south.

Now it is apparent from the map that while water communication between headland and headland is comparatively easy, land communication involves detours of great length around the head of each fjord. In the absence of roads, troop movements could only be carried out by units provided with skis or snow-shoes, for the snow was several feet deep off the roads at this time of year. Therefore, on the face of it, it was apparent that any disembarkation which aimed at speedy success must be made as close to Narvik as possible. The further the troops landed from Narvik the more their difficulties would be multiplied.

The Norwegian troops in the neighbourhood consisted of the 6th Division, under General Fleischer, an able and energetic commander. A battalion of this division had been surrendered intact on the morning of April 9th, when the Germans occupied Narvik, by its commander, Colonel Sundlo, Quisling's friend. But about 200 men under the second in command, Major Omdahl, had slipped away to the mountains to keep up the resistance, and General Fleischer mobilised what he could of the rest of the division. But at no time did it reach full strength.

After seizing all the key points in Narvik the first action of General Dietl, the German commander, had been to despatch a force, about 500 strong, to occupy the divisional depot and training-ground at Elvegaard near the head of Herjangsfjord. This diversion of force proved fully justified. It resulted in the capture of 8,000 rifles and 315 machine-guns, as well as quantities of uniforms, munitions, and stores. The Norwegian uniforms were later used, by the Germans' own admission, to clothe the sailors who came ashore from the sinking destroyers after the second naval battle of Narvik.

It was a rich haul, and the unexpected windfall of machine-guns greatly increased the ability of the force to withstand an ordinary infantry attack. This factor should be remembered when the pros and cons of a landing at Narvik are taken into account. Equally important was the denial of these weapons to the Norwegian forces.

Dietl now spread his men out to the north and east of Narvik, rapidly occupying tactical points which would enable him to secure his flanks and rear and establish a defence in depth among the mountain heights. On the south he contented himself with the occupation of the Ankenes peninsula, just across the Beisfjord from Narvik, and did not attempt to advance further in this direction. To the east his troops advanced along the railway line towards the Swedish frontier. For a week the small Norwegian forces fought delaying actions back along this line. Unfortunately, they waited too long before carrying out demolitions. The Nordal bridge, about four miles from the border, was an exceptionally vulnerable point, but its destruction was left until the vanguard of the German troops eventually arrived within rifle range on April 16th, and then it was too late. Some damage was done when the charge was exploded but it was repaired by the German engineers within a few hours. In the course of that same day the enemy made good their advance to the frontier and cleared the whole of the railway line.

To the north, the trained Austrian ski-troopers were fanning out rapidly over the snow-covered mountains between Herjangsfjord, the most northerly of the five 'fingers' and Gratangenfjord, the next inlet to the north. By April 12th they had established machine-gun posts along the southern shore of the latter fjord, and, according to a report received from Norwegian sources late that evening, their patrols were even operating in the direction of the two still more northerly fjords of Lavangen and Salangen.

General Fleischer's Norwegian forces were meanwhile concentrating in the neighbourhood of Bardufoss, fifty-two miles N.N.E. of Narvik, where there was a good grass-covered landing-ground for aircraft, at present under deep snow.

Such was the information available on the morning of the fateful Saturday, April 13th, when the British force, which had sailed at noon on the previous day, was crossing the North Sea and approaching Narvik.

Unfortunately there had been no liaison between Admiral of the Fleet, the Earl of Cork and Orrery, who commanded the naval side of the expedition, and General Mackesy, who was in charge of the land forces. Lord Cork had sailed at noon on April 12th in H.M.S. *Aurora* from Rosyth; Mackesy had sailed at the same hour in H.M.S. *Southampton* from Gourock.

Nor can the instructions given to the two officers be easily reconciled. Mackesy, as we have seen, was specifically informed that it was not intended that he should land in face of opposition, though this directive may be regarded as modified by the personal letter from the C.I.G.S. Lord Cork, on the other hand, writes in his despatch: 'My impression on leaving London was quite clear that it was desired by H.M. Government to turn the enemy out of Narvik at the earliest possible moment and that I was to act with all promptitude in order to attain this result'.

As the plan stood, a naval reconnaissance party was to land at Harstad, while the advance party from H.M.S. *Southampton* should disembark on the northern side of the Salangen fjord or at the seaward end of the Lavangen fjord, fully thirty miles across country from Narvik.

It was a decision perhaps justified in view of the information, largely unconfirmed, which was available at the time. This seemed to indicate that the German force, about 2,000 strong, based on Narvik, had spread north almost to Salangen, while their destroyers were still in control of the five 'finger' fjords around the port. The necessity of landing well out of range of their guns and the desirability of making early contact with General Fleischer's Norwegian forces indicated a preliminary disembarkation to the north, since Salangen itself, at the head of the fjord of that name, was no great distance from Fleischer's temporary headquarters and was connected with it by an adequate road. Moreover, the news that the German patrols were believed to be approaching this neighbourhood might be taken to imply that they were in effective control of the fjords further south and would therefore be in a position to oppose any landing not made in strength.

That was the situation which dictated the landing of the first detachment of troops at a point so remote from Narvik, despite the manifest disadvantages of this course.

But while these decisions were being made for the disposition of the troops, the Navy was acting with swiftness, decision, and shattering force, and, in the course of a short three hours that afternoon, had radically altered the position. While the commanders of the military expedition were sitting in conference, discussing and selecting the points of disembarkation, a British naval force, under Vice-Admiral W. J. Whitworth, sailed majestically into Narvik fjord. It consisted of the battleship *Warspite* and nine destroyers, *Icarus*, *Hero*, *Foxhound*, *Kimberley*, *Forrester*, *Bedouin*, *Punjabi*, *Eskimo*, and *Cossack*. The Germans had still eight large destroyers available for action, though one or two were not wholly seaworthy and all were short of ammunition. A German submarine lurking at the entrance to the fjord was driven off by depth charges and, led by *Icarus* and *Bedouin*, the British destroyers with *Warspite* in support, passed into Ofotfjord, the approach channel to Narvik. Shortly after noon a German destroyer was encountered lying up in the small bay of Djupvik, not far from the entrance to Ofotfjord. Her torpedo tubes were trained to cover the approach channel, but concentrated fire from the leading destroyers supported by a couple of salvos from *Warspite*'s main armament, soon accounted for her. Against the British destroyers supported by the 15-inch guns of *Warspite* the enemy had little chance. An attempt to manœuvre under cover of a smoke-screen was unsuccessful, as there was sufficient breeze to scatter the smoke. After a running fight lasting for about an hour and a half the German destroyers were almost entirely out of ammunition. One drifted on to the northern shore of Herjangsfjord and was blown up by her commanding officer; another, after receiving many hits, was abandoned by her crew near Narvik; yet another, damaged in the battle of April 10th and firing from a stationary position alongshore in the harbour, was repeatedly hit and finally blew herself up. The remaining four withdrew beyond the narrows into the Rombaksfjord, from which there was no possibility of escape. One of these succeeded in blowing off the bows of *Eskimo* with a torpedo but soon afterwards, on fire fore and aft, ran aground near Sildvik and capsized. The remaining three withdrew to the furthest extremity of the fjord. Here, with their ammunition exhausted, they were scuttled, the crews abandoning them and going ashore to join with the land forces under General Dietl.

By 5.30 p.m. it was all over. Without loss of a British ship the eight German destroyers had all been despatched, together with a submarine which was sunk by the aircraft from *Warspite*. The German fleet at Narvik was annihilated and our own warships could now cruise at will up and down the fjords and toss their shells into the town or on to the neighbouring coast with nothing worse to fear than the fire of German machine-guns from the shore. The German troops were now streaming out of Narvik in disorder. Even officers were tearing off their badges of rank and inquiring of civilians as they passed 'Which is the way to Sweden? Which is the way to Sweden?' At that moment they were a morally beaten force.

Theodor Broch, the young Mayor of Narvik, has described how, even before the end of the naval battle when the issue was still in doubt, he had seen German troops straggling out of the town and back into the hills.

'When we told them that their number was up, they only smiled forlorn smiles and muttered "Kamerad". They were certainly no longer *blitz* men. They looked rather like half-drowned cats nestling close to one another in order to keep warm. Nor were they any longer condescending in their attitude towards their "racial brethren" who had been so tragically led astray by the decadent democracies. Now they wished to be accepted because they were human beings like us and because it was good to be alive. They had lost contact with their officers and their morale was gone.

'Bands of beaten Germans continued to drift through the town and up Fagernes mountain. Laboriously they trampled a path for themselves, zigzagging their way up the steep slope. Their dark rows stood out against the snow wall like curving snakes.'

When the anxious watchers in the town had seen one German destroyer after another sunk or beached and had heard the firing gradually die away, and when it became clear that the German fleet in the fjord had been annihilated, Broch had gone round the town and finding a few German troops still in occupation of the telegraph building had told them that the British were already disembarking and had persuaded the corporal who was in charge to give up his arms and to march away with his troops into the hills. For the moment Narvik was quite clear of German troops, and that night Mayor Broch and his adherents spent in the City Hall singing 'Tipperary' and waiting hourly for the news of the British landing.

Strategically, the enemy position at Narvik now appeared untenable, well-nigh hopeless. They were cut off by hundreds of miles from the nearest German troops, they had lost all their warships and all their supply ships and had been driven out on to the snow-covered and inhospitable mountain slopes. Dietl's situation was further weakened by the dangerous dispersal of his forces. They were spread out over thirty miles of mountain country to the north, largely in isolated 'penny packets'. Dietl's enterprise, justifiable provided that his ships could hold their own in the fjords and protect him from seaborne attack, involved him in exceptional risks now that he had lost command of the Narvik inlets.

The German flight from Narvik had begun around 3 p.m., when the full scale of the defeat suffered by their ships began to be apparent. But as early as 7 p.m., seeing that no landing had yet been made, the first of their troops began to trickle back again, and the process of re-infiltration continued during the night.

Following the naval victory in the fjord, Admiral Whitworth, who had flown his flag in *Warspite* during the action, contemplated putting a landing-party ashore from the ships to seize Narvik. But he had no more than 200 men available for this purpose, and in view of the probability of a counter-attack, once the Germans realised the weakness of the landing-force, it would have been necessary to keep *Warspite* close offshore to provide covering fire. Since a dozen German aircraft had been sighted overhead during the afternoon and at least one German submarine was known to be still at large in the fjord, he decided against exposing his flagship to the danger of both air and submarine attack in these narrow waters; and, in a signal to the Commander-in-Chief of the Home Fleet despatched at 10.10 p.m., recommended that the town be occupied without delay by the main landing force. He announced his intention to visit Narvik again next day in order to maintain the moral effect of the presence of *Warspite* and to accept the air and submarine menace involved by this course of action.

At 10.27 a.m. Sunday, replying to an Admiralty message asking for the strength of the German forces in the Narvik area, Admiral Whitworth reported his conviction that Narvik could be taken by direct assault, without fear of meeting with serious opposition on landing. He considered that the main landing force need only be small, but that it must have the support of Force B[1] or one of similar composition.

This message was passed on to Lord Cork, but his signal proposing the diversion of H.M. ships *Southampton* and *Aurora*, to take advantage of the naval victory, was not received by *Southampton* (in which General Mackesy was travelling) in time to take appropriate action, owing to difficulties in wireless transmission.

Lord Cork had suggested that, in view of the victory, the troops from H.M.S. *Southampton*, two companies strong, should be landed in daylight at Narvik on the following morning (April 15th) under cover of the guns of *Warspite* and the other British naval units. General Mackesy replied that the troops referred to had already disembarked at the pre-arranged points (both near Salangen, well over thirty miles in a direct line from Narvik) between 10 a.m. and noon that morning and that it would be impossible to re-embark them and again disembark them next day at Narvik. He suggested that the troops in the transports which were following could carry out this plan, though he himself doubted its feasibility. In the course of the evening he was confirmed in his opinion by learning that Narvik harbour was now strongly held by German infantry with machine-guns.

Whether the troops could or could not have been re-embarked in time to carry out the Narvik landing successfully in accordance with Lord Cork's suggestion is a matter which probably can never be settled. Lord Cork believed that it could be done; Mackesy was convinced that it could not. It was certainly unfortunate that the convoy should not have sailed until April 12th. Had its departure been advanced by one single day it would have been close at hand to take advantage of the victory gained by the Navy. It is quite clear that the liaison between the military and naval chiefs and between both and Whitehall was insufficiently close. The two commanders had never met previously. They sailed from different ports in different ships, and when they met for the first time on April 15th they found that they had received very different instructions. Mackesy's force had been embarked as for a peaceful landing out of range of the

[1] The force under Vice-Admiral Whitworth, consisting of *Warspite* and the nine destroyers.

German troops at Narvik; Cork was under the impression that offensive action at the earliest possible moment in order to expel the Germans from Narvik was required.

In Whitehall the prospective fall of Narvik was regarded as being immensely facilitated by the naval victory. In consequence, the decision, was taken on that same evening of April 14th to divert *Chrobry* and *Empress of Australia*, carrying the 146th Brigade, southward to Namsos to form part of the force about to operate against Trondheim. The clearing up of Narvik and its neighbourhood would now be left to the 24th (Guards) Brigade, subsequently reinforced by two battalions of French mountain troops, a brigade of the Foreign Legion and a Polish brigade.

By nightfall Harstad, which was to serve as our base, had been cleared. Two companies of the Scots Guards, who had been landed near Salangen, had made contact with the Norwegian forces, whose forward elements were fighting the Germans a dozen miles further south at Fossbakken.

The previous day, General Dietl's acutely threatened troops had received a welcome reinforcement. A dozen JU 52s succeeded in making a landing on the frozen Lake Hartvig, ten miles north of Narvik, bringing a complete mountain battery. The German force already disposed of one such, which was engaged in the mountains to the north, and the newly arrived guns were despatched to the railway sector, where Norwegian troops were, at that date, still blocking the line at Hundalen. As the force possessed, in addition, the guns brought ashore from their own destroyers, as well as those captured on April 9th from the British armed merchantmen lying in the port, their armament was becoming more formidable. The German air superiority being what it was, every day of flying weather would give the opportunity for further airborne supplies to be rushed to this remote northern outpost of aggression, thereby further modifying the balance of strength between the opposing forces.

The naval victory off Narvik, followed by the news of the German evacuation of the town and reports of the landing of British forces in the neighbourhood, helped to substantiate the belief, held for several days in Allied and neutral countries, that Narvik had actually been re-captured. It was a matter of something more than days before the Allied and neutral public learned definitely and finally that the port was still in German hands.

## 2

### *The Indirect Approach*

The greater part of the 24th (Guards) Brigade were disembarked at Harstad in the course of April 15th with thirty-five miles and a decent width of water dividing them from Narvik. Mackesy reported back that German positions around the town were very strong. They held pill-boxes and a trench system covering the landing-places and he believed that Narvik could not be directly reduced either by a landing-force or by naval bombardment.

In consequence, the British commander favoured a wide turning movement from the region of the Salangen and Lavangen fjords through the mountains of the north down towards the Narvik railway. Whatever may be urged against the immediate direct attack upon Narvik itself, which was favoured by both the authorities at home and by Lord Cork, the naval commander on the spot, there were many difficulties inherent in this alternative. Even in peacetime the crossing of the thirty or forty miles of mountain and snowfield that separated the British landing-places from Narvik would have been quite a formidable undertaking. But with trained German mountain troops establishing themselves at the intervening key points the operation promised to be slow, harassing and, perhaps, costly. General Mackesy, moreover, considered that the French Chasseurs Alpins, with their training for mountain warfare, were essential for a successful advance across country of this nature, and their absence, therefore, increased the difficulties of taking the long way round.

By 4 p.m. on April 16th the 2nd South Wales Borderers—the last of the three battalions of the 24th (Guards) Brigade to land—had completed their disembarkation at Harstad. The brigade received orders that night to be ready to cross to the mainland. They would subsequently take up positions at Skaanland, whence they would move by road to Bogen on the northern shore of the Ofotfjord. The troops would be ferried across from Harstad by the small steam-launches known to our men as 'puffers', with the exception of the two companies of Scots Guards in the remote northern fjord of Salangen, who would remain in position there and be progressively reinforced by Chasseurs Alpins whenever the latter should arrive.

The War Office and the Admiralty were becoming concerned at the slowness of 'Avonmouth' to follow up the naval victory and the remoteness of the landings from the strategic objective of the expedition. Accordingly a signal was sent on the morning of April 17th urging an immediate assault upon Narvik. It was pointed out that the Chasseurs Alpins would not be available, and that *Warspite* would have to be called away within two or three days.[1]

Lord Cork and General Mackesy again held different views upon the feasibility of the operation. The former considered that, with his force of one battleship, two cruisers and eight destroyers available to give covering fire, the troops could be landed with little loss and he counted on the shelling breaking enemy morale and reducing resistance to a minimum. He was prepared to risk what he recognised as a hazard of war. Mackesy, however, demurred. His troops were not trained for fighting in snowbound mountainous country and he needed the French Chasseurs Alpins, without whom his attacking force would be numerically inferior to the enemy. Nor could the largely untrained Norwegian troops be relied upon. But, above all, he was convinced that to send the assaulting troops ashore in the ships' boats (the only form of landing-craft we possessed) would be suicidal in the face of well-concealed machine-guns.

The next day was passed in fruitless discussions. Lord Cork felt bound to stress that they were being urged to undertake an early assault upon Narvik and that for his part he was prepared to take a chance on it; but Mackesy continued in his refusal. His original instructions had precluded a bombardment liable to cause large-scale loss of life among civilians and damage to property, and he drew attention to the unfortunate situation of the 5,000 Norwegians still understood to be remaining in Narvik. Lord Cork was likewise bound by his instruction that no attack should be launched except in concert with the military commander. Mackesy did, however, agree to keep his troops at hand and land them following a naval bombardment, if it seemed feasible. The outline of a plan was drafted by the Commander-in-Chief for submission to the Admiralty, but another day had been lost in the process.

On the next day, April 19th, the weather broke—decisively. An icy blizzard swept the coast throughout the morning, to be followed by days of heavy and continuous snow. For a week there was no intermission whatever in the steady fall. It prevented all serious tactical movement by the troops on either side, but the Germans being the men in possession were more easily able to consolidate their position, while our troops were in no situation to threaten them. When the weather at last began to mend, about April 26th, it was too late for any swift *coup de main* against Narvik.

[1] Both were required for the projected attack against Trondheim.

General Mackesy had departed upon the morning of April 19th for a two-day personal reconnaissance of the hostile coast. What he saw did nothing to convince him of the feasibility of the undertaking. Nor was his force, which he judged inadequate to carry out a *coup de main* with any prospect of success, well fitted to undertake a war of attrition. He still lacked both anti-aircraft and field artillery. He had no fighter airfield available as yet to provide air cover for his troops. There was a grave shortage of mortar ammunition. Before departure on his reconnaissance he signalled that his general objective now was to move the British troops gradually forward along the northern shore of the Ofotfjord, in close co-operation with the fleet, while the Norwegians were to be encouraged to operate southwards. His signal concluded with the announcement that no tactical movements by his troops could take place for some weeks owing to the snow.

On this day the War Office changed the code name for the force under his command from 'Avonmouth' to 'Rupertforce'.

Returning at a very late hour in the evening from his reconnaissance, carried out under appalling conditions in blinding snowstorms, Mackesy felt more than ever dubious of the prospects of a naval bombardment and considered that, even if successful, its effect upon the local populations would be most prejudicial to his relations with Norwegian authorities. He himself felt that the responsibility, if it were taken, should be that of the Cabinet.

The reply of Whitehall on the following day (April 21st) was to vest the supreme command in the joint operations at Narvik in Lord Cork. The latter thereupon prepared a plan for the bombardment of military objectives on both shores of the Herjangsfjord and the Rombaksfjord and on the tip of Narvik peninsula. Following the attack by the ships' guns the troops would land, not at Narvik itself but on the east shore of the Herjangsfjord between the villages of Oyjord and Bjerkvik. This would still leave the long though narrow Rombaksfjord between them and their objective, but it would bring them very much closer to the town, would increase the chances of cutting the railway to the rear, and would at least facilitate a later hop on to Narvik peninsula itself.

In pursuance of this policy the Norwegian official radio, now established at Tromsö in the extreme north, whither the King and Government were shortly to follow, began broadcasting a series of messages at two-hourly intervals to civilians in Narvik urging them to evacuate their homes before the bombardment began, a measure which, however humane in its intention, was scarcely calculated to improve the chances of surprise for the assault.

It was 7 a.m. on April 24th, the sixth day of continuous snowfall, that the bombardment opened against Narvik and Ankenes. *Warspite*, *Effingham*, and *Enterprise*, formed a formidable trio, but the thickly falling snow made it difficult to identify targets and the result of the bombardment was generally regarded as disappointing and certainly seemed to justify Mackesy's reluctance to commit his troops.

The only good news that the day brought for the Allies was that a demi-brigade of Chasseurs Alpins (about 4,000 men) had set sail in the afternoon from Scapa and would arrive at Harstad before the end of the week to provide the much-needed reinforcement of mountain-trained troops.

Next day the snow was still falling continuously and there was no improvement in the Allied situation. The Norwegians who had pushed southward from Lavangenfjord on the previous day were driven out of their positions again, and the Germans received reinforcement from a number of paratroops who, despite the appalling weather, were successfully dropped at the head of the Herjangsfjord near Bjerkvik. The prospects of an early capture of Narvik were receding hourly.

All this time the bulk of the British brigade had lain inactive at the western end of the long and irregularly shaped peninsula which forms the northern side of the Ofotfjord. With an improvement of the weather on April 26th two companies of the South Wales Borderers were transferred across to Ballangen at the head of an inlet on the southern side of the fjord nearly twenty miles from Narvik. The following night the remainder of the battalion was ferried across. There were no enemy troops anywhere in the neighbourhood, and on April 29th the battalion was ferried along the shore of the fjord and landed at Haakvik on the Ankenes peninsula again without opposition. The three British battalions were now widely dispersed. One of them lay close up to Narvik on the south side of the fjord, with only a ridge of hills and the narrow mile-wide strip of the Beisfjord separating it from the town; the bulk of the remainder in the Skaanland peninsula to the north of the fjord and well out of contact with the enemy; and two companies far away in the mountains at the head of Lavangenfjord supporting the Norwegian ski-troopers.

April 27th, however, the day on which the evacuation of southern and central Norway was definitely and irrevocably decided, brought welcome aid to our troops in the Narvik sector. The promised three battalions of Chasseurs Alpins were put ashore at Foldvik on the Gratangenfjord and on the southern side of the Skaanland peninsula.

Now, it was hoped, at long last, specialist forces adequately trained and equipped would be available for the long-delayed assault upon Narvik.

This unit had been formed from mid-January onwards and had trained in the Jura area through hard weeks of bitter cold of the late winter for intervention in Finland. After this project fell through, when Finland accepted peace from Russia, the demi-brigade was kept in readiness for possible subsequent operations in Scandinavia, but most of its special winter equipment was returned to the magazines and there had been no opportunity for drawing it again before the troops sailed for Scapa and Norway in April. The training of the troops unfortunately was by no means adequate for the type of fighting in which they would have to engage in Norway. Every man should have been a specialised ski-trooper; instead, the number of *skieurs* was limited to thirty in each battalion. Thereby the role of the Chasseurs Alpins was greatly restricted. Instead of whole battalions which could move rapidly across snowfields their few *skieurs* must be carefully husbanded for reconnaissance and patrol work. Of the rest, some had snowshoes and some had not; their training and equipment, though far better than that of the British troops for the purposes of a campaign among Arctic mountains and snowfields, was probably inferior to that of the Germans who had been selected for this specific purpose.

On the morning of April 28th, General Béthouart, who commanded the French force (he had previously been second-in-command to General Audet at Namsos) arrived at Harstad and went into conference with Lord Cork and General Mackesy. The admiral still favoured a direct attack against Narvik, with the troops landed as close to the town as possible under cover of the ships' guns. With the improved weather better results might be expected from the naval bombardment than had been achieved by the shelling four days earlier.

Béthouart gave careful consideration to the difficulties of either course—the strength of the enemy's machine-gun emplacements around Narvik on the one hand, and the great distance which must be traversed from the Salangen area if Mackesy's plan of a wide turning movement were to be adopted. It meant fifty miles across mountain and snowfield, a slow and tedious business, with the enemy fighting delaying actions all the way back to Narvik. After a thorough reconnaissance of the fjords he favoured an immediate landing close to Narvik, to be developed with all the force at their disposal.

This plan he submitted to Mackesy. It was turned down by the British general who held to his view that it was better to continue the movement by land from north and south.

Meanwhile, the failure of the attempt against Trondheim and the impending evacuation of Aandalsnes and Namsos had resulted in an important modification of the strategic situation at Narvik. This would now become the main, in fact the only, front. Reinforcements of British, French, and Norwegian troops, might be expected to strengthen the Allied position. On the other hand, the Germans would now be freed for an advance northward along the coast, or by sea, from the Trondheim-Namsos area to relieve the menaced garrison at Narvik. Though the great coast road from the south comes to an end at Bodö nearly 150 miles short of Narvik (much more, if one allows for the detours round the heads of the fjords) there was little doubt that German resolution and ingenuity coupled with German air strength would be sufficient to surmount the final obstacle. It was clear that a force must be detached to parry the German advance from the south while 'Rupertforce' finally liquidated the obstinate resistance of Dietl's Narvik garrison.

It was with this object in view that General Carton de Wiart was requested to supply a detachment for withdrawal by land from Namsos to Mosjöen. When he found himself unable to comply, the Scots Guards were ordered, as a preliminary move, to despatch one company to Bodö, where an enemy airborne landing was feared. This was the beginning of the process by which the whole of the 24th Brigade was gradually fed into the 'parrying front' between Mosjöen and Bodö, as the German threat from the south progressively developed.

The fate of this force will now be briefly discussed before we return to the final phase of the Narvik campaign.

## 3

### *Mosjöen: Mo: Bodö*

The scratch force despatched to protect the southern flank of the Narvik landings and to deny the enemy the ports of Mosjöen, Mo, and Bodö, had a somewhat thankless task to perform. The scales were progressively tipping further and further against them, and the German air superiority, which inflicted grave losses upon our warships and transports, together with the shortening nights, rendered the problem of supply increasingly acute. In a series of fighting withdrawals, which bear a good deal of resemblance to the retreat of 'Sickleforce' up the Gudbrandsdal from Lillehammer to Aandalsnes, they succeeded in holding the Germans off from an approach to Narvik throughout the whole of the month of May. During this time they were gradually forced back from positions in advance of Mosjöen through Mo to Bödo—a distance of nearly two hundred miles.

The British force never exceeded 3,500, while the Germans had at least 4,000 troops committed before the close.

This otherwise rather depressing operation, however, represents something of a landmark in the development of the British armed forces in the Second World War. In these operations a number of specially trained Independent Companies were employed, which were the genesis of the future Commandos—renowned for their daring and initiative in the later years of the war.

Ten such Independent Companies had been hastily formed, primarily with a view to the employment of harassing guerrilla tactics against German aggression in Norway. By the end of April five were ready for overseas service. Each company was composed of 20 officers and 270 other ranks. All were volunteers, with the exception of a few officers seconded from the Territorial Army, and some had been specially selected on account of their experience in irregular warfare on the mountainous North-West Frontier of India. Those who arrived in Norway were better equipped than any troops whom we had yet despatched there. They were provided with snowshoes, special Arctic boots, sheepskin coats, and Alpine rucksacks, and they habitually carried a five-day ration of pemmican. They had no transport, for the essence of their role was that they were to be 'ship-based'; but they were provided with an adequate staff organisation equivalent to that of a brigade. They were almost ideally trained and equipped to play the role of a harassing force supporting an army which had already established a solid position in a mountainous sea-bound country. The desperate situation of the Allies in Norway, however, compelled this force of specialists to be employed as troops of the line, fighting a series of hopeless rearguard actions. But it was a beginning, and the experience gained in the disheartening campaign among the northern mountains was of great value when, under Mr. Churchill's electric inspiration, the commando idea developed to full stature.

The first of these Independent Companies disembarked at Mo on May 4th and took up defensive positions to the south around the villages of Ytteren, Ildgrubben, and Finneid. They found a company of Scots Guards from Narvik had arrived at Bodö four days earlier in response to a request from the C.I.G.S. and these had been joined two days later by a hundred Chasseurs Alpins and a section of a British light A.A. battery which had arrived by sea from Namsos.

For some days all was quiet in this area, and by May 9th three more Independent Companies had been landed at Mosjöen and Bodö, and Colonel C. McV. Gubbins took command. He promptly reconnoitred south to make contact with the remnants of the retreating Norwegian forces. These he found, in a state of disintegration around the village of Fellingfors, about twenty-five miles beyond Mosjöen. Since our withdrawal from Namsos the Norwegians had lost heart and in the opinion of their commander there was no longer any hope of holding a front around Mosjöen. Gubbins could do no more than post his forward company at a position about a dozen miles south of Mosjöen in the hope of delaying the German advance as long as possible.

Early the next morning the attack developed along the road from the south. It synchronised with a sea-borne landing at Hemnes, on the coast in the next large fjord to the north of Mosjöen, during the afternoon and the dropping of parachutists on either flank of the new landing. With his forward troops acutely threatened in front and rear, Gubbins decided that Mosjöen was no longer tenable and drew his troops back in the course of the night. The Germans followed up closely and, after their advance party had been skilfully ambushed and had lost about sixty men killed, entered Mosjöen at daybreak on May 11th.

The early loss of this port impressed the commanders at Narvik with the need for greatly strengthening the parrying force, which now bore the name of 'Scissorsforce'. Even at the cost of seriously weakening our striking power before Narvik, it was necessary to despatch troops and guns to Bodö and Mo; otherwise the Germans from the south might be expected within a week or two to link up with the troops in Narvik and the dismal story of Trondheim would be repeated.

It was decided in principle that the 24th (Guards) Brigade, with the exception of the South Wales Borderers, should be fed into 'Scissorsforce' by stages. They would be supported by a troop of field guns, by two troops of light A.A., a Royal Engineer company, and a field ambulance, and a troop of three tanks. The whole would be under the command of Brigadier Fraser. The general objective was to establish them firmly in control of Bodö and the long fjord on which it stands and to deny Mo to the enemy as long as possible. By the afternoon of May 12th, despite heavy and repeated air attacks on Mo throughout the day, the four Independent Companies and the battalion of Scots Guards were established at various points along the coast and the main road from Bodö to Finneid which is to the south of Mo.

But the force was widely extended and had not the means of concentrating against a sudden attack on any one of its units. Moreover, the enemy's air-power was beginning to threaten its supply line. The Irish Guards, who sailed from Harstad on the morning of May 14th, with the engineers and ambulance detachments and three tanks, were attacked by air during the day and the big transport *Chrobry* was sunk. The troops were rescued by the escorting destroyers and brought back to Harstad, but the three tanks were lost—a serious matter in those days of scarcity of armament. H.M.S. *Somali*, one of the escorting destroyers which was carrying Brigadier Fraser, was damaged by a near miss and compelled to return to Scapa for repairs.

A second attempt to reinforce the troops in the Bodö-Mo area by sea met with similar misfortune. This time H.M.S. *Effingham* was despatched, carrying the South Wales Borderers and the ambulance detachment, with an escort of destroyers. She was harried during the passage by persistent bombing and eventually ran aground and had subsequently to be sunk to prevent her falling into enemy hands. The troops were rescued with some of their equipment and brought back to Harstad.

It took the Germans just a week to advance from Mosjöen to Mo. Employing the familiar tactics of a holding attack in front and a turning movement with their superior numbers on the inland flank, and assisted by the dropping of parachutists, they forced the Scots Guards back from the position they had taken up covering Mo, which was reached by the enemy in the afternoon of May 18th. Their troops, too, were becoming dispersed in the course of the advance, but with a striking-force of some 2,000 in the van, combined with their superiority in the air, they proved quite adequate to the task of forcing the British steadily northwards.

Brigadier Gubbins[1] was by this time becoming convinced that with the greater mobility enjoyed by the Germans and their capacity for effecting turning movements by the employment of small coastal ships, seaplanes or parachutists he must retain a strong force at his base at Bodö for effective counter-action. He had at last received the

[1] He had been appointed to the command in succession to Brigadier Fraser, who had been invalided home on May 17th, as a result of wounds suffered near Narvik a fortnight earlier.

remainder of the 24th Brigade, the South Wales Borderers having arrived at Bodö on May 20th and the Irish Guards on May 21st. But Bodö itself was being heavily and repeatedly raided—the Welshmen arrived in the midst of an air raid, when German planes were flying low over the houses and riddling the streets with machine-gun fire—and the troops had necessarily to be dispersed along the shores of the fjord, which rendered their subsequent concentration a difficult matter.

Meanwhile Gubbins selected three defensive lines across the 150-mile watershed between Mo and the head of the Salt fjord on which Bodö stands. On the map they appeared to be positions of reasonable strength, but it was the old story. The troops available were inadequate to cover all points in sufficient strength, they were liable to be out-flanked and they had not the mobility off the road or the supporting arms to enable them to counter or repel the German attacks. Above all, they were subject to the same paralysing influence of the enemy air-power. Had the tanks which went down in *Chrobry* been available they must certainly have delayed the advance; they could scarcely have brought it to a permanent halt.

The German vanguard forced Line A on the evening of May 21st and, following through immediately, delivered one of their rare 'night' attacks against Line B in the small hours. But it scarcely grows dark at all in this latitude at this time of year. In the course of the next day the enemy manœuvred the Scots Guards out of Line B, and Line C was abandoned during the night of May 22nd–23rd, the whole battalion withdrawing to the northern side of the watershed. Aided by two Norwegian battalion groups they had fought all the way back from their original position at Stien, south of Mo, during a whole week, and it was fortunate that the Irish Guards had arrived in time to relieve them, otherwise the position of 'Scissors-force' might have become desperate.

This latter battalion deployed at Pothus, about fifteen miles south of the head of the Saltdal inlet on May 25th to fight the last action of British troops in Norway. It had the support of two of the Independent Companies and some Norwegian patrol troops. For two days a stubborn rearguard action continued, our men giving as good as they got and only being forced back by the combination of air attack with flanking movements through the hills on the east. But on the evening of the first day Brigadier Gubbins received a signal from the Headquarters of the North-West Expeditionary Force informing him that the decision had been taken to evacuate the whole of Norway. Following the second day's action at Pothus Gubbins accordingly disengaged his force and withdrew it rapidly to the northern shore of the long Saltdal fjord. Considerable support was given to the troops during the later stages of this withdrawal by two Gladiators which had arrived in the Bodö area; but after giving protection to the rearguard they were summoned back to cope with a violent enemy air attack upon Bodö itself.

For the Germans saw a real opportunity to destroy the dangerously isolated British force, and they determined, as a preliminary move, to deal with Bodö as they had dealt with Namsos. During May 27th their planes attacked the town in great strength, dropping several hundred high explosives and incendiary bombs which destroyed the field-artillery ammunition dump and large quantities of bulk petrol and rations. The two Gladiators did their best against overwhelming numbers and succeeded in bringing down four German machines before they were themselves destroyed. The anti-aircraft guns were knocked out one after another and the airfield so damaged and cratered that with such labour as was available it would probably have taken some weeks to repair.

That was the end of Bodö as a base. There was scarcely a building of any sort left standing. The raid had been a grimly effective example of what German air striking power could accomplish, and it pointed the need for an immediate evacuation, since the supply situation, with half a division concentrated along the fjord, was likely to become acute, though even now Brigadier Gubbins reckoned that, if no further serious diminution of his stocks occurred, he could hold out for another five days.

The Germans, whose follow-up had been so cautious and restrained on the eve of the Aandalsnes and Namsos evacuations, seemed determined not to let the British slip through their fingers for a third time. 'Scissorsforce' withdrew west along the good road on the northern shore of the fjord during May 29th, blowing bridges and leaving covering detachments to hold off the pursuit. Embarkation began at 11 p.m. that night and continued for two more nights, five destroyers ferrying the troops to the *Vindictive* or to Harstad. Lacking air cover, for nothing could be spared from the Narvik sector, the destroyers which carried out the evacuation ran considerable risks in the narrow waters, and it was fortunate that Bodö lay at the entrance and not at the head of the fjord, otherwise we could scarcely have avoided loss from the enemy attacks. The last of the troops, a company of Scots Guards, held an isthmus ten miles from Bodö until the morning of May 31st and then, with the German vanguard close on their heels, withdrew to the landing-stage of the ruined port and successfully embarked. All the guns had to be left behind, but they, with the remaining transport vehicles, were destroyed by our rearguard before embarkation. On this last day two Gladiators and two Hurricanes gave much-needed air cover during the final run.

The 24th (Guards) Brigade and the Independent Companies had received a somewhat thankless assignment which could no more be carried out satisfactorily with the means at their disposal than could the Namsos or Aandalsnes operations. It was, therefore, perhaps not surprising that relations with the local Norwegian command should have been somewhat strained. Certainly the liaison left something to be desired.

Nevertheless, 'Scissorsforce' had not wholly failed in its task. Though driven back two hundred miles, it had kept the field for a month—time enough to enable the troops further north at long last to capture Narvik. (It fell on the day before the Bodö evacuation began.) The extrication of the troops under Gubbins's command was achieved without interruption from the German ground forces, which had followed up closely in a determined attempt to prevent or embarrass the embarkation. Finally, the withdrawal by sea was carried out without involving the Royal Navy in any further losses—which at that crucial stage of the war it could very ill have afforded.

These achievements are necessarily of a somewhat negative nature, but in the history of the Norwegian campaign, where the balance weighed so heavily against us, even negative achievements are worthy of record.

## 4

### *Narvik: The Last Phase*

At Narvik, following the rejection of Béthouart's proposal for a direct assault, the Allied force continued to develop the policy of attrition, fighting their way slowly by each laboriously won spur, through the mountains far to the north of Narvik.

It was not a stimulating prospect. It involved operations through extremely formidable country, carried out by troops only partially equipped for this type of warfare and opposed by an enemy who, though locally outnumbered, had been given plenty of time to select and strengthen his defensive positions. And with improving weather the Germans took more and more advantage of their supremacy in the air for they flew in both supplies and reinforcements.

So far from being equipped for mountain warfare the French Chasseurs Alpins were provided with arms identical with those carried by the infantry. Their patrols were handicapped by the lack of a light easily manageable weapon in their combats with the enemy outposts. They badly needed something similar to the machine-pistol with which the Germans were plentifully supplied. In this warfare among trackless mountain ridges adequate numbers of ski-troops were essential. The French had seventy to every 1000 men.

The maintenance of the forward troops was a constant headache to the quartermaster's department. An adequate supply of mules would have provided the most satisfactory solution, but when the Finnish plan was dropped the number of mules allocated to the Chasseurs was cut by a half, while they were given in replacement an increased supply of small, light lorries, which, designed for use in the flat country around Petsamo, were utterly useless in the very different territory of Narvik. And so mules were largely employed for evacuating the wounded from the mountains while supplies had usually to be carried up on the backs of the advancing troops.

It is, perhaps, not so surprising that no measures had been taken to issue a special concentrated ration of high calorific value that could be easily carried in great quantities; nor to provide the troops destined for mountain warfare with the double-sheeted 'isotherm' tents which the Norwegian troops possessed. The French troops were supplied with heavy boxes of tinned rations; and to avoid frost-bite during the bitter nights in the mountains they were compelled to build themselves snow igloos.

And from the beginning of May there was the further threat from the force advancing from the south upon Mosjöen, Mo and Bodö.

With the last day of April the thaw began, adding its own quota of difficulties to the movements of troops and vehicles, just as the snowfalls earlier in the month had done. Movement at first became more difficult than ever in the valleys, while the risk of avalanches among the mountain heights compelled extra precautions. And, inevitably, the clear sky brought German planes to bomb and machine-gun the whole area from Harstad to our forward positions near Narvik. They had now an estimated strength of twenty-nine air squadrons in Norway, based mostly on Oslo, Stavanger and Vaernes (the airfield of Trondheim), apart from the planes operating from Denmark. Nevertheless, with the British forces at Namsos and Aandalsnes on the verge of evacuation and with the abandonment of our own attempts at a *coup de main* at Narvik, rumours were again persistent that the Germans were on the very point of surrendering this northern outpost. They were understood to be demolishing the quays, the railways and all the industrial plant in the town and port. When the German commander very properly shifted his headquarters from Narvik town to Sildvik, about ten miles back along the railway, this perfectly sound and sensible move was reported—via Stockholm—as 'the mysterious disappearance of the German commander and his staff'. Finally, the expulsion of between two and three hundred Norwegian and British prisoners, to save feeding them any longer, was taken as an indication that the surrender of the garrison was now only a matter of days.

At the beginning of May the British Cabinet, bearing in mind the changed situation caused by the evacuation of central Norway, once more urged the pressing of the attack against Narvik itself. The message concluded with the admonition that every day that Narvik remained untaken, even at severe cost, imperilled the whole enterprise.

This was certainly true enough, and seemed to assume that a direct assault was sooner or later inevitable, for the Germans could not be allowed to remain in Narvik with impunity. Their air attacks upon our troops and shipping were daily becoming more frequent and the weight of bombs was increasing; moreover, the planes were now bombing from a height out of reach of our A.A. guns. And reports from Denmark spoke of German troop-carrying aircraft being made ready to leave for the north. The snow was running out fast now from the Arctic hour-glass.

The attack had been provisionally fixed for May 8th, but following a reconnaissance of the Narvik coast, General Mackesy and his subordinate commanders were agreed that the operation must fail in the face of absolute German air superiority. The Bardufoss airfield was still under snow and could not be ready to receive our planes for some days; the *Ark Royal* had however arrived on May 6th to give some fighter protection during the interim.

And so, in face of this concert of military opinion, the operation was postponed, first until the night of May 10th–11th and then altogether; and the French Chasseurs Alpins, together with the Norwegian troops on their left, continued their hazardous and wearisome progress through the mountains to the east and south of the Gratangenfjord. The only British troops in contact with the enemy were the South Wales Borderers in the Ankenes peninsula to the immediate south of Narvik.

Reinforcements were arriving—two battalions of the French Foreign Legion on May 6th and a brigade of Poles on May 9th. They were needed, for the German threat to Mo and Bodö necessitated the progressive transference of the entire British brigade to that sector.

On May 13th Lieut.-General Auchinleck arrived at Harstad as G.O.C. of the North-West Expeditionary Force, with authority over all the Allied land forces and the air component. The appointment had actually been made on May 5th, but it had not been intended that it should become valid until Narvik had either been taken or the operation abandoned.

Auchinleck brought a fresh eye to the whole situation. In spite of the Namsos and Aandalsnes evacuations it was still the policy of the Supreme War Council to maintain a base in northern Norway for the purpose of denying the iron ore supply route through Narvik to the enemy, also to keep a foothold in the country as a seat for the Norwegian King and Government.

The arrival of General Auchinleck coincided with a fresh attempt to short-circuit the wearisome turning movement through the Gratangen mountains by a landing closer to Narvik. Assisted by a bombardment from H.M. ships *Somali*, *Havelock* and *Fame* the French 13th Demi-Brigade of the Foreign Legion was landed on the eastern side of the Herjangsfjord near Bjerkvik. A Polish battalion was to have made a synchronised attack on Bjerkvik by land, but when they arrived after a twenty-mile march the place had already been taken. By the end of the day General Béthouart's men held the Oyjord peninsula on the northern side of the Rombaksfjord and so could look upon Narvik across the narrow strip of salt water.

It was a full month since the Royal Navy had cleared the waters around Narvik.

With his forward troops within two or three miles of Narvik to both north and south, Auchinleck could now apply himself directly to the assault upon the stronghold. In conference with the Norwegian commanders, Generals Ruge and Fleischer, he made it clear that it was his intention to hold off the enemy from Bodö in the south (for which purpose the whole of the 24th Brigade and the five Independent Companies were to be employed) and to continue offensive operations against Narvik until he took it. At the same time he was applying himself to the problem of maintaining his force in Norway and on May 16th he submitted his appreciation of the situation to the Cabinet.

In his opinion, northern Norway could be held, provided that no serious threat of aggression developed from Russia through Finland or from Germany through Sweden. He also hoped that it would be possible to develop a limited offensive southwards to deny to the enemy the use of Mosjöen as a port. (It had fallen to the Germans five days earlier.)

To maintain his position in Norway Auchinleck estimated that he would require a total of seventeen infantry battalions (representing an addition of some five or six to the total which he already had in the Narvik and Bodö areas) together with a machine-gun battalion, a cavalry regiment, a squadron of armoured cars, a mounted infantry unit, five batteries of field artillery, two batteries of medium howitzers, together with an addition of fifty-six heavy and thirty-eight light A.A. guns to those already established in northern Norway.

As a covering force and for the protection of convoys he estimated that four cruisers, six destroyers, four escort vessels, a dozen anti-submarine trawlers and a couple of submarines would be required.

For air coverage and support two squadrons of Hurricanes, one squadron of bombers and one Army co-operation squadron were judged sufficient.

This did not constitute an extravagant list of demands, and the requests in terms of air support appear extremely modest; but the situation had now to be viewed in the light of the campaign which had opened in the West some days earlier. When General Auchinleck was actually nominated to his command Norway was still our only active land front. Three days before he took control at Harstad the German offensive had been launched against Holland, Belgium and Luxembourg. It was in the light of the steadily worsening situation in Flanders and beyond the Meuse, and the likelihood, as it seemed at the time, that the front in France would draw in all our available reserves, that the Chiefs of Staff replied to Auchinleck's signal. Brussels had just fallen, and further south the effects of the calamitous collapse of French resistance on the Meuse were beginning to be realised.

It was not surprising, therefore, that the Chiefs of Staff replied that while he could be guaranteed practically the entire force that he required, with proportionate engineer and supply services, he must accept limitation to less than half the number of heavy A.A. guns and less than two-thirds the number of light A.A. that he had stipulated. Nor could they include any bombers in his air allocation.

Asked for his views regarding the retention of the Narvik foothold under these conditions, Auchinleck replied that, while the land forces would be sufficient, given a minimum of three field batteries and two batteries of mediums, he could not agree that there was reasonable prospect of his being able to achieve his task if less than half his considered demand for anti-aircraft artillery was to be provided, the more so since the destruction from the air of his base at Harstad or his single mainland airfield might rapidly make the whole position of the Allied force untenable. Without a single squadron of bombers at his disposal he would be unable to employ the most effective means of reply to the German air attacks which had begun to cause him serious anxiety.

He concluded with the following observations. The inevitability of the evacuation of northern Norway was entirely dependent upon the enemy's will to avail himself of his undoubted ability to attack. Should the enemy attack, he could not, with the reduced forces that had been suggested, hold himself responsible for the safety of his Force; nor would he pretend that there was any reasonable certainty of his being able to achieve the object given to him in his instructions. If, in spite of this, larger considerations should lead His Majesty's Government to decide that northern Norway must continue to be held with the diminished resources laid down by them, he could not answer for the consequences; but every effort would be made to do what was possible with the resources at his disposal.

Having despatched this clear and soldierly summary, the British commander applied himself to the immediate situation at the front, and plans were issued for a direct assault upon Narvik to be launched at the earliest possible date.

In the face of Auchinleck's reply there could be only one decision. The Allied forces in France had by this time been cut in halves, and the Germans had reached the Channel near the mouth of the Somme and were moving rapidly northwards to occupy Boulogne and Calais. The possibility of unprecedented disaster for the whole of the British army in France was now horrifyingly imminent. Under these circumstances, during the night of May 24th–25th, orders were received at the Allied headquarters at Harstad that northern Norway was to be evacuated as speedily as possible.

In truth there could be no alternative to this decision. Norway, already a sideshow, became an unjustifiable and highly unprofitable luxury at a time when every man and every gun, every ship and every plane we possessed might soon be needed for the direct defence of our own shores. There were now rather more French than British troops in northern Norway, but, with the Germans on the Somme and the Aisne, the case for their withdrawal was still stronger. Under any circumstances, the report by the Commander-in-Chief had shown that we should soon be faced with the choice of evacuating Norway or being blasted out of it.

Nevetheless, Auchinleck determined to carry through the operation against Narvik, while arranging the preliminaries of the evacuation. The belated occupation of the port would at least ensure the maximum destruction of the facilities for shipping the iron ore to Germany; moreover, it would be an effective method of concealing our intention to evacuate. And if all went well there was always a possibility that, deprived of Narvik, the enemy force, which was composed of elements of some ten battalions[1], might be compelled to surrender.

And so the news of the impending evacuation was communicated at first only to General Béthouart, head of the French contingent. For several days it was concealed from the Norwegians and subordinate commanders.

It was just before midnight May 27th–28th that a British force of three cruisers and five destroyers steamed into the Rombaksfjord and opened a close range bombardment of Narvik and the positions round it. To watchers in the town 'the overwhelming fierceness of this attack was beyond either expectation or description. The night was one long continuous explosion. The British ships ran in from both sides of Narvik peninsula. . . . House after house in Narvik was hit and took fire. Soon the burning houses formed a continuous wall of flame along the shore.'

And under cover of this bombardment troops of the Foreign Legion and 6th Norwegian Division began to cross the Rombaksfjord to the peninsula immediately to the north of the town at midnight, while the Polish brigade opened a converging attack across the hills of the Ankenes sector in the south.

This time the Allies had at last struck with sufficient troops, sufficient fire-power—directly at their target. There was hard fighting for some hours, particularly in the Ankenes sector, where the Germans fiercely counter-attacked the Poles and temporarily recovered some ground, and the two or three tanks which had been employed to support the advance in either sector proved of little use; those that did not promptly break down were soon knocked out by enemy fire. But by evening it was all over. Narvik had been cleared of the enemy in the course of the day and at 10 p.m. General Béthouart was able to report that the town was firmly in French hands, together with the shore-line on either side of it and about 350 German prisoners. During the course of the night the Poles who had smashed their way up from the south-west made contact with the French at the head of Beisfjord.

[1] They had received a further reinforcement by air on May 15th and still more troops arrived immediately before the assault.

But the capture of Narvik did not lead to any weakening of the German resistance. With dogged determination from which it is impossible to withhold our admiration, this indomitable force retired slowly backwards along the line towards Sweden. They had been anticipating this moment and had for some days been preparing supply dumps and even an airfield at Björnefell close to the Swedish frontier. Norwegians, French and Poles pressed forward along the railway, but it was soon clear that there would be no wholesale surrender and that the Germans would fight back mile by mile to the border. Time could not be spared for the barren satisfaction of thrusting them into a probably only temporary internment in Sweden, and the Allied command now began to push ahead its plans for evacuation.

It needed, as it ultimately transpired, only one heave more. The German force, now amounting to about 6,000 men since the reinforcements of mid-May and a further reinforcement just before the attack on Narvik, was almost at its last gasp. It had fallen back upon Björnefell, which was only three miles from the Swedish frontier. Dietl, with his back to the snow-wall, was beginning to note signs of serious indiscipline among his hard-pressed troops. Information to this effect reached the French lines and was a contributory factor in the request made by General Fleischer at this time that two or three French battalions should be left at Narvik, in the belief that, together with the Norwegian forces, they would be sufficient to inflict the *coup de grace* upon the Germans.

It would not have been worth while. There was never any question of Dietl's force surrendering to the Allies. When the vanguard of Chasseurs Alpins, Legionaries and Norwegian troops eventually thrust them from their last stronghold on the Björnefell they must simply have retired across the Swedish frontier into internment. Little glory would have accrued to the Allies in this operation; and, in view of the pressure which Germany was able subsequently to exercise upon Sweden, there is little doubt but that she could have insisted upon their repatriation at any time she wished.

On June 1st Sir Cecil Dormer, British Minister to Norway, after a visit to Harstad, informed the Norwegian Government of our intention to evacuate. The Government in turn passed on the news to the Norwegian High Command, General Ruge and General Fleischer who continued to co-operate loyally to the end.

The withdrawal of our troops began at 10 p.m. on the night of June 3rd and was spread over five days and nights, the last convoy leaving only on the morning of June 8th. It had none of the dramatic quality which had distinguished the Dunkirk evacuation during the previous week. The weather was generally unfavourable for air attack and the Germans only launched one serious raid during this period, and that was directed against Narvik town. On the very last night of the evacuation a small party of enemy parachutists landed near Ballangen on the southern side of the Narvik fjord, too late to hinder our departure.

As a result it proved possible not only to evacuate the whole of the 25,000 troops in the area but also to get away more stores and equipment than had been hoped. A fair proportion of the badly needed A.A. guns were saved, and ten Hurricanes and Gladiators were flown away to the aircraft-carrier, *Glorious*. Every scrap of war material and equipment was going to be urgently needed in the grim struggle that lay ahead in defence of our own shores.

There was a tragic postscript to this otherwise successful evacuation. The German Naval Staff, convinced that what remained of their fleet could provide a valuable relief to the hard-pressed forces of General Dietl, ordered out *Scharnhorst* and *Gneisenau*, together with *Hipper* and their only four available destroyers to attack our naval base at Harstad and shipping in the Harstad-Narvik area. The enemy had no hint that evacuation was taking place, and when the German admiral learned that a large British convoy was at sea he determined to attack it. The troopship *Orama*, which was carrying German prisoners, was sunk, and later on the same day (June 8th) *Glorious*, which was sailing independently of the convoy, was caught and destroyed together with her two attendant destroyers, *Ardent* and *Acasta*. As some compensation for these lossess, *Acasta* succeeded in torpedoing *Scharnhorst* and inflicting damage which kept her out of action for several months.

The total British forces evacuated from the Narvik area amounted to 817 officers and 12,284 other ranks. Our casualties over a period of nearly two months had totalled 45 officers and 461 other ranks. These losses were mostly incurred on the southern ('Scissorsforce') front during the series of rearguard actions from Mosjöen to Mo and Bodö in the month of May.

The French, who by mid-May had about 11,700 troops ashore, lost 170 killed and 360 wounded or missing. Norwegian battle losses were reported as approximately 4,000.

For the whole of the Norway campaign British casualty figures therefore total 150 officers and 1,915 other ranks, much the greatest number of these having been suffered in the course of the operations from Lillehammer back to Aandalsnes.

The official German casualty list gave 1,317 men killed, 1,604 wounded, and the relatively high figure of 2,375 missing, the last figure including those lost at sea. No evidence has emerged since the cessation of hostilities which gives any reason to doubt the German figures for their own losses.

It is a somewhat ironical commentary on the whole Narvik episode that by far the most effective sabotage of port installations and of the plant of the Swedish Iron Ore Company at Narvik was carried out by the Germans prior to their evacuation of the town on May 28th. The demolitions on the railway effected by the Norwegian troops during the first days of the campaign proved a comparatively easy matter to repair. Thanks to the employment of a quantity of civilian labour, working for ten hours a day, the line was open again only three weeks after the Allied evacuation. The damage done at the port proved very much more serious, and the British estimate that a year's work would be necessary to repair the port installations before the iron ore could be shipped in any appreciable quantity proved rather on the conservative side than otherwise.

Not until January 1941 did it prove possible to begin shipping even the smallest quantities of ore. In the twelve-month period that followed, the quantity of shipments averaged little more than nine per cent of the pre-war annual figure of 7,000,000 tons, and although the total climbed during the succeeding months, its peak point, in the early part of 1943, was only twenty-seven per cent of the pre-war figure.[1] After that, owing to the demands made upon German shipping in other quarters, the figure began progressively to decline until the end of the war. German thoroughness in demolition had overreached itself, and it may well be doubted whether the Allies, amateurs in sabotage as in so much else in modern war at that period, could have done anything like so effective a job as that which was done by the Germans themselves.

If only for that reason, it had been worth while persevering until Narvik was taken.

[1] Figures supplied to the author by a representative of the Swedish Iron Ore Company in Narvik, May 1947.

NARVIK : THE APPROACH TO THE HARBOUR

*Photo: Imperial War Museum*

THE CONSTRUCTION OF SKAANLAND AIRFIELD

*Photo: Imperial War Museum*

# Epilogue

THE story of the Norway campaign is largely one of disappointment and failure. In early 1940 the policy of the Allies was still influenced by their initial unpreparedness, material and psychological, for a major war; and perhaps both Britain and France were slow to appreciate the skill with which German aggressions were planned and the thoroughness with which they were carried out. At this time the enemy possessed by far the better war machine and knew how to make the fullest use of it.

Scandinavia had occupied our attention almost from the outbreak of the war when we had first been confronted with the enemy's abuse of Norwegian neutrality in the transit of Swedish iron ore shipped from the port of Narvik to Germany. We had contemplated an expedition to Scandinavia as part of the policy of bringing aid to Finland; we had contemplated it as a means of protecting Norway from the consequences arising out of our mine-laying in her territorial waters. This operation did not, of course, provoke the German invasion, for that had been in preparation for many weeks past. It was largely a coincidence that the far reaching and swiftly executed German thrusts followed so promptly upon our own very limited effort which our naval, military and air-power were not held ready to support.

What occurred within twenty-four hours of our mine-laying operation was merely the development of Germany's own act of aggression into which she had been tempted, rather against the will of the High Command, and at first of Hitler, by the fear of our appearance in this theatre. In other words, it was a strategic retort to the presumed Allied plan of opening up the war in the north rather than a tactical retort to our establishment of mine-fields in Norwegian waters. The Germans, having struck first, left us with the moral advantage of coming into Norway as her defenders. Britain—and France no less—were bound to intervene, for they had entered the war in defence of the rights of small nations. The very faith which they held demanded action against the aggressor, even though such action should be to their own disadvantage.

The Royal Navy, under conditions of extreme hazard, landed the troops in Norway and brought them away again. There is particular cause for pride in such naval achievements as the stirring episodes of the two sea battles of Narvik. Our losses in ships and those of the enemy have been recorded in these pages; it should also be mentioned that by the end of June the enemy's surface fleet had been so reduced by our action as to cause some easement of the Navy's task of protecting our sea communications.

It would be idle to speculate upon the chances of success if the projected naval attack upon Trondheim had been allowed to proceed, and it does not appear that the occupation of Trondheim would have gone far to solve our difficulties. It is true that only by its capture could we have obtained the use of an adequate airfield, but the possession of one or two airfields is no guarantee against air attack so long as the enemy possesses a large superiority in planes and an ability to reinforce his air strength more swiftly and with greater frequency. These were the conditions that prevailed. When, after the naval attack was cancelled, it was seen that our detachments which had disembarked at Namsos and Aandalsnes could not even threaten Trondheim from the landward side, the case for the prompt evacuation of central Norway was complete.

If, from the military angle, the chief satisfaction in the campaign lies in the successful disengaging of our forces and their subsequent withdrawal by sea, due credit must be given to the local commanders and their troops. The handicaps under which the commanders laboured have been described; and it must be remembered that some battalions had received only elementary training, while none had been trained, or were equipped, for mountain warfare amid the snow. For the most part, close support weapons and artillery were lacking, and there was little or no counter to enemy air attacks. The French and Polish contingents suffered to a great extent the same disadvantages.

During their long retreat from Lillehammer to Aandalsnes General Paget's force was obliged to fight a series of rearguard actions. On nearly all these occasions the troops held their positions for as long as had been planned, and the later actions were, on the whole, more skilfully conducted than the earlier ones. At Namsos, a German landing from the sea turned the flank of the Steinkjer position, but our troops were extricated and continued the retreat with negligible loss. At Bodö, when the enemy made a determined effort to destroy the British force, Brigadier Gubbins got his troops clear after being very closely engaged. Taken all in all, we succeeded in withdrawing our various contingents from Norway with far smaller losses than might have been expected.

Norway was not, and could never have developed into, a major theatre of war. Given the limited forces and material at our disposal, the ever present prospect of active operations in France and Belgium, and the need to guard the Middle East, Scandinavia was bound to be, as Mr. Chamberlain described it in the House of Commons on May 7th, a side-show. To the Germans, no less than to ourselves, it was a side-show. They looked upon it as an undertaking that offered certain valuable and tangible benefits, but an undertaking to be indulged 'on margin' since it was eccentric from the all-important and already frequently postponed campaign which was soon to be launched against the main armies of the Allies. But the Germans did expend a total effort in the sense that they demanded and received the maximum from the forces which they employed. What they flung into Norway was committed up to the hilt in terms of enterprise and energy, in terms of imaginative planning and whole-hearted execution.

Once the storm had broken in the Low Countries the Norwegian campaign became, to some extent, an irrelevance so far as the three major combatants were concerned. With the German Panzer divisions sweeping down upon the Channel ports it became abundantly clear that the fate of Norway would be settled elsewhere than on her own territory. Almost from the moment that the French line was broken on the Meuse it became a question of cutting our losses in Scandinavia and extricating our Narvik force as soon as it had carried out its object of doing the maximum damage to the port and railway upon which Germany depended for the shipment of her iron ore.

The interruption to the enemy's supply of this essential raw material can be counted as one advantage gained by the Allies from their intervention in Norway. To the Germans went a valuable prize: possession of the whole Norwegian seaboard from the Skagerrak to beyond North Cape.

# THE COMMANDOS

# CHAPTER I

# Shock Troops in Action

## 1

### *The Commando Idea*

'In co-operation with the Royal Air Force naval and military raiders yesterday carried out successful reconnaissances of the enemy coastline. Landings were effected at a number of points and contact made with German troops. Casualties were inflicted and some enemy dead fell into our hands. Much useful information was obtained. Our forces suffered no casualties.'

*British official communiqué. June 26th* 1940.

'Reconnaissance attacks of weak enemy forces on the north French coast during the night of June 24–25 were repulsed without difficulty.'

*German official communiqué. June 26th* 1940.

BY the end of June 1940 Great Britain stood alone. Poland and France, the two allies with whom she had entered the war in the previous September, had been successively beaten down. The smaller countries that lay in the path of Germany's aggressive designs had suffered the same fate. And as France staggered to catastrophic defeat Italy had entered the war on the side of Germany to claim her share of the spoil. By good fortune, by the heroism of the Royal Navy and of the R.A.F. and perhaps through the providential stubbornness of Herr Hitler, the British Army in Flanders had been snatched from what appeared certain annihilation on the beaches of Dunkirk.

The men lived to fight again, but it seemed that for a long time they must fight defensively to preserve the safety of our Island and the links with our Dominions and Colonies. At some date, unimaginable during the course of that tragic June, it might be possible for the men who had been flung incontinently out of Europe to return as liberators. And meanwhile much must and could be done to strengthen our Middle East base on the Nile until it could be used as a means of striking back in the Mediterranean against the weaker of our two enemies. But for the present the troops in Britain must largely remain an army on the defensive.

It was not the first, though it was the gravest, crisis of this nature in our history. We had faced invasion and subjugation from Philip of Spain when the great Armada sailed up the Channel and the seasoned veterans of the Duke of Parma lay just across the sea in that same Low Country around Dunkirk and Bruges and Brussels awaiting the arrival of the ships that were to transport them to the shores of Kent. We had faced invasion and subjugation from Napoleon of France when the Grande Armée lay encamped on the cliffs above Boulogne and the flat-bottomed transports assembled in the ports below. On each occasion Europe had seemed closed to our forces, with every power either dominated by or in alliance with the tyrant.

It was the historic challenge and it was met in the historic manner. It was not enough that the Battle of Britain should be won in the air by the young men of the R.A.F. as the earlier Battle of Britain had been won in the Channel and in the North Sea by the young sea captains of Drake and Lord Howard of Effingham. We must find some means of taking the offensive with forces inferior in numbers and in a situation that appeared to offer few advantages of any sort. The island stronghold might be a City of Refuge; it was important that it should not become a prison. If we could not keep the field—and we were as incapable of doing so in 1940 as in 1794—we must devise a means of harassing and weakening the enemy. More beards might be singed than that of the King of Spain.

Basically, that was the idea behind the formation and development of the Commandos. It implied the maintenance of the tactical offensive at a time when we were condemned, possibly for years, to the strategic defensive. The many raids that followed that earliest Commando action, so laconically reported above, were less important for what they achieved, in terms of losses inflicted upon the enemy and information obtained, than for the lessons which they taught in the development of new techniques of attack and, above all, for their effect upon the psychology of the troops involved on either side. Perhaps in the truest sense of the term they represented a form of 'psychological warfare'. Not only did they provide confidence and battle experience—both sorely needed—to our own men; they contributed to maintain the enemy garrisons across the water in a state of tension and uncertainty, wondering whether anything would strike them suddenly from the sea or from the air; wondering when, where, and in what manner it would strike.

For that purpose a special force was needed, shock troops, volunteers trained to a high pitch of toughness, endurance and battlecraft. We have already seen the Commandos in their embryonic state as the 'Independent Companies' which, designed for harassing and guerrilla operations in conjunction with a regular force in the field, had to be committed to the thankless task of delaying the German advance northwards upon Narvik after our evacuation of Namsos and Aandalsnes. These Independent Companies were the fore-runners of the Special Service Battalions which were training in Scotland and which were soon to win world fame as the Commandos.

The amphibious tradition in warfare has been nobly maintained by the Royal Marines; but what was required after the conquest of Europe compelled us to 'look to our moat' was the creation of small detached, independent units capable of being rapidly shifted from one point to another and of carrying out lightning raids upon the enemy coastline. A raiding technique was required rather different from the particular responsibilities and aptitudes of the Marines.

The whole coastline of Europe from Narvik to Bayonne was now under German control, and before many months were past the whole coastline of the Mediterranean from Genoa almost to the Dardanelles and from Tripoli to Salum was to pass into the hands of the Axis. But the very extent of the enemy conquests provided just the opportunity that we needed—the opportunity to strike back now here now there at weakly held positions, for even the *Wehrmacht* could not be equally strong at all points, the opportunity of making use of the special topographical and military information which we might expect to receive from members of the fighting forces of the Allied nations in England.

The Commando idea at its inception owed much to the enthusiasm with which it was received by the Prime Minister, whose historical sense and grasp of strategic realities rendered him quick to appreciate the possibility of delivering amphibious strokes similar to those employed, so effectively, by the elder Pitt during the Seven Years War. But for the genesis of the idea we must look to a Staff officer whose name has scarcely broken above the surface of history.

On June 4th, when the evacuation from Dunkirk had just been completed and Mr. Churchill delivered his great 'fight on to the end' speech to a crowded and enthusiastic House of Commons, Lieut.-Colonel Dudley Clarke, G.1 to General Sir John Dill, then Chief of the Imperial General Staff, had set himself, as he walked home from work in the light summer evening, to ponder the means by which British forces might still continue to maintain the offensive spirit and even exercise a tactical initiative. Reflecting upon the occasions in recent history when small mobile armed bands had successfully harassed hostile forces of many times their own number, and considering above all the activities of the Boer Commandos in the later phases of the South African War, he began to feel that the same type of result might be achieved by means of amphibious Commandos which, taking advantage of our continued command of the sea, might operate successfully in mobile hit-and-run raids across the Channel.

'Before I went to bed I tried to marshal my ideas into the outline of a plan jotted down in note form on a single sheet of writing-paper.'[1]

Other minds were working in the same direction during those brilliant and tragic June days. The following evening General Dill himself informed his G.1 that he wanted a means of fostering the offensive spirit in the army until such time as it was possible to resume offensive operations. He showed immediate interest in the suggestion propounded by Colonel Clarke, undertook to put it up immediately to the Prime Minister, and was able, on returning from a Chiefs of Staff meeting on the following morning, to inform his subordinate 'Your Commando scheme is approved, and I want you to get it going at once'.

In the evolution of his idea and in the choice of a name Colonel Clarke has stated that he was influenced by memories of a boyhood spent in South Africa and by reading Colonel Denys Reitz's book *Commando*. The existing conditions, however, imposed two considerations which did much to limit the scale on which the Commandos were organised and the range of their activities.

It had to be taken as axiomatic that no existing army units could be made available by diverting them from home defence.

In view of the wholesale loss of British armament at Dunkirk, the utmost economy in the matter of weapons must be employed. Here again, home defence must necessarily and rightly have priority.

This implied that the Commandos must inevitably be content to operate as it were on the exiguous margin that remained after the evident and clamorous needs of our Homeland, Empire, and ocean communications had been satisfied. There would not be many men

[1] Dudley Clarke, *Seven Assignments*, p. 207.

available for the operations envisaged by Colonel Clarke, and they would have, at the start, exceedingly little material with which to operate. But the idea went forward, and it is a tribute to the dynamism and long-term vision of the Prime Minister that not ten days after the last men had been snatched from the beaches of Dunkirk the first step should have been taken towards re-creating the offensive spirit, however minor and modest might be its earlier manifestations.

On June 12th Lieut.-General Sir Alan Bourne, Adjutant-General of the Royal Marines, was appointed to the command of raiding operations, with the immediate task of getting together volunteers from the Army to train for the execution of these raids and from the Navy to provide the crews and the shipping to convey them to and from their objectives.

It was the same day on which Madame Des Portes, bursting in upon the French Prime Minister, M. Reynaud, while he was in conference with his newly appointed War Minister, General Charles De Gaulle, insisted that an immediate end be brought to the hopeless and pointless struggle against Germany.

It was the same day on which M. Reynaud made his fatal decision to withdraw the seat of Government not to Brittany, where it would remain in contact with the unbroken will and the inflexible decision of the British Prime Minister and the British nation nor yet to North Africa, but to Bordeaux, where it was at the mercy of every defeatist element.

It was the same day on which General Weygand issued his historic one-line order for the general retreat of the French forces to the south, abandoning Paris without a struggle.

That was the time and those were the circumstances under which the Commandos were formed.

The instructions given to General Bourne implied the adoption of tip-and-run tactics which would compel the German defenders to disperse their forces along their immense coastline (thereby conceivably contributing to hamper the maximum concentration for purposes of invasion of our Island) and would also inflict a certain amount of damage upon enemy installations.

There is nothing surprising in the double origin of the Commandos, stemming out both from the theory of Colonel Clarke in Whitehall and the practice of the Independent Companies in Norway. The new ways of war which were being developed with such devastating success by our enemy demanded new methods of counter-action. The Commandos were part of the answer. They were trained, pre-eminently, for amphibious warfare, for the task of landing with secrecy on a hostile coast, engaging in swift and tough fighting ashore, usually accompanied by planned sabotage, and re-embarking again. Stress was therefore laid on night operations and upon the development of craft and subtlety. Discipline was to be no less intense than in Regular units, but it was to be combined with the development of personal initiative. There was to be an absence of the 'nursing' methods by which the private soldier in the Army has so much of his thinking done for him. The men were to receive a billeting allowance and were then left to find their own accommodation. Their physical fitness was to be that of a trained athlete. They learned endurance by lengthy route marches; they were taught to scale cliffs, to swim rivers in full kit or to cross them by means of bridges of toggle rope easily carried on the body. They learned comradeship by being trained to work in pairs—a development of a very old principle of warfare. They learned to endure extremes of fatigue, of cold and heat, to experience sudden and unexpected demands upon their vitality and ingenuity as when, coming off parade at 3 p.m. they would abruptly be informed that the next parade would be held at a point some sixty or seventy or more miles distant at 6 a.m. on the following morning and that they must find their own means of transporting themselves and reporting punctually.

And with all this went intensive training in the use of every form of close-quarter weapon, every form of sudden and stealthy physical assault. For the Commandos were trained as the shock troops of warfare, the experts in daring offensive action, the virtuosi in killing.

Yet certain criticisms of the Commando idea must squarely be faced. The historian examining the records of Commando operations is repeatedly struck by the extreme and remarkable contrast between the intensity of the training and preparation and the comparative insignificance, of the objective.

This applies not to such few really major operations as were carried out (e.g. St. Nazaire) nor yet to those in which the Commando formed a part of a greater whole (e.g. the bridgehead over the Litani during the Syrian campaign in 1941, the bridgehead over the Orne in Normandy in 1944), but rather to the numerous undertakings, many of them unreported in the press, in which a landing was made by perhaps a dozen men, a sentry or two killed, a prisoner or two brought back. On these occasions the damage done and the loss of life inflicted were as negligible as the information obtained. In the terse reports sometimes published stress was put on the importance of such operations and hints were given that the information obtained had been valuable. As an attempt to create uneasiness in the hostile camp such announcements had their merits when we had learned next to nothing. When important information really was obtained, as for instance in the Bruneval raid, our communiqué was careful to make no reference to the fact.

These smaller attacks invite criticism on the grounds that they constituted a policy of pinpricks. They can scarcely be regarded as conforming to the conception of the Prime Minister who noted that he considered it 'unworthy of such a large entity as the British Empire to send over a few cut-throats'. But for some weeks, even months, the few cut-throats represented very nearly all that we could do in the way of offensive action, and if the *Wehrmacht* remained supremely contemptuous of such gnat-bites as we might succeed in inflicting, no other means existed at the time of operating offensively out of Britain. The mistake, if mistake there was, lay in the tendency to prolong the pinprick raids beyond the period when they formed the only offensive potential of our ground-troops against north-western Europe.

A further and by no means negligible argument may be advanced in this connection. Most of the raids, while quite insufficient to cause the enemy serious concern or adversely affect his morale, were yet on a scale that impelled him to devote more attention to his western defences than might otherwise have been the case. The celebrated West Wall was the natural corollary to Hitler's turning away from the contemplated attack upon Britain to unleash his forces against Soviet Russia. Yet the intensity with which this work was undertaken and the speed and thoroughness of its construction were naturally conditioned by the degree of probability of attack. In that connection there is evidence that the various Commando raids against the German-held coast in the west were generally followed by a period of intensive digging and wiring in the sector which had been the object of our attack. It might almost be true to say that to prod at any part of this coastline was to ensure that any neglect of the defences in that sector would speedily be remedied. In other words, if we kept ourselves on the alert by such methods it is pretty clear that we did precisely the same for our opponents.

Nor can too much importance be attached to the battle practice which these operations provided. It was battle practice under highly specialised conditions. There was a rigid time-limit, usually of a very few hours; as a rule, only close-range weapons were involved on either side—no field artillery, no tanks. The attacks being for the most part planned against fixed and static positions were not specially appropriate as a preparation for the war of movement which it was to be hoped might follow the invasion of the Continent from the west.

Yet another aspect should be considered. While it was desirable that the enemy defending the West Wall should be accustomed to the grim if stiffening realisation that at any time and at any point he was liable to attack, yet the tension so created could be and was visited upon the local inhabitants. In this respect, of the two countries habitually visited by the Commandos from the United Kingdom, Norway seems to have suffered more severely from enemy reprisals than did France, and consequently the Norwegian reception of our raiders was frequently more restrained. The sequel to the first raid on the Lofoten Islands, when our Commando accomplished its task with smoothness and despatch, was the arrest by the Germans of large numbers of Norwegian officers. Many arrests of British sympathisers occurred in Svolvaer and other towns. When the Commandos returned nine months later on the occasion of the second raid they were told, 'You are heartily welcome if you come to stay, but we don't want another Svolvaer'.

Ideally, of course, the Commando raids were not intended to involve the local inhabitants. The intention was that the raiders should slip in and out, take what they had to take, destroy what they had to destroy, and kill whom they had to kill without interruption or interference; ideally, no fighting was implied in the smaller raids, or only fighting of such a one-sided nature that the German defenders died or disappeared without ever knowing what had hit them. This, of course, was an ideal not often achieved; but it should be noted that the more smooth and successful our operation the more likely would the enemy be to jump to the conclusion that it had been assisted and abetted by local civilians. Against the importance of the objectives to be achieved by the raid had to be set the retrospective German counter-measures.

All this must not be taken as a condemnation of the Commando idea or of the technique and methods employed. The training and evolution of shock troops for special tasks is a recognised feature of modern war. But it is important that the tasks should be commensurate with the training and preparation. As our offensives grew more spacious and more ambitious (North Africa, Italy, Normandy) the Commandos themselves came to be relied upon for co-operation in the general plan by taking on the more particularly difficult and hazardous tasks as a part of a greater whole. For this became the true function of the Commandos once the country had survived by heroism and bluff the great crisis of 1940–41. When Lovat's men swarmed ashore near Courseulles at dawn on June 6th, 1941, they were the spearhead of a mighty army, carrying out a long and deeply conceived plan.

## 2

### 1940: *The Early Raids*

It does not fall within the scope of this book to produce a minute and detailed account of every Commando raid undertaken during the six years of war, but rather to select the more important and more symptomatic, and to note the general trend of Commando activities. Certain operations undertaken by troops other than Commandos are appropriately included.

Perhaps the night of June 24th–25th, 1940, represents for Britain the very nadir of the war. The armistice signed by France in the Forest of Compiégne was due to come into force on the following morning, and Britain would thenceforth stand absolutely alone in arms against the might of Hitler's victorious Germany to which had been added the almost unblooded strength of Fascist Italy. On that midsummer night of high tragedy and yet higher defiance and resolution the first Commando raid was launched.

It was not a very elaborately prepared raid. It could not have been, for it was only twelve days since a Directorate of Raiding Operations had been formed, and in that intense month of June those who controlled the Armed Forces of the country had many and more pressing matters to consider. The scale of the raid was modest, though not so modest as many which subsequently followed. A force of 200 men was to be landed at various points on the French coast south of Boulogne to obtain information about the nature of the German defences and to bring back prisoners. It was most unlikely that the German High Command, which confidently expected a British surrender in a matter of some three weeks, would have taken any elaborate steps to fortify the French coast against a British counter-invasion, and the enterprise, therefore, could have little but a psychological effect. But it was a beginning.

Inevitably the raid was characterised by a good deal of improvisation. It was uncertain what shipping would be available. Defects were found in the craft that were allotted, and at the last moment eight fast, light motor-boats manned mainly by civilian crews were substituted. But only sufficient were obtained to convey 115 officers and men of No. 11 Independent Company. This party set sail before dark towards a mid-channel rendezvous. Major R. J. F. Todd of the Argyll and Sutherland Highlanders was in charge of the landing operation with Lieut.-Commander J. W. F. Milner-Gibson as Senior Naval Officer. Colonel Clarke, in whose brain the Commando idea had germinated, also accompanied the expedition.

Landings were to be made shortly after midnight at four specified points on the twenty-mile stretch of coast between Boulogne and Berck-sur-Mer. The four parties would pick up information, destroy any enemy installations they might happen across and bring back what prisoners they could. It was not intended that they should remain ashore for more than an hour—which scarcely gave sufficient time for any very detailed reconnaissance.

The four parties met with somewhat varied fortunes. One of them went ashore among the sand dunes which fringe much of this coast, made no contact with the enemy and duly withdrew after penetrating successfully some hundreds of yards inland. A second was frustrated in its approach by discovering that the point where it had been detailed to land was being used as a German sea-plane anchorage. It was hoped that it might be possible to take advantage of this chance to try and destroy some of the sea-planes. But as one of the boats drew in close to shore a sea-plane was observed to take off and hum overhead, only a few feet above the boat. It was clear that the Germans at this point were thoroughly on the alert and since the chance of surprise was lost the troops wisely did not land.

The third party, which included both Colonel Clarke and Major Todd, made their reconnaissance ashore without encountering any Germans, but during the withdrawal a small number appeared and shots were exchanged, one of which struck Colonel Clarke a slight glancing blow behind the ear—the only casualty sustained by any of the landing-parties. The fourth group met with more success. Landing at Merlimont Plage, between Le Touquet and Berck, they took unawares a couple of German sentries and killed them both. It occurred to no one to search the bodies for documents.

The return partook of the nature of an anti-climax. The boats straggled back independently, and one of them was refused admission to Folkestone harbour since no one on board was successful in establishing his identity. It lay off the boom for some time before the occupants were permitted to land.

This was not a very auspicious beginning. Clearly planning, training, and equipment, would all require far more prolonged and detailed attention for the tasks which lay ahead.

COMMANDO TRAINING: A LANDING

*Photos: Imperial War Museum*

COMMANDO TRAINING: MOUNTAINEERS

LOFOTEN ISLANDS: OIL BURNING AT STAMSUND

*Photo: Imperial War Museum*

The summer and autumn of 1940 saw a continuance of the policy of small pin-prick raids upon the occupied coast of France. Their tactical importance was not great. The most interesting, in the light of after developments, one may well feel, was that which was carried out on the night of September 27th–28th on the coast of Normandy. The two points selected for attack by detachments of No. 1 Commando were St. Vaast on the eastern side of the Cherbourg peninsula and Courseulles on the coast of Calvados, north-east of Bayeux and north-west of Caen. St. Vaast is a few, a very few, miles to the north of a beach which the men of General Bradley's First American Army were to name Utah, where they swarmed ashore at daybreak on June 6th four years later, and it was at Courseulles that the 3rd Canadian Division of the Second British Army went ashore on that same tremendous morning. One is tempted to wonder whether Adolf Hitler or Keitel, Von Rundstedt or Rommel, as they sought feverishly to read the mind of the Anglo-American command during those late spring days of 1944 ever scanned the records of a trifling incident nearly four years earlier when two weak troops of Commandos landed and stayed ashore twenty and twenty-five minutes respectively at St. Vaast and near Courseulles and killed three Germans in the process.

On a larger scale was the raid carried out against Guernsey, which with the other Channel Islands had been occupied by the German forces soon after our evacuation of the mainland of France late in June. The object on this occasion was primarily sabotage, only secondarily the gathering of information. Elements of No. 3 Commando (under Major J. F. Durnford-Slater) and No. 11 Independent Company (Major R. J. F. Todd) amounting to a total of 32 officers and 107 other ranks were to land at three points on the east and south-east of the island and destroy such petrol stores, workshops and aircraft as they might find on and around the aerodrome of Le Bourg. There was a more direct military logic behind this raid than in the case of either of the other two that have been mentioned. Since the grand invasion of England was imminently expected in that month of July, 1940, it was probable that the Luftwaffe would attempt to establish forward fighter bases as speedily as possible, and the advanced and exposed situation of the aerodrome on Guernsey seemed to offer an unique opportunity for a swift spoiling attack.

On the night of July 14th the force set sail in two destroyers, H.M. ships *Scimitar* and *Saladin*, accompanied by seven motor-boats which were to transfer the troops to the beaches. The distance to be

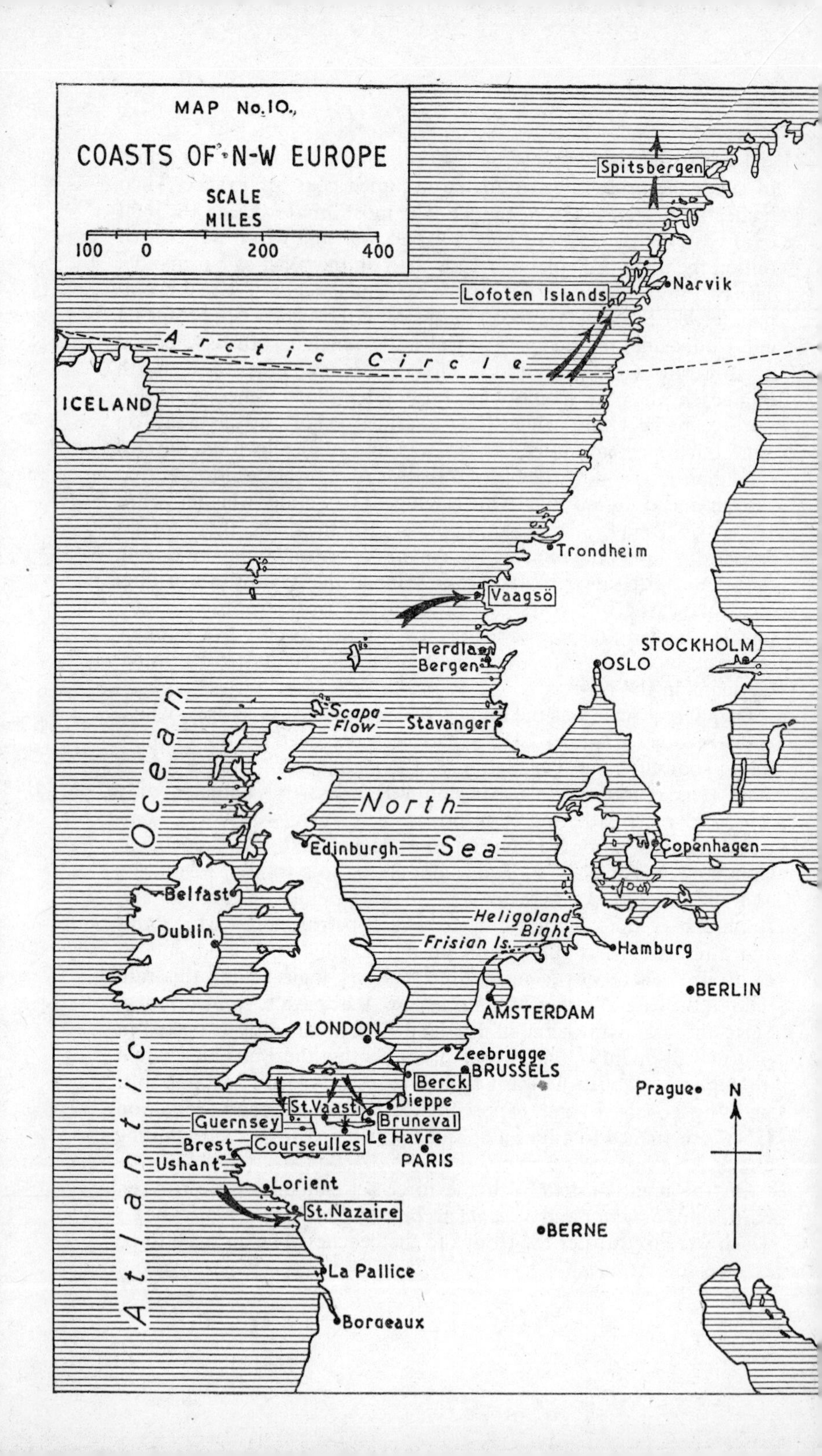
MAP No.10.
COASTS OF N-W EUROPE
SCALE
MILES
100 0 200 400
Spitsbergen
Narvik
Lofoten Islands
Arctic Circle
ICELAND
Trondheim
Vaagsö
Herdla
Bergen
STOCKHOLM
OSLO
Scapa Flow
Stavanger
Atlantic Ocean
North Sea
Edinburgh
Copenhagen
Belfast
Dublin
Heligoland Bight
Frisian Is.
Hamburg
BERLIN
AMSTERDAM
LONDON
Zeebrugge
BRUSSELS
Berck
Prague
N
Dieppe
St.Vaast
Bruneval
Guernsey
Le Havre
Brest
Courseulles
PARIS
Ushant
Lorient
St.Nazaire
BERNE
La Pallice
Bordeaux

traversed was considerably greater than in the case of the Boulogne-Merlimont raid three weeks earlier, and there was a distinct possibility of attack by enemy submarines, E-boats or aircraft. It was also not unlikely that the expedition might have to face attack from French surface craft, since the unhappy Oran incident had brought the two former allies to the verge of declared hostilities.

As on the occasion of several other raids during this early period, difficulty was experienced in striking land at the intended points. One party drifted completely astray, their compass failing them. They arrived off an unfamiliar shore with high cliffs and no beaches, which they believed to be the island of Sark. The second group also failed to make land; they had difficulties with the engines of their motor-boats and eventually turned about and set a course for home. The third party met with more success. Forty men under the command of Major Durnford-Slater touched down on time. The sea was choppy and, since the boats could not come close in owing to the rocks, the men waded ashore up to their waists in water. A reconnaissance of the south-east corner of the island, known as the Jerbourg peninsula, revealed the fact that no steps had yet been taken to render the aerodrome operational and that the barracks where it had been supposed that the enemy might be found were empty. The process of combing the peninsula took longer than had been expected and little information of a positive nature was gleaned. Moreover, the rising swell made re-embarkation exceedingly difficult, and four men who were not strong swimmers had to be left behind and were eventually captured by the Germans.

The scale and achievement of the above raids makes it clear that Commando activities exercised no significant effect upon the course of the war during 1940. It was not to be supposed that they would. These first months were a period of training and preparation interrupted only by occasional minor raids carried out by small improvised forces with an even more improvised armament. It was not until 1941 that the raids began to develop in scale and importance.

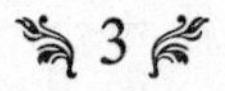

## 3

### *The Mediterranean*

On July 17th, 1940, Admiral of the Fleet, Sir Roger Keyes (later to be Baron Keyes of Zeebrugge and Dover) was appointed Director of Combined Operations, succeeding Lieut.-General Bourne who loyally undertook to serve as his second-in-command. No figure stood higher in the public imagination as a symbol of the daring offensive traditions of the British armed forces. It was Sir Roger who had conducted the brilliant St. George's Day raid upon Zeebrugge in 1918, the outstandingly successful amphibious operation of the earlier war. His re-appointment to active service, and the particular rôle for which he was selected were an indication of the importance that the War Cabinet attached to the development of the Commando idea not merely as representing a potential 'nuisance weapon' but rather as a direct factor in our strategy. For Sir Roger Keyes was not a man with whom it was possible to associate half-measures.

By the beginning of 1941 the pattern of the war with Germany and Italy was already very different from that which it had presented at the time when the Directorate of Combined Operations had been formed six months earlier. On the one hand the prospect of an armed invasion of Britain, though it had by no means passed, had immensely decreased as the result of the great autumn victory of the R.A.F.; on the other, we now had a land front very much in being in northern and eastern Africa, where the meagre and thinly spread forces under General Wavell were dealing vigorously with Italian armies nearly ten times their number. At the same time Mussolini's ill-calculated aggression against Greece had brought to our side a new and heroic ally, who was engaged in belabouring the armies of the Fascist dictator in the mountains of Albania. In less than six months the war had taken a most remarkable turn for the better.

Fascist Italy had been shown to be militarily feeble—far feebler than had ever been supposed—and something less than half-hearted in its enthusiasm for the war. The question now was how this could best be capitalised, how could the weak southern flank of the Axis be so assailed that Italy might, perhaps even in 1941, be knocked out of the war, or at least her armies be driven from Albania and Libya. It was with the object of hastening this process that the decision was taken early in 1941 to deliver an airborne attack upon the great Apulian aqueduct in southern Italy.

This great engineering achievement provides the main water supply for the 2,000,000 inhabitants of the province, including the towns of Taranto, Brindisi, Bari, and Foggia, the three first-named places being ports of embarkation for Albania and the Balkans. It was supposed, a trifle optimistically, that the cutting of this source could be so effectively carried out that it would take a full month to repair. As a result it was not impossible, so ran the argument, that the Italian Government, already struggling with its difficulties in both Albania and

Libya, might be less inclined to persevere with one or both of these campaigns.

It was a distant hope; but since the number of men involved was small, and the possible gain was very great there would seem to be full justification for the attack. At the very least it provided an opportunity of trying out newly trained parachutists in an offensive operation with a clearly defined objective. That was justification enough.

The operation has especial interest as being the first British airborne operation in history. By comparison with later undertakings its scale was minute and its degree of success very modest; but it is the first milestone on the road which is marked by such mighty enterprises as the Normandy airborne landing, Arnhem, and the airborne crossing of the Rhine. For that reason the parachutist action against the aqueduct in the neighbourhood of Monte Vulture on February 10th, 1941, is assured of its place in history. It was a beginning, and no beginnings are without significance.

From the host of volunteers who swarmed to apply when it was known that some form of parachutist action against the enemy was intended, seven officers and thirty-two other ranks were finally selected. Under the command of Major T. A. C. Pritchard (Royal Welch Fusiliers) the party was composed partly of Royal Engineers, under Captain G. F. K. Daly, to whom would fall the task of blowing up the aqueduct, partly of infantry who would provide the covering party. This number included two Italian anti-Fascists who would act as interpreters.

On the night of February 7th–8th, Major Pritchard and his men were flown to Malta, the base from which the attack would be launched, in six Whitleys, which would carry them over their target. The photographs received that day indicated not one but two aqueducts, 200 yards apart, clearly outlined against a background of snow in the wild and desolate country south-west of Monte Vulture. The site selected for the demolition was sufficiently remote to suggest that there was a good chance of carrying out the operation unimpeded. After that the group would scatter and make its way as best it could through the sparsely populated southern Appenines to the mouth of the Sele, on the west coast of the peninsula near Salerno (at the very spot where British and American troops were to go ashore two and a half years later). Here a submarine would lie in waiting to take them off on the night of D+8 and again on the night of D+15. In view of the surprise nature of the action, the probable absence of any very serious defence forces from the neighbourhood, and the distraction of Italian attention elsewhere, there seemed a reasonable hope that the men might be able to carry out their task and subsequently to make their escape undetected.

At dusk on February 10th, eight Whitleys took off from Malta. Six of them carried the parachutists and were detailed to drop them over the target area; the other two would carry out a diversion by bombing the large airfield of Foggia.

The night was clear, with a full moon throwing into relief the snow-covered heights below, when five of the six troop-carrying Whitleys arrived over their target about 9.45 p.m., a quarter of an hour after zero hour, and proceeded to drop their load of men and containers from a height of about four hundred feet.

The drop was tolerably accurate, some of the parachutists landing within fifty yards of their objective and none further than three-quarters of a mile away. Major Pritchard assembled his men, only to discover that the passengers in the sixth Whitley had not arrived.

This plane had been delayed at the start, owing to last-minute engine trouble, and when it eventually took off it lost its way. It arrived slightly off course and about an hour and three-quarters late. The six parachutists whom it dropped landed, in consequence, in the wrong valley, much too far away to take part in the night's proceedings. Most unfortunately this party included Captain Daly and some of the engineers.

There was nothing to be gained by delay, and Pritchard accordingly began to organise the collection of the containers, with the assistance of a dozen farm hands who were rounded up in a neighbouring building. These latter went obediently about their task in the phlegmatic manner of peasantry all over the world, one of them remarking that whereas nothing had ever happened before in their valley, now they would have something to talk about for the rest of their lives.

Lieut. G. W. Paterson, the senior sapper officer, had meanwhile examined the pier of the aqueduct, which was found to be constructed not of masonry, as had been supposed, but of concrete, which would present a much tougher problem. However, 800 lb. of explosive were available, though some of the containers had failed to leave the aircraft, and Paterson thought that this would be sufficient for the task in hand. A small covering force was formed under the command of Lieut. A. J. Deane-Drummond, while the sappers went to work packing the dynamite against the west pier of the aqueduct and its abutment. Soon after midnight all was ready. The Italians were shepherded into a farm building, warned that if they attempted to escape they would be shot, and at 12.30 the main charge was fired.

When the descent of debris had ceased, Paterson examined the results. The pier had collapsed and the water was already beginning to flood down into the valley. Meanwhile a minute or two later Lieut. Deane-Drummond, with such dynamite as remained over had blown up, for full measure, a small bridge crossing the Genestra stream nearby.

Leaving their one casualty (a broken leg incurred in landing on the hard ground) in a neighbouring farmhouse, the party now made off for the mouth of the Sele, fifty miles distant. They had ample time to cover the distance, since the submarine was not due for a week. But, as they wore uniforms, detection could only be avoided by travelling at night and lying up by day. Major Pritchard divided the thirty-three men into three groups, each with an officer in charge. His own group, moving off westward, was compelled gradually to edge up towards the mountains and when dawn broke on February 12th, after their second night of travel, they found themselves above the snow-line. They took refuge in a cave, but inevitably their traces were all too visible. A farmer noted them and gave the alarm. From their hide-out the parachutists had the sombre experience of watching the preparations for their capture. Three bloodhounds led the way, followed by a miscellany of village dogs; next came a gaggle of village children drawn on by curiosity, followed in their turn by pursuing mothers, endeavouring to bring them back; behind the mothers came the fathers, similarly entreating, and behind the fathers came the local gendarmerie. In this tragi-farcical situation there was no choice left for our men. They had little ammunition left, and no opportunity to use it. Major Pritchard was accordingly compelled to surrender.

The same day saw the rounding up of the other two parties concerned in the blowing up of the aqueduct. Captain Daly's little group, however, enjoyed rather a longer run for their money. They had heard the sound of the explosions and realised that the work had been accomplished. They broke away west and remained at large until February 15th. By that time, however, they were still about eighteen miles from the Sele mouth, and running short of food. They endeavoured to bluff their way through by claiming to be German airmen in urgent need of a car. The bluff was called and they were requested to show their papers. That was the end.

The material results of the raid fell some way short of expectations. So far from taking a month to repair the aqueduct appears to have been in use again after two and a half days and before the local reservoirs in the towns which it served had run dry.

More important, however, was the moral effect. The affair gave the Italian rulers a bad fright. If it did nothing else, it at least demonstrated the value that lay in the Commando principle of compelling the enemy to feel that we were in a position to strike at him at any time and in any place. The neighbourhood of the aqueduct was barred off from neutrals, more stringent air raid precautions were introduced and something in the nature of a Home Guard began to be formed to combat future enterprises of this nature. This was all to the good, inasmuch as it compelled the Italians to withdraw manpower from the armed forces or from the production of war material.

But perhaps the most valuable effect was political. Two anti-Fascists had been among the party, and the Italians feared that there might have been others who had not fallen into their hands. Henceforth the possibility that further exiles might be parachuted into the country to sow disaffection towards the Fascist regime was an ever-present fear for the authorities. Many Italians hated the Fascists and their German allies; the incident of the Apulian viaduct, unimportant in its material achievement, might be taken to represent the writing on the wall.

During the second half of 1940 it had become clear that the Middle East must be the principal area of operations for our land forces for some considerable time to come. It was natural, therefore, that steps should be taken at an early stage to form local Commandos in that theatre of war and to despatch from Britain what could be spared from raiding operations directed across the Channel and the North Sea.

Two Commandos (Nos. 50 and 52) were formed in the Middle East, and three more (Nos. 7, 8 and 11) were despatched to the same area early in 1941. At that time plans were afoot for these to be used in co-operation with the 16th Brigade, together forming the 6th Division, to launch a full-scale attack upon the Dodecanese.

Even before the turn of the year the plan had come under consideration, and it was formally approved by the Defence Committee on January 21st. Since the entry of German troops into Rumania in early October and the Italian attack upon Greece at the end of the same month, it seemed clear that the next phase of the war would be fought out in the Balkan peninsula; and since British aid to Greece was envisaged at this early date it was obviously desirable to clear the flank of our sea communications with Piraeus and Salonika. Moreover, the conquest of the Dodecanese would eliminate the air threat to the Suez Canal, would give our shipping undisputed command of the eastern Mediterranean and would constitute an added inducement to Turkey to enter the war on our side.

The operation, which was planned with considerable care, was to have started in mid-April with a direct attack upon Rhodes and Scarpanto. The troops earmarked for it were supplementary to those who were to be despatched to Greece in accordance with the agreement reached in the Tatoi and Athens conversations in February–March; and in view of the state of Italian morale at this date there were good prospects of success. But the reverse suffered in Cyrenaica in the first days of April, caused General Wavell to cancel the operation only a fortnight before it was due to take place. This was just as well, for even had we taken the islands we could not have held them after the German conquest of the mainland, and they must have suffered the same fate as Crete. Only on the assumption that General Maitland Wilson's army had a reasonable prospect of remaining on the mainland of Greece would this diversion of force have been justified.

The whole question of the proper employment of Commandos in the Middle East was never satisfactorily settled. Nos. 50 and 52 Commandos were fed into Crete at a late stage of the battle and compelled to make use of their training in offensive tactics to conduct a defensive action covering the retreat of the main body. In the process they lost seventy-five per cent of their strength killed or captured.

Immediately following this disaster a Composite Commando was employed to secure the crossing of the Litani river in the opening phase of the Syrian campaign; this action has been described by Lord Keyes as 'the one really successful Combined Operation carried out in the Middle East',[1] but again the losses were heavy—about a third of the men committed.

Thereafter, the part played by the Commandos in the Middle East waned in importance. On the whole, G.H.Q. in Cairo never took very kindly to the idea. The reason is not far to seek. It had always one, frequently two, and at one critical stage four campaigns on its hands. And the troops in the field, as can be seen from a study of the campaigns in Greece and Syria, were never sufficient for the tasks they were called on to perform. The strained planners in the vast block of flats on the fringe of Cairo's Garden City had to devote much of their time to the exacting task of trying to make two ends

[1] *Amphibious Warfare and Combined Operations*, p. 91. Lord Keyes of course was referring to Commando actions as such and not to major operations: the Anglo-American landings in North Africa and Sicily, etc.

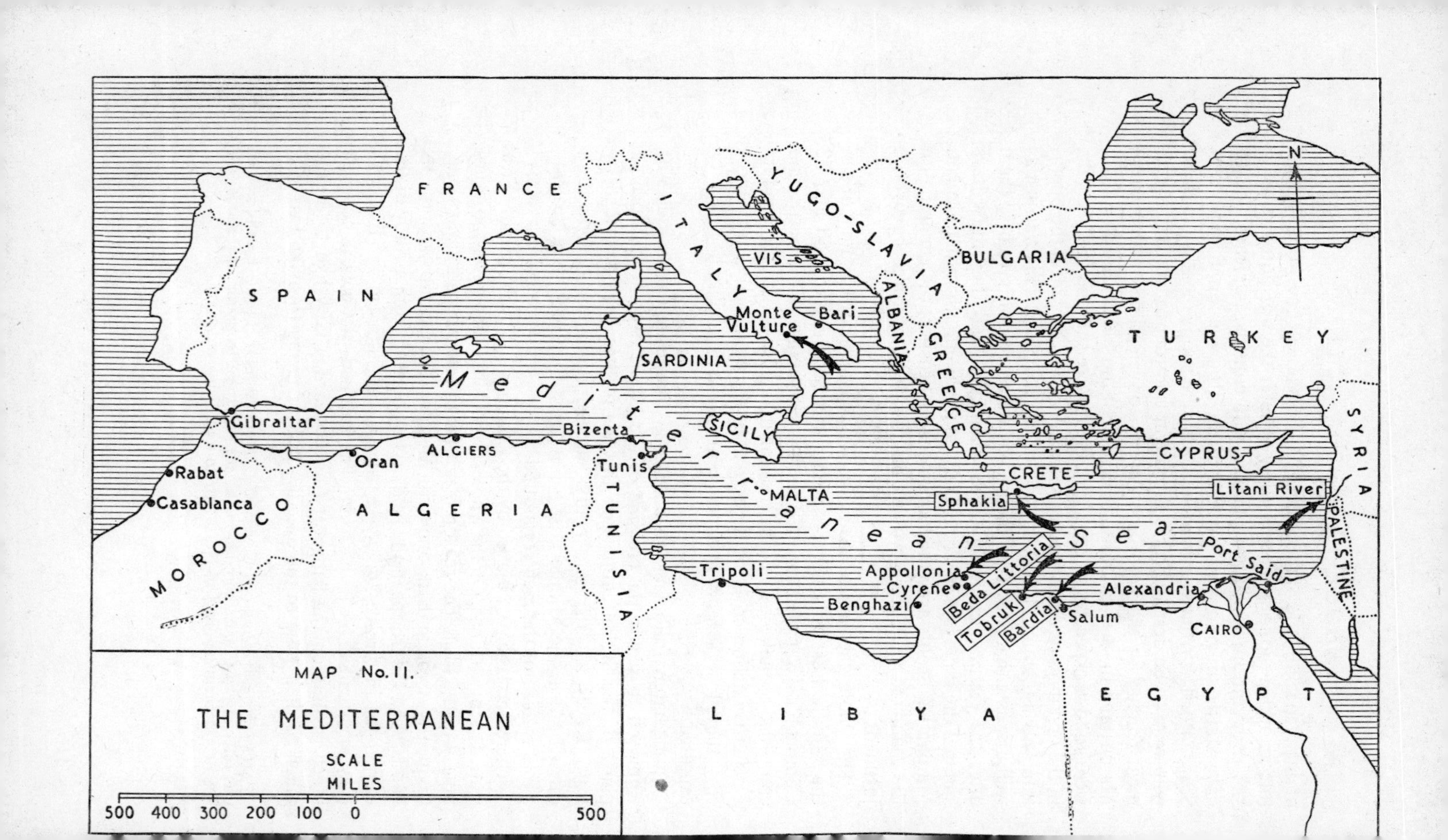

MAP No. 11.
THE MEDITERRANEAN
SCALE
MILES
500
400
300
200
100
0
500
FRANCE
SPAIN
ITALY
YUGO-SLAVIA
BULGARIA
ALBANIA
GREECE
TURKEY
SYRIA
PALESTINE
MOROCCO
ALGERIA
TUNISIA
LIBYA
EGYPT
Mediterranean Sea
Gibraltar
Rabat
Casablanca
Oran
ALGIERS
Bizerta
Tunis
SARDINIA
SICILY
MALTA
VIS
Monte Vulture
Bari
Tripoli
Benghazi
Cyrene
Appollonia
Beda Littoria
Tobruk
Bardia
Salum
Sphakia
CRETE
CYPRUS
Litani River
Alexandria
Port Said
CAIRO
N

meet, trying to stretch each brigade to do the work of three. It was therefore quite naturally felt that any additional troops that might become available could be profitably employed in supplementing our chronic shortage of infantry on one of the main fronts rather than in engaging in what were regarded as no doubt lively but not very relevant side-shows.

Nor was there the same psychological need as existed in England for maintaining the offensive spirit. For here it was no question of toning up an army condemned to wait through weary months that dragged on into years for the opportunity of putting its training to the test. Here there was a front in being and direct contact with the enemy; there was no English Channel between and our troops did not have to get into boats when they wanted to find him.

Only two independent Commando raids were carried out in the Mediterranean during this year, and both of these belong properly to the story of the ebb and flow of the desert war. The earlier one was directed against Bardia, which had recently passed back into enemy hands, on the night of April 19th–20th. The whole of No. 7 Commando was employed with the object of surprising and destroying enemy concentrations in the neighbourhood of the town. Tactically the assault was a failure, for our information proved out of date. Bardia itself was found to be completely empty and there were no enemy concentrations in the neighbourhood. Nevertheless, some strategic advantage resulted. Rommel, who had been pressing us hard on the Egyptian frontier, though with an unsubdued Tobruk on his flank, grew concerned at the prospect of further menace to his communications. He could not risk seeing a British force established at Bardia as well as at Tobruk. Accordingly, troops were diverted to adopt a watching rôle against further attempts of this nature. The effect of this move on the course of the campaign cannot be assessed with certainty.

The second raid was still more closely integrated into the strategy of the desert war. General Auchinleck in the autumn of this year was engaged in planning his offensive which aimed at destroying the German Panzer divisions and reconquering Cyrenaica. He aimed at preceding it with a stroke at the nerve centre of the enemy—Rommel's Headquarters at Beda Littoria, 250 miles behind the battle front. Here it is sufficient to say that, despite the great gallantry shown by the Commando detachment which carried out the attack, it failed of its main purpose. Our information proved faulty, for it was subsequently learned that the house attacked was not Rommel's headquarters. Of the fifty-nine men despatched on the expedition only

Brigadier Laycock himself and one other man returned. It was a bold and courageous stroke, but the chances of laying by the heels so mobile a commander as Rommel were never excessive.

Even before this raid took place the Middle East Commandos had been largely broken up. A detachment of No. 8 Commando had taken part during the summer in the defence of Tobruk, but 'Layforce', following its heavy losses in Crete, ceased to exist.

So far as Africa was concerned that was practically the end of Combined Operations in the more specialised sense (save for one unsuccessful raid upon Tobruk, at that time in German hands, in September 1942) until the great venture of the North African landings so profoundly altered the whole course of the war. With Greece and Crete constant contact was retained, and British liaison officers were continually put in or Greek patriots withdrawn by submarine with little interference from the enemy. Particularly effective was a raid on Crete at the beginning of July 1943, as part of a deception scheme aimed at inducing the enemy to believe that Crete and Greece were the designed objectives at a time when our invasion fleets were actually on the point of departure for Sicily.

Whether the Commandos could have been used with greater effect in the Middle East will no doubt always be open to question. There were those who like Lord Keyes, believed that this theatre of war was admirably suited to their use, and those who regarded them as a mere luxury to be indulged when no really pressing operations impended.

On the one hand the number of objectives of vital importance within reach of our amphibious forces; the peculiar nature of the enemy's line of communications to his armies in Africa, which had first to cross the Mediterranean and then to run parallel to the sea along the coast of Libya; the existence of smouldering rebellion against the Axis in both Yugoslavia and Greece—all these seemed to offer opportunities more favourable in many respects to the Commando technique than were presented by the German-held coasts beyond the Channel and the North Sea.

But to set against this was the chronic shortage of shipping in the Mediterranean, intensified by the necessity of keeping Malta permanently, and Tobruk through eight vital months, adequately supplied. More decisive still in inhibiting Commando activities was the desperate need of manpower. Even after the successful completion of the subsidiary Middle Eastern campaigns (Iraq, Syria, Persia) during the summer of 1941 it was still necessary to maintain a considerable military establishment to protect these three countries against possible invasion from the north. The German attempt at conquest by infiltration had been foiled in 1941, but the danger of conquest by direct attack through the Caucasus or Turkey was a very real one almost to the end of 1942.

For these reasons the 'luxury theory' prevailed. Commandos, it was decided, were all very well for toning up training, for providing battle experience and for maintaining the offensive spirit in the armies at home. But here in the Middle East and Mediterranean there was always one front permanently *in esse* and two or three others continually *in posse*. Here there were better ways of employment for picked troops than to dissipate them in a succession of haphazard uncoordinated tip and run raids, such as appeared, viewed from the angle of Cairo—or Alamein—to be the practice at home.

Was there then no scope for an irregular raiding force operating against the enemy's rear and lines of communication and demanding the exercise of the same qualities of courage, endurance and quick imaginative thinking that were encouraged among the Commandos? There was scope for such a force. Already, before the first Commandos arrived in the Middle East, in the Long Range Desert Group the answer had been found. It was not trained precisely along Commando lines, and it was not an amphibious force. It did not need to be, for in the Middle East it was not necessary to get into boats in order to attack the enemy. But the activities of these mobile forces roving far out across the North African desert were the natural counterpart to the spoiling raids carried out across the waters by the picked troops of the beleagured garrison of the United Kingdom.

## 4

### *In Northern Waters*

The raids which were carried out against Norway were primarily economic in object. For geographical reasons Norway was never a 'starter' as a possible region for the opening of the so-called 'Second-Front'—if only because the invasion of Norway involves a further amphibious expedition before Germany or Central Europe can be entered.

The first important overseas Commando raid was directed against the Lofoten Islands, off the north coast of Norway in March, 1941. Its objectives were economic in the first instance, secondarily political, only indirectly military. These remote islands, situated in practically the same latitude as Narvik, were of particular importance on account of the herring and cod-oil factories in the four ports of Stamsund, Henningsvaer, Svolvaer, and Brettesnes, which supplied glycerine for the making of munitions (also for the Vitamin A and B capsules, used by German troops). The destruction of these four factories, which between them provided fifty per cent of Norway's output of fish oil, would therefore have much the same effect as would a highly successful air-raid upon a German industrial target. In addition to this primary objective, the Commando, besides capturing or sinking any enemy ships that might be encountered, would be able to carry out additional subsidiary functions not possible for aircraft. The opportunity was to be taken to bring off recruits for the Norwegian armed forces, to round up notable quislings in the neighbourhood and any Germans whom we might happen to encounter on the spot, and to distribute such comforts as coffee, sugar, and clothing to the local inhabitants.

This like other Commando operations whose objectives were economic, aimed at accomplishing its purpose as far as possible without engaging in action with the enemy.[1] Yet, though it was improbable that any strong German force would be stationed at so distant a northern outpost, and although our Commando raids had hitherto been confined to the French coast and the Channel Islands, planning had to take place on the assumption that the landing would be opposed and that we might be involved in hard fighting by both sea and land. The force despatched consisted of some 500 men made up in equal parts from No. 3 Commando (Lieut.-Colonel J. F. Durnford-Slater) and No. 4 Commando (Lieut.-Colonel D. S. Lister) together with a detachment of Royal Engineers for demolition work and a platoon of fifty-two Norwegian troops. The whole was under the command of Brigadier J. C. Haydon.

A strong naval contingent, fully adequate to deal with any force likely to be encountered in these waters, was despatched under the command of Captain C. Caslon, R.N. It consisted of five destroyers—*Somali*, *Bedouin*, *Tartar*, *Eskimo*, and *Legion*—escorting two converted Dutch ships acting as troop-carriers, *Princess Beatrice* (Commander J. Brunton) and *Queen Emma* (Commander C. A. Kershaw). The last-named officer had won fame in a very different field as England's scrum-half in international Rugby football matches twenty years earlier.

[1] The distinction between those types of Commando raid which specifically sought out enemy forces and those which deliberately avoided them is an important one. The Bardia raid is an example of the former, Lofoten of the latter.

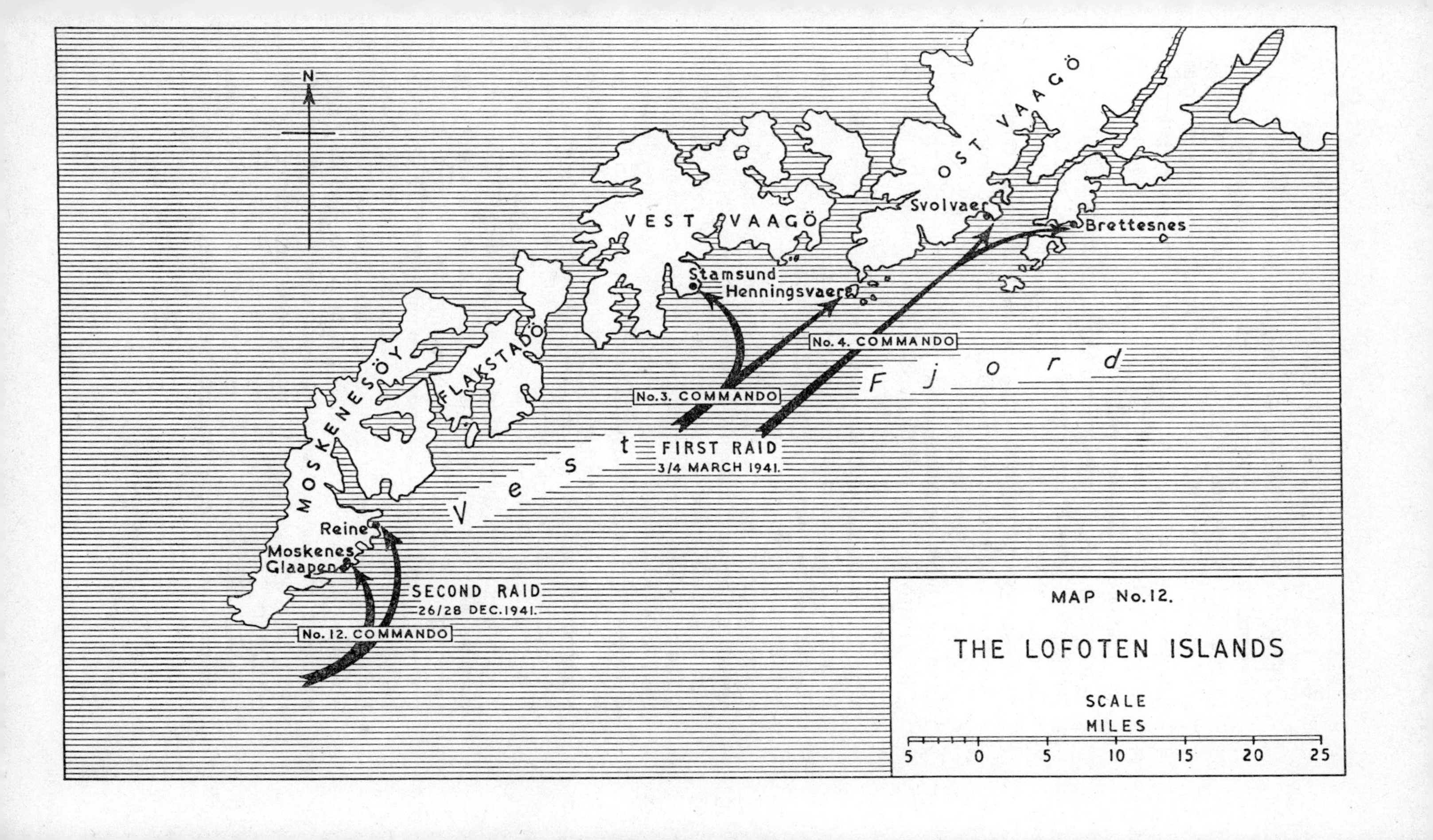
N
VEST VAAGÖ
OST VAAGÖ
Svolvaer
Brettesnes
Stamsund
Henningsvaer
No. 4. COMMANDO
No. 3. COMMANDO
FIRST RAID
3/4 MARCH 1941.
Vest Fjord
FLAKSTADÖ
MOSKENESÖY
Reine
Moskenes
Glaapen
SECOND RAID
26/28 DEC. 1941.
No. 12. COMMANDO
MAP No. 12.
THE LOFOTEN ISLANDS
SCALE
MILES
5 0 5 10 15 20 25

The possibility of German air action had also to be taken into consideration. For that reason the operation was originally to have place as early as January since it was most unlikely that German bombers would be available or ready to operate in the far north at that season of the year. But the Dutch ships, which were needed for carrying the troops, could not be rendered serviceable before the end of February, so a later date had to be chosen.

After remaining a week incommunicado the raiders sailed at the beginning of March and entered the Vest Fjord, the approach channel to the islands, on the night of March 3rd. The weather conditions were perfect with no sign of a swell, and it appeared that surprise was complete, for as the ships drew close towards the Lofotens they noticed the navigation lights all burning brightly. It was a good omen for success.

In the early morning twilight the landing-craft pushed off from the two transports towards the shore. No. 3 Commando was to go ashore at Stamsund and Henningsvaer, No. 4 at Svolvaer and Brettesnes. The Svolvaer landing party, taking advantage of the clear sky overhead and the absence of swell, actually anticipated zero hour by half an hour; the other three landed on time at 6.45 a.m. Nowhere was any opposition encountered. The Engineers went methodically about their business. Eleven fish-oil factories were blown up, one electric light plant, and oil tanks containing 800,000 gallons in all.

The only opposition came from a single German armed trawler, the *Krebbs*, which after bravely engaging the destroyers, was hit, driven aground and later sunk. Demolition parties destroyed four small merchant ships, and a fifth, ss. *Hamburg*, of nearly 10,000 tons, was hit and set on fire by H.M.S. *Tartar*. The total tonnage sent to the bottom amounted to over 18,000.

By 12.45 p.m. all the troops were back on board the transports. They brought with them 225 prisoners, including a dozen local quislings. The Germans were partly taken off the merchant ships, partly captured ashore. They had put up no sort of fight and appeared relieved that they were not to be put to death. 'It was public knowledge in Germany', they said, 'that the captain of the *Cossack* had shot the whole crew of the *Altmark*.' In addition to the prisoners, 314 Norwegian volunteers, including eight women, and the English manager of the firm of Allen & Hanbury, were successfully brought away. Not a single casualty of any sort was suffered by our expedition.

The Lofoten raid is a classic example of the perfectly executed Commando raid. Specific objectives were chosen, and in every case success was gained. Apart from the fact that the *Hamburg* might well have been, and nearly was, seized and carried away instead of being sunk, it is impossible to find any flaw in the execution of the operation.

The economic gain was clear-cut and measurable. That the Germans had hopes of developing the Lofoten oil factories is clear from the fact that the Svolvaer branch which had been closed down from lack of business in 1936 had just re-opened for war purposes and had been reconditioned and repaired in the course of the winter months. 'So we could say to Hitler: "Open a factory in the Lofotens on Monday, and we'll blow it up for you on Tuesday". '[1]

Despite the excellent weather conditions the Germans had made no attempt to attack our ships from the air at any stage in the proceedings, though it appears that they were sighted at sea by a German reconnaissance plane twenty-four hours before their arrival off Lofoten. The presence of the convoy was three times reported to German Air H.Q., but no action was taken upon this information. The German communiqué dealing with the raid confined itself to announcing that our force had made a brief landing on some remote northern islands followed by a speedy departure. The enemy showed his concern however by the reprisal arrest of a number of Norwegian officers and by taking steps to station a bomber detachment at Bardufoss on the mainland to the north of Narvik. Without this, so ran the official appreciation of the results of the raid, the defence of Lofoten and Narvik would become impossible.

The German attack upon Soviet Russia in June, 1941, brought into temporary prominence the still more remote northern islands of Spitsbergen which lie 370 miles to the north of the most northerly point of Norway.

Lord Macaulay, whose imagination had been fired by the contemplation of black men fighting one another on the coast of Coromandel and red men scalping one another by the Great Lakes of North America, as the outcome of the territorial greed of Frederick the Great in Silesia, would surely have been fascinated at the range of a war which could bring the armed forces of Canada to Spitsbergen as the result of the megalomania of an Austrian house-painter and the somewhat ambiguous status of the port of Danzig. For if ever any part of the globe must have seemed safe from the incursion of the Second World War it was surely Spitsbergen. The lost tribe of Indogirka in northern Siberia managed to live through the second

[1] Evan John, *Lofoten Letter*, p. 46.

decade of the present century without ever having heard of the First World War; the inhabitants of Spitsbergen in the fifth decade were less fortunate.

The navel cord which linked the archipelago with the struggle against Nazi Germany was composed of coal. Norwegian companies for forty years, Soviet Russia for ten years, had exploited the coal deposits in Spitsbergen. Now, in 1941, the bulk of the Russo-Norwegian population, apart from a few trappers, depended upon the produce of these mines.

In mid-July, M. Molotov had approached Sir Stafford Cripps, then British Ambassador in Moscow, with a proposal for joint action to occupy Spitsbergen and to expel the Germans from northern Norway. The British Government, on the advice of the Chiefs of Staff, approved the first half of this plan, but upon consideration decided that a garrison permanently established at so distant and desolate a spot would represent nothing but a useless and unstrategic dispersal of force and that the coal deposits could be more effectively denied to the enemy by the landing of a small force for the demolition of the mine installations and the evacuation of the population.

The Norwegian Government's approval for this proposal was obtained. A force of 46 officers and 599 other ranks, drawn from the Edmonton Regiment and the Saskatoon Light Infantry with the 3rd Field Company Royal Canadian Engineers, a few British R.E. personnel, and Norwegian troops attached, set sail under Brigadier A. E. Potts commanding the 2nd Canadian Brigade in the *Empress of Canada* bound for Spitsbergen. This was the only active operation in which Canadian troops took part during 1941.

The naval escort, commanded by Rear-Admiral P. L. Vian, consisted of two cruisers and three destroyers.

As in the case of the Lofoten expedition earlier in the year preparations had been made for an opposed landing, since it was not known whether or not the Germans had occupied the islands. But when the Canadians stepped ashore on August 25th they found that they had stolen a march on the enemy. No German troops had yet arrived on any of the islands. Once again the engineers got methodically to work. Essential parts of the mines machinery were removed or blown up; 450,000 tons of coal that had been raised to the surface and were awaiting exportation were set on fire and 275,000 gallons of fuel were similarly destroyed. It was a saboteurs' picnic. Whether the German High Command, as it contemplated its armies grinding inexorably across the rich industrial area of the Ukraine towards the oil wells of the Caucasus, had ever given a thought to distant Spitsbergen is another matter, but the sappers enjoyed themselves. Two wireless stations were also destroyed after having issued a number of bogus weather reports, recording fog and unfavourable flying conditions in order to discourage enemy reconnaissance aircraft from venturing near the island while our troops were ashore. This piece of deception proved entirely successful, and the Germans seem to have had no inkling of what had occurred until at least three days after the departure of our expedition.

Meanwhile, having deprived the inhabitants of their means of livelihood our expedition set to work at the task of evacuating them. The 2,000 Russians were to be withdrawn to the Soviet Union, the 800 Norwegians to Great Britain. On the whole these unfortunate persons, so untimely caught up in the vortex of war, accepted their lot with philosophic resignation. One of the Norwegian managers registered a bitter protest at the destruction of his mine, and the Russian consul at the town of Barentsberg could only be dislodged after he had imbibed the contents of a bottle of Caucasian brandy and two bottles of Caucasian champagne. He was eventually brought on board on a stretcher.

The 2,000 Russians, with an uncovenanted quantity of baggage, were trans-shipped to Archangel. After disembarking these folk, the *Empress of Canada* was able to take on board 192 officers and men of the French army who had escaped at various times from German prisoner-of-war camps into Russia and who now were anxious to rally to the forces of General de Gaulle. It was possibly the most satisfactory aspect of the operation. They were taken on board and conveyed to Britain together with the 800 Norwegian miners and trappers.

On October 27th, 1941, Captain Lord Louis Mountbatten succeeded Sir Roger Keyes as Director of Combined Operations. A few months later he was promoted to the rank of Acting Vice-Admiral (his title being changed to that of Chief of Combined Operations) and he was granted the honorary rank of Lieutenant-General in the Army and Air Marshal in the Royal Air Force. There was more than mere symbolism in these appointments. No major change of policy was involved; pinprick raids of dubious value continued intermittently against the coast of France and the Channel Islands. But in the larger raids that followed—Vaagsö, Bruneval, St. Nazaire, and finally Dieppe—there was an increasing tendency to integrate the functions of all three services into a more closely knit and therefore more efficient unity.

The first of these raids took place against Vaagsö, an island off the Norwegian coast between Trondheim and Bergen, at Christmas, 1941. The operation resembled that delivered against the Lofotens in the previous March in that its aim was again mainly economic—the destruction of fish-oil factories and shipping. It differed from the earlier raid inasmuch as it was a planned attack against a position known to be fortified with coastal batteries and garrisoned with German troops. At the Lofotens we sought successfully to avoid contact with the enemy; at Vaagsö we invited it.

The point was selected not only on account of the fish-oil and canning factories in the neighbourhood but also because it was situated on the channel known as the Indreled between the garland of islands that fringe the Norwegian coast and the mainland. Coastal shipping habitually passed up and down this channel and there tended to be certain natural assembly points where ships were liable to congregate during heavy weather before passing across the stretches of open sea that formed gaps in the channel. One such point was that part of the Indreled known as the Ulvesund. The island of Vaagsö forms, as it were, the outer wall of this channel, with the towns of North and South Vaagsö on its inner side. At a point where the channel is no more than half a mile wide lies the tiny island of Maaloy, 500 yards long but scarcely more than 200 wide.

Four coastal guns were sited on Maaloy in addition to anti-aircraft batteries, and there were known to be German troops both on Maaloy itself and in the town of South Vaagsö. There was therefore no prospect of an unopposed entry. It was clear that landings must be made on both islands and the German troops vigorously assailed: Maaloy island and South Vaagsö town must both be taken and held long enough to allow the saboteurs to do their job. That meant action. We could count (probably) on surprise and (possibly) on the hang-over effects of Christmas festivities, for the attack was timed to go in on the morning of December 27th.

The force despatched was similar in size and composition to that which had carried out the unimpeded raid upon Lofoten ten months earlier. The total of 51 officers and 525 other ranks under the command of Brigadier Haydon was made up of parts of No. 2 Commando (Major J. M. T. F. Churchill) and No. 3 Commando (Lieut.-Colonel J. F. Durnford-Slater) together with parties of engineers, of R.A.M.C., and with a Norwegian army detachment under Major Linge who had led a similar contingent at Lofoten.

The naval contingent under Rear-Admiral H. M. Burroughs,

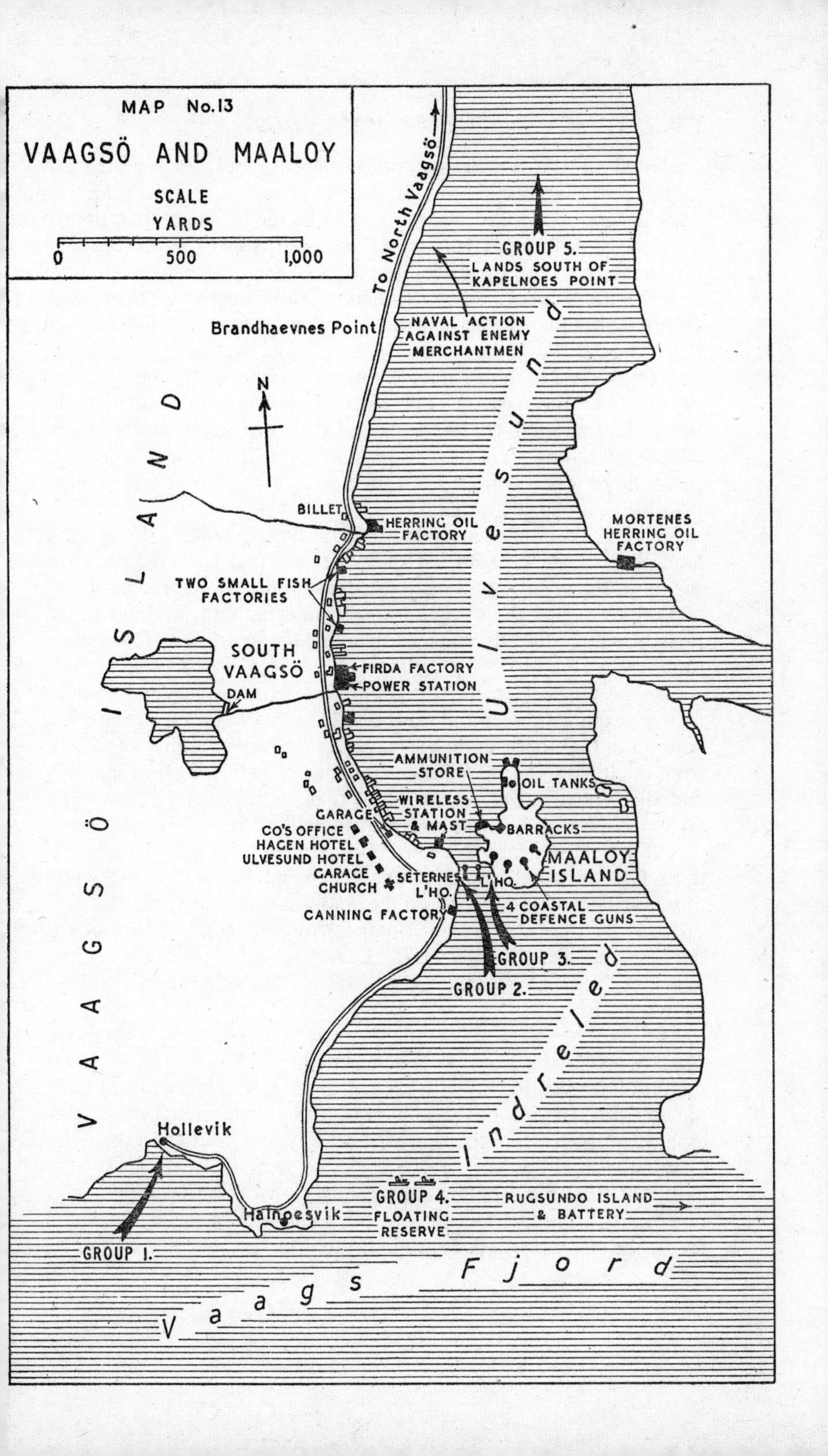
MAP No.13
VAAGSÖ AND MAALOY
SCALE
YARDS
0
500
1,000
To North Vaagsö
GROUP 5.
LANDS SOUTH OF
KAPELNOES POINT
NAVAL ACTION
AGAINST ENEMY
MERCHANTMEN
Brandhaevnes Point
N
VAAGSÖ ISLAND
Ulvesund
BILLET
HERRING OIL
FACTORY
MORTENES
HERRING OIL
FACTORY
TWO SMALL FISH
FACTORIES
SOUTH
VAAGSÖ
FIRDA FACTORY
POWER STATION
DAM
AMMUNITION
STORE
OIL TANKS
WIRELESS
STATION
& MAST
GARAGE
CO'S OFFICE
HAGEN HOTEL
ULVESUND HOTEL
GARAGE
CHURCH
BARRACKS
MAALOY
ISLAND
SETERNES
L'HO.
L'HO.
4 COASTAL
DEFENCE GUNS
CANNING FACTORY
GROUP 3.
GROUP 2.
Indreled
Hollevik
Halnoesvik
GROUP 4.
FLOATING
RESERVE
RUGSUNDO ISLAND
& BATTERY
GROUP 1.
Vaags Fjord

consisted of the 6-inch gun cruiser *Kenya* and four destroyers, together with a couple of landing-ships.

A feature of the undertaking was to be the close co-operation of the R.A.F. A force of Hampdens would attack the land objectives immediately before the disembarkation of the Commandos. Fighter cover would be provided by Blenheims and Beaufighters; the nearest German airfield—Herdla, north of Bergen—would be attacked; and there would be a demonstration against the large airfield of Stavanger. It was more than eighteen months since Dunkirk and twenty since the fiasco of our Norwegian campaign, and our air-power had strengthened and expanded to a degree scarcely to be conceived in those dark days of 1940. We were therefore in a position to employ the air arm on a far greater scale than would have been possible at an earlier date.

Sailing from home waters at 4 p.m. on Boxing Day the force made landfall in the darkness of the following morning. The wind had been high and the sea rough during the days immediately preceding, but conditions during the actual voyage were calm, and the ships nosed their way into the Ulvesund and the landing-craft were lowered on time.

For the purposes of the operation five separate groups had been formed, each with a separate and clearly defined task. Group 1 would land on the southern shore of Vaagsö island, about a mile and a half from the town of South Vaagsö, clear one or two villages in this area and then move up along the coast road as operational reserve to Group 2. Group 2 would land immediately south of South Vaagsö would attack and take the town and carry out the planned demolitions. Group 3 would attack and capture Maaloy island. Group 4 was to remain as floating reserve on the landing-craft, ready to be thrown in wherever the need arose. Group 5 would be conveyed on board the destroyer *Oribi* further up the Ulvesund and landed between the towns of South and North Vaagsö where it would establish itself as a covering force.

At 8.48 a.m. the naval bombardment of the German positions on Maaloy was opened by the 6-inch guns of H.M.S. *Kenya*, and two minutes later the destroyers joined in the fire, which continued until nine o'clock. In view of the smallness of the target area it must rank as a very intense bombardment, and it seems to have taken the German garrison by surprise.

In that brief ten minutes shells rained down upon Maaloy at the rate of fifty a minute, blotting out the island with their smoke, shattering the barracks and destroying three of the four coastal guns.

Under cover of this storm of fire, Major Churchill and his men moved towards the island in their landing-craft. They came ashore dry-shod and promptly formed up for the attack on the barracks. Despite the weight of the preliminary fire from the ships' guns, and the low-level attack by Hampdens with smoke-bombs which immediately followed, the Germans put up considerable resistance, in the course of which Major Linge, who commanded the Norwegian detachment, was killed. By 9.20, however, it was all over. The island was completely in our possession and twenty-five prisoners had been taken, including the German commanding officer. Group 3 had completed its allotted task.

Across the strait on Vaagsö island the fighting was tougher and more prolonged. Group 1 had landed at the southern end of the island and speedily cleared the villages in the neighbourhood. Colonel Durnford-Slater and Group 2 meanwhile had gone ashore close to the outskirts of South Vaagsö and had immediately become engaged in severe fighting. Though taken by surprise the Germans had rallied quickly, and they began to fight back inside the town from house to house like the good soldiers they were, while a detachment on the hillside above kept up an enfilading fire upon the Commandos. As a number of the factories and buildings which it was hoped to demolish lay near the further end of the town our men had to reduce one little strongpoint after another, fighting grimly all the while against time, since there was a fixed hour by which the demolitions must be completed and they must be back on board. Accordingly at 10 a.m. Brigadier Haydon decided to throw in his floating reserve, Group 4. They had scarcely arrived on the scene before they were joined by Group 1, coming up from the south. And while these additional troops were battling their way through the town part of Group 3, having completed its task on Maaloy island, crossed the narrow strait and entered the fight.

By 11 a.m., therefore, no less than four of the five groups had been sucked in to battle at the focal point of South Vaagsö, while the fifth, which had duly sailed some little distance up the Ulvesund, had landed further north and was holding the ring, having blown craters in the coastal road to prevent enemy reinforcements being hurried from North Vaagsö to the scene of action.

No. 6 Troop of No. 3 Commando, under Captain Peter Young, who had previously taken part in the raid on Guernsey, was in the van of the advance and by a series of bold rushes, covered by tommy-gun fire from the windows of captured houses, managed to set ablaze the principal German strongpoint, a warehouse near the water-side. For the courage and resource which they displayed in respectively organising and leading the advance, Colonel Durnford-Slater received the D.S.O., and Captain Young the M.C.

While the Commandos were shooting their way from doorway to doorway through the town and along the waterfront, the Navy and Air Force were heavily engaged. Following the heavy bombardment to cover the landings H.M.S. *Kenya* directed her fire against a battery on the island of Rugsundo, four miles to the south-east. The Hampdens had done good work by 'smoking' it, thereby masking its fire, but it repeatedly opened up again and not until the duel had lasted for more than four hours and a direct hit had been scored on our cruiser was it finally silenced. The destroyers meanwhile had entered Ulvesund. A number of merchant ships, as was expected, were found in the straits as well as an armed trawler. These were promptly engaged. In all, nine were sunk, totalling some 15,000 tons. No loss was suffered on our side. As at Lofoten the ships proved more than adequate to deal with all they found in their way.

No previous Commando operation had received the assistance of anything like the same degree of air co-operation as was provided in the skies above Vaagsö and over the neighbouring fjords. Following the dropping of smoke bombs to mask the German shore batteries while the assault went in, Blenheim and Beaufighters maintained a fighter screen over the scene of action, and over the ships during the first stage of the withdrawal, for nearly seven hours. They were intermittently attacked and lost two Beaufighters and a Blenheim but destroyed four Heinkel 111's in the engagements that took place. Most important of all, they were successful in preventing a single bomb-hit being scored on any of the ships. And while they were engaged in providing this essential 'umbrella' a squadron of Blenheim bombers attacked Herdla airfield at noon, blowing large holes in the wooden runways and causing the destruction of at least one ME 109. A further squadron carried out the diversionary attack upon Stavanger port and aerodrome.

Thanks to these well planned and well synchronised activities of the two sister Services the Commandos were able to carry on their fight on Vaagsö without interruption from sea or air—conditions unbelievably different from those in which British troops had fought among Norwegian mountains and fjords some twenty months earlier. The Germans in South Vaagsö were never entirely mopped up, but their force was sufficiently weakened and dispersed to allow our sappers to go ahead with their tasks without interference other than from occasional snipers. On Maaloy the destruction was total. The barracks, all four coastal guns and every German installation on the

VAAGSÖ AND MAALOY : FIRES AND EXPLOSIONS

*Photo: Imperial War Museum*

VAAGSÖ AND MAALOY: GERMAN PRISONERS

*Photo: Imperial War Museum*

MAALOY: SEARCHING FOR GERMANS

*Photo: Imperial War Museum*

*Photo: Imperial War Museum*

RAIDERS OF BRUNEVAL

island were demolished. On Vaagsö the job was almost as thorough. All the German offices and the huts inhabited by the soldiers, all the fish-oil factories, the wireless station, and the lighthouse, were destroyed. When the short mid-winter day ended, about 150 Germans had been killed, and we brought back 98 as prisoners, while 71 Norwegians accepted the offer of a passage to England.

About 3 p.m. when darkness had already closed down, the withdrawal took place, quite ineffectively harassed, despite the bright moonlight, by a small number of Heinkels. It had been both a successful and an instructive raid. Successful, because the material objects which had been assigned to the attacking party had been achieved, with insignificant exceptions; instructive, because for the first time in an operation of this nature all three Services had been woven together in one harmonious pattern and because it had demonstrated that, given these conditions, a well-defended enemy strongpoint could be assaulted and overcome. Therein lay promise for the future.

These days of December, 1941, provided a further development in that for the first time two entirely independent Commando raids were carried out simultaneously. The second raid on Lofoten was, however, little more than the *ridiculus mus* emerging from a much more ambitious conception.

The opening of the Russo-German campaign and the decision taken by the British War Cabinet to send all possible aid to Russia had thrown into relief the importance of the northern sea route to Murmansk and Archangel. As we have seen, the Russian suggestion to undertake operations for the expulsion of the Germans from northern Norway found no favour in our eyes. Since, however, the long seaboard of Norway lying parallel to this route provided convenient air bases and its deep inlets afforded lurking places for German surface raiders against our convoys, attention was given to a plan for establishing a quasi-permanent base for our own raiders either at Bodö on the mainland or on one of the islands. The dangers and difficulties of maintaining so remote and isolated a post are abundantly clear, and they were not less obvious to the planners than to the *ex post facto* wise-acres.

The scheme was eventually whittled down to the much more modest project of landing 300 men in the Lofotens to do as much damage as they could to the local shipping and fish-oil industry for as long as they could.

The force was under the command of Lieut.-Colonel S. S. Harrison, and included 223 officers and men of No. 12 (Irish and

Welsh) Commando, the balance of the 300 being made up by Norwegian volunteers. The landing ship, s.s. *Prince Albert* was escorted by H.M. cruiser *Arethusa* and eight destroyers, two of them Polish, and a number of minesweepers and corvettes, all under the command of Rear-Admiral L. H. K. Hamilton. At 6 a.m. on Boxing Day after an uneventful North Sea crossing the Lofotens were reached and the troops, white robed and white hooded, camouflage against the background of snow, put ashore successively in the most southerly of the islands at the villages of Reine and Moskenes by the single landing ship that was available. There was only a handful of Germans in the neighbourhood and these were not looking for trouble and were easily rounded up. Rather surprisingly it was found that they had not consumed all their Christmas ration of pork, wine, chocolate, and cigarettes and these delicacies were accordingly distributed among the local inhabitants. A German armed trawler was sunk and two Norwegian coastal steamers were taken but had to be abandoned through lack of coal to fuel them back to England.

The welcome extended by the population was warm so long as it appeared that our troops were making preparations for a prolonged and possibly permanent stay. Since there were no Germans in these islands apart from one or two observer posts in the north, while the season of the year made air attack improbable (the sun does not rise above the horizon in this latitude between December 10th and January 3rd), Admiral Hamilton began to contemplate the possibility of establishing himself for some time in the southern Lofotens. On the morning of December 28th, however, a German aeroplane flying overhead dropped a bomb perilously near to the *Arethusa*. This fore-warning of what might be in store was confirmed when intercepted enemy signals revealed that a considerable force was being assembled to expel us. Accordingly, Admiral Hamilton took the decision to withdraw during the afternoon, since the advantage of remaining a short time longer in these waters could not outweigh the danger to his ships that might result from dive-bombing attacks from hostile aircraft. Having blown up two wireless stations and evacuated 266 Norwegian patriots besides taking 29 German prisoners and a few quislings, the expedition withdrew. In a modest way it had achieved its immediate objectives, but it may be doubted whether the trifling advantages of the raid balanced the disillusion caused to the Norwegian inhabitants who for the third time saw a British expedition sail away from these waters leaving them still under Nazi control.

## CHAPTER II

# Bruneval and St. Nazaire

### 1

THE year 1942 saw in some sense the fruition of the Commando idea. Though the small-scale efforts continued intermittently, the year is distinguished by two raids of major importance—Bruneval and St. Nazaire—and then Dieppe. Bruneval and St. Nazaire were each carried out with a definite objective: at Bruneval to seize and carry away a German radar installation; at St. Nazaire to ram the lock gates and block the channel of entry and exit for large ships. Each of these raids depended, to a greater extent than previously, upon the closely knit co-operation of all three Services. Each represented a mounting scale of attack. At Bruneval the assault party was carried in a dozen bomber planes and amounted to 120, while a couple of destroyers, four gunboats and an L.S.I. stood by to take the troops off. The St. Nazaire operation involved over twenty ships, including the escorting destroyers, and more than 600 men took part in the assault. At Dieppe and thereafter, in the great Combined Operations of the next two years, the Commandos are merged into a mightier whole. They play their part as shock troops allocated to certain tasks for which their training has fitted them. Their rôle is not less but more important than when they were engaged on carrying out spoiling raids on their own account, but their independent function disappears.

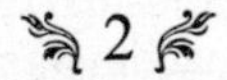

### 2

*Bruneval*

Like two boxers, poised and ready but each waiting for his opponent to lunge, the Armed Forces of Britain and Nazi Germany had watched one another across the intervening moat of the English Channel since midsummer 1940. Following the German defeat in the Battle of Britain cross-Channel raiding by air had been spasmodic on either side. British attacks upon the embarkation ports and British fighter sweeps over northern France had been answered by German tip-and-run raids against our south-coast towns. And meanwhile, on either side of the moat, science, harnessed to new methods of attack, was harnessed also to the detection of attack by means of the development of radio-location or radar. Posts of this nature were established at intervals along the Channel coast designed to give warning of the approach of hostile aircraft or shipping. Originally the enemy had been far behind us in research and achievement in this respect, but by the end of 1941 it was known that they had made considerable progress, and it was thought important that we should obtain some check on the nature and extent of their development.

The best method of doing so would be by means of a sudden swoop upon one of the radar installations whose location was known to us from the excellent air photography of the R.A.F. photographic reconnaissance units. One such post was known to exist close to the village of Bruneval, on the Normandy coast twelve miles north of Le Havre. It was known to be an installation of the newest type, and its situation was such as to give a reasonable hope that it might be seized by a sudden and unexpected assault.

The objective was contained in a shallow pit standing only a hundred yards from the edge of the cliffs and between them and a single isolated modern villa in which lived the radar specialists, believed to be not more than ten in number.

The possibility of an attack from the sea was considered but rejected. The cliffs are more than 300 feet high at this point, and the only approach, the steep and narrow gulley leading up to Bruneval village half a mile away, was adequately covered by machine-gun posts and pill-boxes. A landing-force would necessarily be caught in this gulley and would almost certainly be completely wiped out. On the other hand, for trained airborne troops the task was a good deal more simple. The country in the neighbourhood of Bruneval was quite suitable for parachute landings, the adjacent lighthouse of Cap d'Antifer provided a capital land-mark, the isolated position invited a surprise attack, and the machine-gun posts covering the gulley could be simultaneously assaulted from the rear with much better prospect of success. Parachutists of the newly formed but still largely embryonic 1st Airborne Division were therefore selected to deliver the attack; they would be conveyed to the scene of operations by bomber aircraft and brought back after the action by units of the

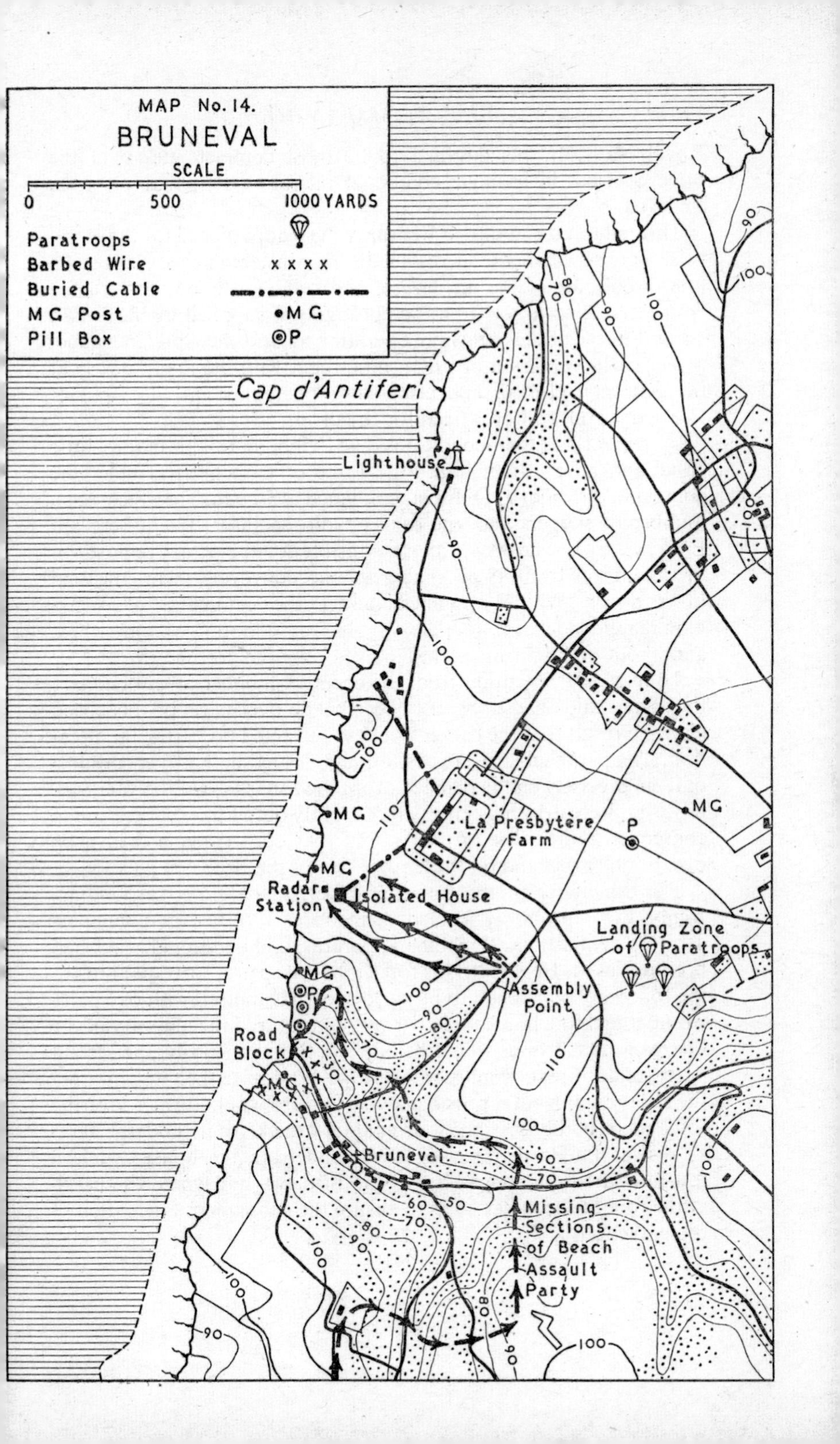
MAP No. 14.
BRUNEVAL
SCALE
0
500
1000 YARDS
Paratroops
Barbed Wire
Buried Cable
MG Post
Pill Box
Cap d'Antifer
Lighthouse
La Presbytère Farm
MG
P
Radar Station
Isolated House
Landing Zone of Paratroops
Assembly Point
Road Block
Bruneval
Missing Sections of Beach Assault Party

Royal Navy. It was destined to be most complete tie-up of the three Services in a single combined operation that had yet been achieved.

Throughout the month of February the troops picked for the enterprise were rehearsing their roles with the considerable assistance of a first-rate model of the pit, house, and neighbourhood, constructed with extreme accuracy from the photographs supplied by the R.A.F. As in the case of the parachute operation against the Apulian viaduct a year earlier a period of bright moonlight with the moon nearly at the full was selected, and after some postponement the night of February 27th–28th was fixed for the drop.

In perfect weather conditions—no wind, a bright moon, little cloud and a very light haze—the force of parachutists, under the command of Major J. D. Frost, emplaned at 10 p.m. They included a number of sappers and one expert radio engineer, Flight-Sergeant E. W. F. Cox, who would be responsible for the actual removal of the apparatus from its pit. The machines conveying them consisted of a dozen Whitley bombers under the command of Wing-Commander Pickard. The short flight was smoothly accomplished, and about midnight the planes arrived over the dropping zone.

To mask our intention from the enemy a number of diversionary low-flying raids had previously been made over parts of this coast, with the result that the dozen Whitleys attracted no particular attention. The parachutists were cast off and floated down to earth most of them precisely on the planned dropping zone. Two of the Whitleys, however, were driven by enemy flak slightly out of their course and in consequence the score of men whom they carried made their drop over a mile away and on the further side of the Bruneval gulley.

The remainder of the force, however, made a perfect landing, Major Frost promptly formed them up as soon as the containers carrying demolitions, signalling apparatus, and additional arms, had been retrieved. He divided his force into four parts, corresponding to the four rôles which had to be performed. He himself with one party would attack the house, where it was conjectured the majority of the German radar troops would be billeted. Simultaneously, the second party, under Lieut. Young, would attack and seize the pit, capturing the radar equipment if possible intact. A third would form a covering force against the possibility of counter-attack from the large farm known as La Presbytére, slightly inland from the house; while a fourth cleared the approaches to the Bruneval gulley and the beach at the foot of the gulley so as to ensure the subsequent evacuation of the parachutists.

But a part of the covering party and a part of the force which was to have cleared the gulley and the beach was far away on the further side of Bruneval.

Since nothing could be gained by awaiting the arrival of the missing parachutists, Major Frost promptly led his troops at the double to the attack. With his men immediately behind him he rushed the house, finding the door open and only a single German within. He was killed trying to defend one of the upper rooms. Leaving a detachment to hold the house, Frost then hurried to the radar post in the garden, where confused sounds of fighting and explosion were now audible. Here, too, surprise had been complete. Five of the six Germans found there were killed; the sixth, attempting to escape, was captured on the cliff-edge and under immediate interrogation stated that there were about 100 German troops posted in and around La Presbytére.

Already this force was making its presence felt by a brisk fire directed against the neighbourhood of the radar pit, and Flight-Sergeant Cox, who was busily dismantling the apparatus with the assistance of the sappers, found his work enlivened by a stream of machine-gun bullets, two of which struck parts of the machinery while it was actually in his hands. However, he continued unperturbed with his task. The equipment was removed from the pit and loaded on to a collapsible trolley, which had been dropped by air for this purpose, and the force around the house and pit began to withdraw over the open downland towards the gulley and beach. Before leaving they blew up the site of the radar installation, for it was an important part of the scheme that the enemy should suppose that our object had been limited to destruction rather than to removal of the apparatus for the purposes of examination and comparison with our own.

There was need of haste now, for the lights of German vehicles had been observed moving down the road in the direction of La Presbytére. Reinforced, the German troops in the farm might well sally out to attack; moreover, it was to be supposed that the machine-gun posts all along this part of the coast would now be fully on the alert. Everything depended upon the success of the party attacking the gulley defences.

Frost and his men moved along the downland in the moonlight towards the gulley, some 600 yards distant. They knew of the existence and precise location of the German strongpoints, but they had reason to think that these might not be fully or adequately manned. As they drew near, a voice cried out in English:

'The boats are here. It's all right. Come on down.'

At that moment a machine-gun opened up from across the gulley. What had happened was that the pill-boxes and machine-gun posts covering the gulley and beach had not yet been taken, as the party detailed to carry out this part of the operation had been too weak to attack, owing to the absence of the troops dropped beyond Bruneval. Major Frost accordingly detached a part of his own force to join the attack. It was pushed home, strengthened by the welcome and unexpected arrival of the errant party under Lieut. E. C. B. Charteris, who arrived in time to launch a decisively successful assault against a pill-box overlooking and dominating the beach.

Lieut. Charteris, who acted throughout with great presence of mind, had early realised that he had been dropped in the wrong place, partly owing to certain slight but unmistakable differences in the terrain, partly through observing the other Whitleys still flying on overhead. Rallying his men, he had led them off in what he judged to be the right direction, reassured presently by the sight of the Cap d'Antifer lighthouse, which gave him his bearings. They were compelled to make a considerable detour inland owing to the difficulty of crossing the gulley close to the coast, but their arrival helped to decide the issue. The pill-boxes and machine-gun posts were overrun. The paratroops slipped easily through the barbed wire, which was found to be casually and unintelligently disposed, and the beach was captured.

The whole operation had been carried through inside two hours, and there was some little time to wait before the shipping arrived. But shortly after 2.30 a.m. Major Frost, signalling with a pocket torch, made contact with the landing-craft which were to take the parachutists off the beach. Intermittent fire continued from unsubdued machine-guns about 400 yards along the cliff from the beach, and this served as an additional guide to the shipping. The landing-craft moved in towards the beach. In succession the German radar apparatus, the prisoners, the wounded, and the remainder of the force were taken aboard. The flotilla, under the command of Lieut.-Commander F. N. Cook, consisted of gunboats and an Infantry Landing Ship, escorted by a couple of destroyers. It drew off from the shore and, covered by Spitfires after daylight broke, successfully made port in the course of the morning without having experienced either air or sea attack.

The Bruneval raid was an almost perfect model of the small, controlled combined operation. It may be set alongside the first Lofoten expedition, inasmuch as both achieved precisely what they set out to achieve. Our losses had been infinitesimal: one man killed, seven wounded, and seven missing. For this trifling cost we had obtained the concrete information that resulted from carrying away the radar installation, had killed probably from thirty to thirty-five Germans and had made three prisoner. The result of the gap thus torn in the German system of air-raid detection was quickly felt when only four nights later Bomber Command delivered a raid in shattering force upon the great Renault factory, which was engaged in turning out war material for the enemy, and completely gutted it.

We may here step slightly out of the chronological order of raids to refer briefly to a less successful operation undertaken later in the same year against German radar installations on the Channel coast. The intention was, as before, to create a gap in the enemy radio-location chain, to bring back some of the apparatus and, if possible, German radio-technicians as well. On the night of June 3rd–4th some 250 men of No. 1 Commando, under Major K. R. S. Trevor, landed between Boulogne and Le Touquet, in the precise area where the first of all the Commando raids had probed the German-held coast just two years earlier.

The troops coming by sea, got ashore easily enough, and penetrated some hundreds of yards inland. But the enemy defences were found to be much more on the alert against both sea- and air-borne attack. Our men were greeted, as soon as they made contact, with a burst of fire from mortars and machine-guns firing on fixed lines. A searchlight swept the sky and sea approaches, and showers of Very lights added to the general illumination and helped to impress upon our troops their helplessness in an enterprise of this nature against a fully aroused defender.

Under the circumstances our men were lucky to get off without serious trouble. No enemy strongpoint was assailed. The Commando merely landed, held a bridge-head among the sand-dunes for an hour and then withdrew just before dawn. Only one man was killed and two left behind, but so far as was known no damage was done to the enemy and no casualties inflicted. On the way back, our shipping was attacked from the air and about twenty naval casualties were suffered. Two enemy patrol boats, however, which attempted to attack the convoy were driven off, one being set on fire and probably sunk.

By contrast with the beautifully planned and brilliantly executed operation at Bruneval this expedition had therefore a somewhat sorry outcome. The Prime Minister, though never backward with encouragement where Commando activities were concerned, made the comment:

'I hope these small raids of yours will not have the effect of putting the whole coastline into a state of vigilance.'

That, indeed, was what was beginning to happen as the result of our hit-and-run policy. The toxin was producing a corresponding anti-toxin. But at least these raids served one highly desirable, though indirect, purpose. Inasmuch as so high a proportion of them were delivered against the stretch of coast between the mouth of the Seine and Cap Gris-Nez, they helped to confirm the impression already being formed both at Hitler's personal headquarters and at the headquarters of the German General Staff that when the attack was ultimately launched across the Channel it would be delivered against some part of the sector Calais-Le Havre. An idea of this nature once formed is liable to exercise a conditioning influence upon all subsequent information. And there was plenty of subsequent information that contributed to build up the impression. For that reason the small pin-prick raids in the Pas de Calais sector, so trifling in scale, so trivial in positive and measurable achievement, were not without their importance.

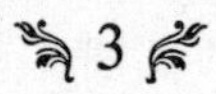

## *St. Nazaire*

The early months of 1942 represent one of the ebb periods, though not the lowest, of our fortunes in the course of the six years of war. The Japanese intervention and the rapid overrunning of Hong Kong, Malaya, Singapore, and the Indonesian islands had seriously altered the whole balance of strength against us, and the corresponding counterweight supplied by having America as an active ally could not immediately be felt. In North Africa the second winter offensive across Cyrenaica, after reaching Benghazi once more, had once more been driven back almost to its starting point. And nearer home grave disappointment had been caused by the escape of the *Gneisenau* and *Scharnhorst*, which had so long lain in port at Brest, up the Channel to Norwegian waters: a movement which seemed to provide a unique opportunity to our naval or air forces to destroy both ships as they ran the gauntlet of the narrow seas.

It was at this depressing season, when the sequence of 'hard and heavy tidings' over long months of failure and disappointment was unbroken and was beginning to seem unbreakable, that an incident occurred which, though its full significance was scarcely appreciated at the time by the public, was to exercise an important influence in our favour upon the trend of the war.

The long-drawn naval war in the seas around our Islands tended to focus on two particular 'battles' (though the word is not specially appropriate to describe these operations)—the Battle of the Atlantic and the Battle of the Arctic Convoys. Each battle was, in essence, a battle for supply; in each we were on the defensive. In the former we were fighting to keep open our supply lines from America, in the latter to protect our convoys to our Russian ally. The one battle was in fact a natural and logical extension of the other.

For the Battle of the Atlantic the German bases for offensive action were the two great Biscay ports of Brest and St. Nazaire; for the Battle of the Arctic Convoys the enemy enjoyed the use of the full length of the deeply indented Norwegian coast and the ports of Bergen, Trondheim, and Narvik. German naval strategy concentrated upon maintaining bases and hideouts on either coast, thereby ensuring their ability to shift naval units from one operational theatre to another. Correspondingly, it was our aim to render these ports as far as possible unusable to the enemy, thereby forcing their ships out into the open or into less suitable and less commodious harbours.

Throughout 1941 this grim and resolutely contested contest had continued, without either combatant being able to claim any decisive advantage. But the proximity of Brest to our bomber bases had rendered it an excessively uncomfortable berthing-place for enemy shipping and the sudden flight of the *Gneisenau* and *Scharnhorst* to Norwegian waters was in part conditioned by the repeated damage inflicted by our air attacks as well as by Hitler's decision to concentrate his surface raiders in northern waters with an eye to the Russian convoys. In the disappointment felt at the failure to intercept and destroy these two ships there was a tendency to overlook the real advantage gained by the fact that we had made Brest too uncomfortable for enemy raiders.

Yet St. Nazaire remained, a first-class port, the only one on the French coast capable of providing a base for a heavy raider such as the *Tirpitz*, which early in the year 1942, had been observed 'shifting restlessly' on the Norwegian coast. Let the *Tirpitz* once reach the sanctuary of St. Nazaire and she would be in a position to intervene with effect in the Battle of the Atlantic. For that reason the decision was taken to make the port unusable for any ship of her size.

It is most important that this should be clearly realised, because in the course of the planning a subsidiary objective emerged, and there has since been a tendency to mistake the subsidiary for the main objective.

Briefly speaking, the main objective was to block the great dry dock known as the Forme Ecluse, which had been specially constructed in 1932 to berth the *Normandie*. The subsidiary objective involved the landing of small parties at various points on the waterfront to carry out a number of specific acts of sabotage with a view to rendering the harbour tidal and impairing its value as a base for U-boats operating in the Atlantic.

The main objective was brilliantly achieved; the subsidiary tasks, though attempted with great courage and pertinacity, were only partially carried through. And because of this, and the quickness with which German propaganda seized upon the more favourable aspects of the operation, from their point of view, the St. Nazaire raid, which in reality was the most brilliantly successful of all the Commando operations, has never quite received the credit which is its due.

The plan shows the characteristic features of the port which determined the nature of the raid. It will be seen that there are three main basins—the Avant Port, which is the most southerly opening from the Loire estuary and connected by the South Lock with the great Bassin de St. Nazaire, on the west side of which the Germans had constructed, with immense industry, a number of concrete submarine shelters. These were capable at that time of affording complete protection to as many as eighteen U-boats simultaneously and were still in the process of being enlarged to take a further ten. The Bassin de St. Nazaire connected in its turn with the innermost harbour known as the Bassin de Penhouet. It was also linked directly with the Loire on its eastern side by a channel known as the Old Entrance.

The capacity and importance of the harbour had been immediately increased by the construction of the Forme Ecluse which connected directly from the Loire estuary to the Bassin de Penhouet. Nearly 480 yards long and 55 yards wide, it constituted the largest dock in the world and was capable of accommodating a ship up to 85,000 tons. Nothing larger than a 10,000-ton ship could pass through the south entrance to the Bassin de Penhouet, and the capacity of the Old Entrance was smaller still. Let the Forme Ecluse only be effectively dealt with, and the value of St. Nazaire as a port would be immeasurably diminished.

With this object in view the planners set to work. The major purpose was to destroy the lock gates of the Forme Ecluse by ramming them with a destroyer charged with explosive, thereby flooding the dock and causing its entrance eventually to become silted up. Combined

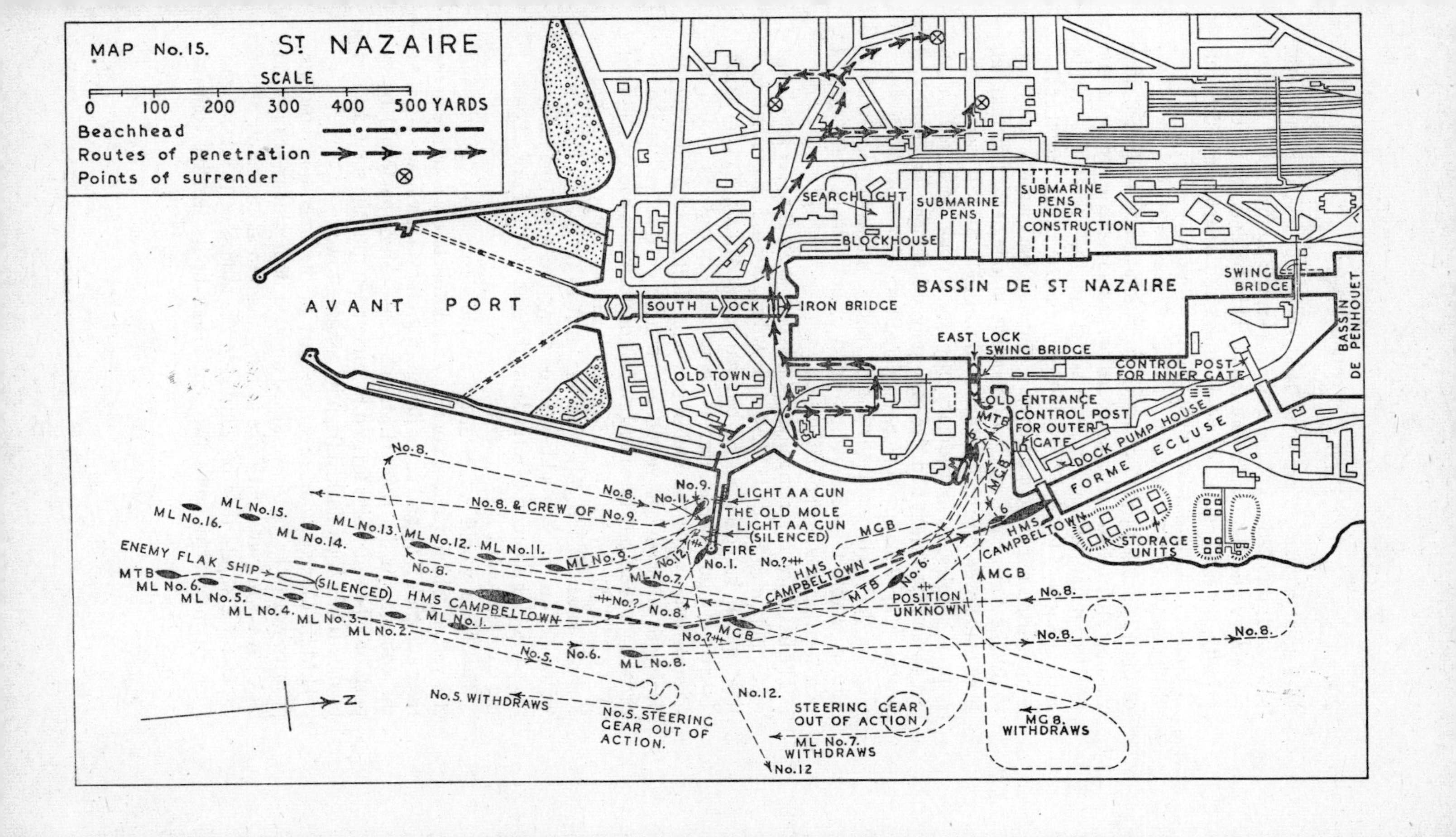
MAP No. 15. ST NAZAIRE
SCALE
0 100 200 300 400 500 YARDS
Beachhead
Routes of penetration
Points of surrender
AVANT PORT
SOUTH LOCK
IRON BRIDGE
BASSIN DE ST NAZAIRE
SWING BRIDGE
BASSIN DE PENHOUET
SEARCHLIGHT
BLOCKHOUSE
SUBMARINE PENS
SUBMARINE PENS UNDER CONSTRUCTION
OLD TOWN
EAST LOCK SWING BRIDGE
CONTROL POST FOR INNER GATE
OLD ENTRANCE
CONTROL POST FOR OUTER GATE
DOCK PUMP HOUSE
FORME ECLUSE
STORAGE UNITS
LIGHT AA GUN
THE OLD MOLE
LIGHT AA GUN (SILENCED)
FIRE
No. 8. & CREW OF No. 9.
ENEMY FLAK SHIP
(SILENCED)
HMS CAMPBELTOWN
MTB
MGB
ML No. 1.
ML No. 2.
ML No. 3.
ML No. 4.
ML No. 5.
ML No. 6.
ML No. 7.
ML No. 8.
ML No. 9
ML No. 11.
ML No. 12.
ML No. 13.
ML No. 14.
ML No. 15.
ML No. 16.
No. 6 POSITION UNKNOWN
No. 5. WITHDRAWS
No. 5. STEERING GEAR OUT OF ACTION.
STEERING GEAR OUT OF ACTION
ML No. 7. WITHDRAWS
MGB. WITHDRAWS
No. 12
N

with this, it was proposed to land small parties to destroy the gates and installations of the other docks, the pumping and winding machinery and the oil storage tanks. Thirdly, and last in order of priority, the landing parties would attack and destroy any accessible U-boats or shipping they might find in the port.

The choice of a destroyer to fulfil a rôle somewhat similar to that of the *Vindictive* in the Zeebrugge operation was only reached after various alternative methods of sabotage had been considered and rejected. It had been at one time hoped that the operation might be carried out by a landing-party of Commando troops, at another that a submarine might be employed. Eventually the decision was taken to use the American destroyer *Campbeltown*, one of the fifty that had been made over to Britain in the autumn of 1940. Since it was in many respects obsolescent for ordinary purposes, it could be spared for this action and its weight and size were judged sufficient for the task. It proved a most happy choice, and credit for this must be given to Captain J. V. Hughes-Hallett, R.N., and Commander J. D. Luce, both of whom throughout the period of preliminary planning had persistently urged its adoption.

The naval force accompanying *Campbeltown*, was under the charge of Commander R. E. D. Ryder. It would consist of a number of light motor launches (to be referred to as M.Ls.), sixteen in all. Twelve of these would carry Commando troops, as would the *Campbeltown*, while the other four would be fitted with torpedoes to deal with such surface vessels as might be encountered in the approach up the Loire estuary. In addition to this, a motor gun-boat (M.G.B. 314), which acted as Headquarters Ship, and a motor torpedo-boat (M.T.B. 74) were allocated to the force. The former would help to provide additional covering fire, while the latter had the particular function of torpedoing the gates of the Forme Ecluse if the *Campbeltown* failed to arrive.

The force would be escorted by the destroyers *Tyndale* and *Atherstone*, which would accompany the flotilla to the entrance of the river and pick it up and cover its return journey a few hours later. At the entrance to the river H.M. submarine *Sturgeon* would be in position when the ships arrived to guide them into the right channel by means of a light flashed from its conning-tower.

H.M.S. *Campbeltown*, to whose part in the operation absolute priority was to be given, would be directed immediately against the lock gates with sufficient force to burst them in as the result of her impact. She would then be scuttled in the mouth of the dock, and after an interval of some two and a half hours the five tons of explosive with which she was loaded would be detonated by delayed action fuses. This provided a treble insurance of damage to the great dock. First the gates would be broken inwards by the nicely calculated force of the destroyer's impact; then the entrance would be blocked by the scuttling of the ship; finally, further damage would be inflicted by the subsequent explosions. The sinking of the ship in itself provided a guarantee against any reasonable likelihood of a German party going on board to remove the charges.

The choice of motor launches to carry the greater number of the troops was conditioned by their shallow draught which enabled them to pass up the Loire not by the deep water channel which was well covered by German coastal batteries but across the mudflats, which were situated somewhat to starboard. At high tide these were just sufficiently covered to enable the motor launches to pass over them, and the *Campbeltown*, too, could cross them after she had been specially lightened. A further advantage lay in the fact that whereas normal troop-carrying vessels would inevitably betray to any roving reconnaissance aeroplane that a raid was in progress, the presence of motor launches, with the troops concealed below deck, would merely suggest an anti-submarine sweep with destroyer escort—quite a normal proceeding in the Bay of Biscay.

Since the fuel supply of the motor launches was not sufficient to enable them to make the double journey, well over 500 miles in all, they were fitted out with extra tanks. As a protection against the air attack which was to be anticipated on the return voyage they were further provided with 20-mm. Oerlikons in place of the 3-pounder which was their normal armament.

The military force consisting of 44 officers and 233 other ranks, nearly all drawn from No. 2 Commando, two troops of which had been present at Vaagsö, were under the command of Lieut.-Colonel A. C. Newman (Essex Regiment). It was disposed in three main groups to correspond with the three selected landing-places.

Group 1 would make the voyage in *Campbeltown* and land from her on either side of the Forme Ecluse as soon as she struck the lock gates. This force was composed of 75 men under the command of Major W. O. Copeland. Their chief tasks would be to destroy the lock gates at the further end of the Forme Ecluse, the operating machinery controlling them at both ends of the dock, and the oil storage tanks on the east side.

Group 2, 85 men under the command of Captain M. C. Burn, would land from the M.Ls. of the starboard column on either side of the Old Entrance. To them was allocated the destruction of two flak towers near the Penhouet Basin, the swing-bridge between the St. Nazaire and the Penhouet Basin and the swing-bridges across the Old Entrance. A perimeter defence would be established to cover the temporary headquarters of the whole force which would be established in a house near the Old Entrance.

Finally, Group 3, of 89 men under Captain E. S. Hodgson, would land at the Mole, two or three hundred yards south of the Old Entrance, to storm the pill-boxes and the anti-aircraft positions and the swing-bridges across the South Entrance which connected the Avant Port with the Bassin de St. Nazaire. A firm bridge-head would then be established at the landward end of the Mole, into which each of the other parties would withdraw when its tasks had been completed and from which the whole force would be evacuated.

These three groups were in turn subdivided into smaller parties of a dozen or fifteen men, each with its specific rôle, whether assault, protection, or demolition. Unfortunately the number of troops was severely limited by the capacity of the motor launches, and in consequence there was practically no general reserve available for clearing up any part of the operation that was found to be unexpectedly 'sticky'.

Since St. Nazaire was a port of such unquestionable value to the enemy the approaches were heavily guarded, and the dual purpose anti-aircraft guns could be used with as much effect against shipping in the river as against hostile aircraft overhead. To counter the formidable German defences our planners depended upon three factors: surprise, diversion, and speed.

The preparations for the raid were shrouded with the utmost secrecy, and it seems certain that no hint of the objective leaked out. Calculated indiscretions contrived to leave the inquisitive with the impression that an anti-submarine sweep in the Bay of Biscay was intended. But since the enemy defences might be expected to be manned and alert, some form of diversion was necessary. This was to be provided by an air attack upon St. Nazaire dock area laid on by Bomber Command with the then considerable total of seventy Wellingtons, which would distract the enemy radar and, it was hoped, drown the noise of the approaching naval craft. This air raid was timed so as immediately to precede the attack from the sea. In consequence, the dual purpose guns, elevated to fire at the aircraft overhead, would be unable simultaneously to deal with the Commando troops, who would be landing in some cases actually within a few feet of the gun sites. It was further calculated that the effect of smoke, burning buildings, blocked streets, and severed communications, would throw the defenders into confusion at the moment of the landing and enable the various assault and demolition parties to get speedily through their respective tasks without excessive interference.

For speed was the essence of this assault. Colonel Newman had impressed upon his men the importance of being 'quick in and quick out'. Each party would move straight off to its assigned job as soon as it got ashore and, having completed it, would withdraw to the re-embarkation perimeter at the Mole. It will have been noted that among the tasks was the destruction of the bridges over the connecting channels between the Bassin de St. Nazaire and the Bassin de Penhouet, the Bassin de St. Nazaire and the Avant Port, and the Bassin de St. Nazaire and the Old Entrance from the Loire estuary. This would have the effect of creating two separate islands, which for the sake of convenience will be referred to as the Isle de St. Nazaire and the Isle de Penhouet respectively. In all, it was intended that the troops should be ashore about one and a half hours, landing as soon as *Campbeltown* struck the lock gates at 1.30 a.m.; and the entire force was to embark again by 3.30 a.m. in order that the ships might be clear of the river and out to sea by the time that dawn broke.

In fixing the date of the attack consideration of moon, tide, and weather, had to be taken into account. A full moon was required and a high tide for carrying out the operation under the most advantageous conditions. This gave a period of about five days in each month. It was decided that the operation should take place between March 28th and April 1st. The most desirable weather conditions would include bright sunny weather at sea and a haze over the land, with an easterly wind. When a spell of this sort of weather began about March 20th it was decided that the opportunity was too good to miss. Since it could not be counted upon to last indefinitely, the operation was timed for the night of March 27th–28th, twenty-four hours before the earliest planned date.

Last minute photographs of the dock area had been obtained by air reconnaissance. They revealed a fresh development of the sort that is always liable to throw the best-laid schemes of mice and planner agley. In the words of Commander Ryder:

'The day before sailing a beautiful series of air reconnaissance photographs were sent to us. This was stop-press news indeed, and we examined them in detail with a large magnifying glass to see if any additional defences had been added. The result was not without humour, as the enemy had chosen that moment to berth four torpedo boats alongside the very place Newman had picked as his headquarters . . . When asked what reserves he had got, he answered "Twelve". I suggested that he would probably need all of them.'[1]

On the afternoon of March 26th the force slipped unostentatiously from the port of Falmouth, where the shipping had been for some time assembled and undergoing the necessary alterations to fit it for the operation. It stood well out to sea, passing nearly a hundred miles to the west of Brest at midnight, and when the haze lifted completely before dawn on March 27th, White Ensigns were hauled down from the ships and German flags hoisted on the destroyers. Nevertheless, there was a danger that the ruse might fail to deceive the enemy and a close look-out was kept for German reconnaissance aircraft.

The day was not without its incidents. Soon after 7 a.m. a submarine was spotted by the destroyer *Tynedale*, which then hoisted the White Ensign once more and opened fire. The submarine crash-dived and may or may not have been hit by subsequent depth-charges. It was afterwards learned that she did indeed make a report to shore, but merely described 'two destroyers steering south-west', an item of information which caused the enemy no particular concern. Around midday two French trawlers were sighted in succession. Since there was a risk that they might carry wireless transmitters and might signal the presence of the flotilla to the enemy, both were boarded, the crews taken off and the trawlers sunk. In each case the Frenchmen showed the utmost friendliness and professed themselves eager to come to England and rally to the Free French Movement. This was not altogether surprising in view of the fact that throughout the occupation the Bretons maintained a magnificent record of resistance to any form of collaboration.

Later in the day the sky became overcast, which greatly reduced the danger of the ships being spotted from the air. Messages were received from the Commander-in-Chief, Plymouth, confirming the presence of five enemy torpedo-boats, off St. Nazaire. They might be encountered at any time, and he was despatching two further destroyers, H.M. ships *Cleveland* and *Brocklesby*, at top speed to help cover the withdrawal on the following day.

After dark the ships altered course, turning east towards the mouth of the Loire. At this time one of the port side motor launches (M.L. No. 10) developed engine trouble and the troops and crew aboard had to be transferred to one of the supplementary M.Ls. This was the only mishap on the outward voyage, and at 10 p.m. the beacon light of the submarine *Sturgeon* was duly sighted off the

[1] Commander R. E. D. Ryder, V.C., *The Attack on St. Nazaire*, p. 37.

mouth of the river. The force was now in cruising order, M.G.B. 314 leading the way in with both the naval and military commanders on board, followed by H.M.S. *Campbeltown*, with the M.Ls. disposed to port and starboard and M.T.B. 74 bringing up the rear. In this formation the flotilla began to move upstream. The destroyers *Atherstone* and *Tynedale* had by this time parted company and were in the process of taking up their patrolling positions to seaward.

From about midnight gun flashes were observed from the north-east and a considerable amount of flak, suggesting that heavy air activity was in progress. This was all to the good and the spirits of the attackers were justifiably high. The ships passed over the flooded mudflats without mishap, and by great good fortune they even slipped by the lighthouse situated in midstream about two miles short of the harbour, without detection from its searchlight.

So far, things had gone with almost miraculous smoothness. Commander Ryder's vessels had sailed all day in the open sea without detection from the air. They had entered the river without encountering booms, minefields or other unexpected obstructions, they had stopped a patrol vessel and now they had passed the principal searchlight tower.

Only a few minutes more and they would be within reach of their goal.

But that moment was the last of undetected serenity that the force was to experience. Though the searchlight had apparently failed to pick up the flotilla, the alarm had in fact been given. The moment had been reached when the wave of battle breaks upon the orderly sequence of planning. From this point onwards two wills and two forces would be directly in contact. The dice had been shaken; now they were about to fall.

It was 1.22 a.m. There were eight minutes to go to zero hour when H.M.S. *Campbeltown* would strike the gates of the Forme Ecluse. Abruptly, every searchlight from either bank of the river leapt to life. The whole flotilla was brilliantly floodlit, and every detail of every craft was clearly outlined to the enemy on shore.

Such a development had been anticipated, and measures had been taken to deal with it. The *Campbeltown's* funnels had been carefully cut on the slant during the weeks of preparation in order to give her a superficial resemblance to the *Moewe* class of large torpedo-boat employed by the Germans on this coast. The M.Ls. with their low silhouettes and dark colouring might also hope temporarily to escape identification.

From a shoreside battery came a challenge. This eventuality, too, had been foreseen. Commander Ryder was provided with a signalman experienced in sending and receiving German morse. While the German flares broke the velvet of the night-sky, Leading-Signalman Pike calmly replied with a long message in clear to the effect that two craft damaged by hostile action requested permission to proceed up harbour without delay. Firing momentarily ceased. Every minute of delay counted now. A similar signal despatched in reply to a station on the southern bank produced a similarly gratifying cessation of fire. Then the guns opened again from the northern shore.

Again the headquarters ship signalled. This time it was the international code signal for ships being fired upon by friendly forces. Again the enemy guns fell silent. The daring bluff had seen the force almost through to its objective. Six minutes to go and *Campbeltown* would strike the gates.

'Those few minutes seemed like a lifetime. Then, without warning, the whole bag of tricks was let loose. The noise was terrific. Tracers of every colour seemed to pour into our fleet—*Campbeltown's* sides seemed to be alive with bursting shells, and from the bridge of the gunboat we could watch the stream of tracer coming towards us, and it seemed as if we could just duck below it as it passed overhead.

'Every vessel answered the fire. Oerlikon, Bren, and mortar fire poured into the searchlights and gun positions. Some of the searchlights were put out, and I'm sure the shooting was doing some good work.'[1]

An enemy flak ship in mid-stream received three bursts from the pom-poms of M.G.B. 314 at 200 yards range and was promptly silenced. Every ship that passed gave her a burst of fire to complete the good work. The air was full of tracer, both sides loosing off all they had; and despite the more heavily protected emplacements of the German guns and their heavier calibre, which ranged up to 88-mm., the skill of our gunners in concentrating upon each emplacement in turn as they passed gave us a temporary advantage.

The speed of the force had now quickened to eighteen knots as it thrust towards the harbour. *Campbeltown* was drawing the bulk of the fire; already she had received several hits and her engine-room was on fire by the time she passed the Mole. M.G.B. 314 pulled sharply over to starboard to enable her to drive ahead.

'She was coming fast and shooting hard. She made a straight dive for the lock gates . . . she was lost to us in the glow of searchlights as we circled round to starboard. The next we saw of her was at the moment of

[1] From the personal account by Lieut.-Colonel Newman.

her striking the lock gates . . . Through the boom she cut without a tremor, and then slap into the middle of the huge iron dry-dock gate . . . There was a grinding crash and the flash of some minor explosion in her fo'c'sle as she came to rest . . . Flying timber, smoke, sparks, and flames, made it impossible to see very clearly, but when these had cleared away, there she was firmly wedged in the centre of the main gate.'[1]

It was 1.34 a.m., just four minutes after zero hour. With royal punctuality H.M.S. *Campbeltown* had kept her rendezvous at St. Nazaire.

From now onwards the turmoil of battle overwhelms the particular details, and it will be simplest to ignore strict chronological sequence and trace in turn the fate of the various shipping units and then of each of the landing-parties before considering the results of the action as a whole.

It was the role of the M.Ls. after moving upstream in double column astern of *Campbeltown* to close with the shore, the starboard column landing its contingent of Commando troops at the Old Entrance while the port side ships landed their men at the Mole. But now the disadvantages of these vessels, which had hitherto done all that was required of them, were becoming terribly apparent. Being constructed of wood and practically without metal plating, they were extremely vulnerable to enemy fire, and it was beginning to appear doubtful whether once the force had been observed and fired upon, they would be able to close to land and put the troops ashore, much less remain afloat long enough to be able to withdraw them.

We may deal first with the M.Ls. of the starboard side (Nos. 1–6). These had the role of landing their men on either side of the Old Entrance. Unfortunately, the leading ship was almost immediately hit. She quickly caught fire, swung athwart the port column and beached in shallow water near the end of the Mole. As a result the next two ships (Nos. 2 and 3) missed their landing-place in the prevailing glare and continued on upstream. Later they turned back, reached the Old Entrance and put their men ashore. These, however, were met with such a hail of fire that they were driven back on to their craft which thereupon withdrew, still under heavy fire. The fourth and fifth ships in the column were both hit, the former going on fire while the latter managed to withdraw, though with her steering-gear badly deranged. M.L. No. 6, undeterred by the fate of her predecessors, managed to pull in to the Old Entrance and successfully landed her troops. She then received a signal to proceed alongside the

[1] Composite account from reports by Commander Ryder and Lieut.-Colonel Newman.

*Campbeltown* and help to take off survivors. She set out on this task but was apparently sunk somewhere near. M.G.B. 314, the Headquarters Ship, had followed her in and also disembarked her troops, among whom was Colonel Newman, the assault force commander, at the Old Entrance.

Thus, in the starboard column, only one M.L. and the motor gunboat succeeded in landing their men without having immediately to re-embark them.

The M.Ls. of the port column were to land their troops, as stated, at the Mole, which, after the various tasks of demolition had been carried out, was to be held as a bridge-head from which the whole landing-force would be re-embarked. It consisted of seven troop-carrying vessels (Nos. 9–15) with a spare launch (M.L. No. 16) astern. On this side also the leading craft (M.L. No. 9) was speedily hit, burst into flames and swung in under the Mole. M.L. No. 10, next in the line, had developed engine trouble near the mouth of the river and had transferred her troops to another launch. M.L. No. 11 duly landed her troops on the Mole but soon after was sunk. M.L. No. 12 closed in to the Mole, but was unable to put her troops ashore and after a gun duel with the defenders withdrew into mid-stream. Nos. 13, 14 and 15 either overshot the mark or found themselves unable to land their troops owing to the heavy and accurate fire coming from the unsubdued pill-boxes on the Mole.

The attempt to land troops on the Mole from the port column was therefore no more successful than had been the similar attempt at the Old Entrance from the starboard craft. Only M.L. No. 11 actually put her men ashore. At each point, however, a number of men managed to scramble to land through the shallow water after their launches had been hit or sunk.

Three other motor launches had been given roving assignments to provide covering fire and shoot up any craft that might attempt to interfere with the landing. These were M.L. Nos. 7, 8 and 16. M.L. No. 7 was hit off the Old Entrance and had her steering gear put out of action but succeeded in pulling out of the engagement. M.L. No. 16, after giving effective covering fire to the troops at the Forme Ecluse, Old Entrance and Mole, was eventually set ablaze and blew up. The most adventurous experience was that of M.L. No. 8. After a well-maintained and effective bombardment of enemy flak positions beyond the three landing places, she had directed a torpedo at what appeared to be the outline of a German destroyer, but had no opportunity of seeing the result. Then, determined to sit well in on the mêlée, she had sailed back towards the Mole where she succeeded in rescuing and withdrawing into safety almost the entire crew of M.L. No. 9, a very fine achievement on the part of Lieut. Boyd, who was in charge of the craft and who subsequently received the D.S.O.

The two remaining assault ships, the motor gun-boat and the motor torpedo-boat, were both involved in heavy action around the Old Entrance. The gun-boat, mingling in the very thick of the battle was repeatedly hit but almost miraculously came through that night of fire bloody but unbowed. The torpedo-boat was less fortunate. Not being any longer required to act as reserve battering-ram to H.M.S. *Campbeltown*, she was ordered to torpedo the lock gates at the Old Entrance, and then to make the best speed she could back to home waters. She carried out the first part of this task with complete success, but attempting to rescue the crew of one of the burning M.Ls. was herself hit and set on fire.

It is now time to trace the fate of the various landing parties.

By far the most successful were those who had been embarked upon *Campbeltown*. The shock of collision was, from all accounts, considerably less than had been expected[1] and the troops under Major Copeland's command lost no time in scrambling ashore, using scaling ladders to descend from the fo'c'sle on to the quays. Promptly, the assault and demolition parties went about their work. Almost all the planned sabotage was successfully carried through. Here, as at the other landing points, the troops were divided into demolition parties and protection parties. The former were to get quickly ahead with the work of destruction while the latter covered them from counter-attack. Both parties together would then withdraw to their pre-arranged points of embarkation. The flak positions on either side of the lock gates were quickly silenced as were two gun positions on the roof of the pumping-house, and protective perimeters were then formed while the demolition troops went about their tasks. One party blasted its way into the pumping-house and destroyed the machinery inside; another carried out an equally good job on the winding-hut at the further end of the Forme Ecluse. Only the oil storage tanks on the right of the lock gates were left intact, and this was due to the accident of the covering party, who had been holding a defence perimeter with great tenacity, mistaking the multi-coloured enemy tracer bullets for the withdrawal signal and retiring before the work could be undertaken. For the rest, the tasks assigned had been carried out with great swiftness and efficiency. Captain Roy, whose party of fourteen men had made the assault on the west side

[1] Men in the engine-room were at first actually uncertain whether they had indeed struck the gates. Ryder, *The Attack on Nazaire*, p. 52.

of the Forme Ecluse, then formed a perimeter through which the remainder of the troops were able to pass towards the Old Entrance, whence they would move towards the final bridge-head at the Mole.

Elsewhere, however, no such good fortune had attended our landing parties. This was due to the excessively vulnerable nature of the motor launches which, as has already been noted, suffered to so great an extent from the raking fire of the shore batteries that they were only able to land a small fraction of the troops who were to have operated on the Isle de Penhouet and the Isle de St. Nazaire. At the Old Entrance only a single one of the motor launches of the starboard column (M.L. No. 6) succeeded in putting its troops ashore at the time of the original assault, and as it happened this party, under Sergeant-Major Haines, was one which had been delegated only for support duties. The two parties under Lieut. Woodcock and R.S.M. Moss, after making a temporary landing a little later, had been forced to re-embark and both craft were later sunk. Of the other M.Ls. Captain Burn, who had been in the leading ship of the starboard column, succeeded in getting ashore alone when it drifted in and sank in shallow water near the head of the Mole. Showing great gallantry and presence of mind he proceeded entirely single-handed to carry out the task which had been allotted to his party of fifteen men. He crossed the St. Nazaire island and pushed on alone, right through to the two flak towers at the further end of Penhouet island. Finding them unoccupied he promptly set fire to them both and destroyed them, an action for which he received the Military Cross.

Meanwhile Sergeant-Major Haines's party had been joined by the Headquarters party. It consisted of Colonel Newman, his adjutant Captain Day and six others. Landing from the M.G.B. they moved straight off in the direction of the house which had been selected to act as temporary headquarters. As they turned the corner of the building they bumped straight into a German emerging from the house. Under interrogation he admitted that the very house chosen by our planners was in fact a German headquarters. The prisoner was ordered to go back and bring out all the men inside with their hands up, but at this moment the small British party began to come under heavy fire from one of the ships in the St. Nazaire basin at a range of something less than 100 yards. Colonel Newman drew back his handful of men and was fortunate, a little later in making contact with the party under Haines. A fierce fire duel now developed, for the enemy were subjecting the score of British troops to bombardment from vessels lying in the harbour, from gun positions on the roof of the U-boat shelters and from a battery on the south side of the river. Against this the Commando troops had only their small arms, and a single 2-inch mortar with which Haines temporarily silenced the guns on the roof of the U-boat sheds.

But the destruction of the M.Ls. had wrecked the plans for demolition in this area. Instead of having ninety-three men (including the Headquarters party) ashore at the Old Entrance there were only twenty-four, and though these were gradually joined by the occasional survivor from one or other of the burning motor launches and progressively by members of Major Copeland's Group from the Forme Ecluse, there was little now that could be done save to hold a fighting perimeter and prepare to withdraw, as planned, to the Mole, about 500 yards downstream, whither the launches of the port column had been directed and where Group 3 under Captain Hodgson should now have been firmly established.

But at the Mole the situation was even worse than at the Old Entrance. As has been seen, only M.L. No. 11 actually put her men ashore according to plan, though a few survivors from the other boats joined them. This small group included two officers of the demolition control party. Both were killed in the subsequent fighting but not before they had made their way across the Isle de St. Nazaire to the entrance lock, and Colonel Newman who later saw two small German vessels sunk at this point, expressed the opinion that these ships were probably sunk by members of the demolition party. The only fighting troops to establish themselves on shore were the small party of six under Captain Watson. These very bravely held a perimeter at the Mole from which it had been intended that the re-embarkation should take place—if motor launches were available.

But no motor launches were available. Apart from two or three which had been forced away from the neighbourhood of the quays the whole flotilla had been destroyed, and with their destruction any hope of extricating the force had vanished.

By the time that the demolition troops from Major Copeland's Group, which had landed from *Campbeltown* at the Forme Ecluse had withdrawn to the Old Entrance, Colonel Newman was beginning to take steps to attempt the withdrawal. Captain Roy's covering force was still in action west of the Forme Ecluse, and since no withdrawal signal was available Lance-Corporal Harrington was sent as a runner. He succeeded in this hazardous mission, although it was necessary to cross and re-cross the bridge near the Old Entrance, which was being subjected to continuous and concentrated fire.

But the withdrawal to the Mole, as a preliminary to evacuation, revealed the grim situation in which the survivors were placed.

'There were no M.Ls. alongside the Mole [writes Colonel Newman] and the general view of the river, so far as I could see presented only a picture of sinking craft. I therefore decided that transport home would not be forthcoming, so calling Major Copeland and Stan Day into a confab by a railway truck I decided to break inland with the idea of making for Spain.'[1]

These few unemotional, even unemphatic, words reveal the quality of the man who had the leadership of the land forces at St. Nazaire. The boats which were to have carried his force back to safety were almost all blazing brightly away in the river; the town ahead was fully alert as a result of the fighting of the past hour; Colonel Newman, with less than a hundred survivors, all of them lightly armed, many of them wounded, planned to fight through to the nearest neutral territory, some 600 miles distant. The boldness of the decision was on almost an Homeric scale.

For greater security the men were hastily organised in groups of about twenty to make their way through the town as best they could and break into the open country, where assistance from the local population could be expected. Intense enemy fire continued while this extemporised plan was being worked out, and on one occasion a stick grenade fell right in the midst of Colonel Newman's council of war without causing a single injury.

'The scene at the bridge-head is difficult to describe. There were several railway trucks, which gave excellent cover for sundry groups forming the perimeter. Fires and smoke were everywhere, and small arms fire was coming from most of the buildings around us.

'Everyone was behaving magnificently and coolly returning the fire with ever-diminishing ammunition. When the group leaders reported, their salutes and bearing might well have been back in Scotland, and the orders to fight a way inland were received with grins which reflected their delight at being able to continue the scrap. Away the parties went, mostly right-handed to try and work their way round to the inner bridge at the main entrance.'[2]

Colonel Newman's own party moved in good order, crossed the bridge over the South Entrance and broke into the town. The bullets were striking the girders of the bridge above their heads as they crossed, and Colonel Newman believes that the Germans in their excitement had forgotten to lower their sights.

'The sequence of events during the next half hour I cannot adequately describe. We seemed to be at one moment jumping over a wall into someone's back garden, then bursting through houses back into the road. I

[1] Personal account by Lieut.-Colonel Newman. [2] Ibid.

remember going head first through a window into somebody's kitchen—there to see breakfast or supper laid out on a check tablecloth and thinking how odd it all was. The next moment we were dashing along a road when an armoured car appeared, spitting fire from the summit on all and sundry—including Germans—but we were lucky to find a small alley to dodge into as she passed. Someone scored a good hit as a motor-cycle and side-car, full of Germans, came dashing across a square. The enemy troops pitched out and the bike crashed into a wall. Major Copeland found a lorry which he tried to start. This he was unable to do and only succeeded in putting on the headlights, to be met with a universal cry of "Put those bloody lights out!"

'By this time ammunition was running out. The wounded who had kept up with us marvellously were very weak and had lost a lot of blood . . . I felt that the time for a halt wasn't far away. Every cross-road by now seemed to be picketed with an enemy machine-gun, and movement was very difficult. [Eventually the party took refuge in a house] in which we found a very convenient air raid cellar complete with mattresses on to which we piled. As far as possible wounds were dressed, and well-earned cigarettes were smoked. A watch was kept at the stair-head, and I decided that here we should stay until night-time when we would set out in pairs for the open country. I also decided that if we were found in the cellar I would surrender, as the wounded were in a pretty bad way and a single hand grenade flung down the stairs would see the lot off. Sergeant Steele was at the stair-head when we heard Germans in their heavy boots enter the building. We heard them go upstairs and then what sounded like them leaving again. Just as we thought we were safe somebody shouted something in German and I knew it was all up. I dashed upstairs and tried to indicate that we would surrender. We were hustled out into the street with the ignominious feeling of having our hands up and marched across the road to a lighted house—German Headquarters!'[1]

And gradually from different directions the remnants of this brave force were rounded up and brought in during the course of the day. Only three of the whole number managed to avoid capture and, after a succession of remarkable adventures, made their way back to England.

It is time to return to the fortunes of the naval contingent. While the motor launches burst, one after another, into flame, the gun-boat, which had served as Headquarters Ship and which still carried Commander Ryder, continued to give support to the attacking troops. After having run in to the quayside and disembarked Colonel Newman and his party between the Old Entrance and the Forme Ecluse Commander Ryder determined to see for himself exactly what had happened to the *Campbeltown* since no accurate account could

[1] Ibid.

be obtained from the survivors who were now rapidly being rushed on board the gunboat. Accordingly, accompanied by a single seaman armed only with a broken bayonet, he stepped ashore, was promptly challenged by one of the Commando with a tommy-gun, gave the password, which happened to be his own name, and was permitted to proceed. Having satisfied himself that the scuttling had been effectively carried out and that the explosions continually occurring in the neighbourhood were an indication that the demolition work on shore was proceeding merrily, he returned on board. The M.G.B. now moved off in the direction of the Mole, which was found to be still in enemy hands. From a pill-box the enemy were keeping up a deadly short-range fire against the motor launches as they attempted to berth. The pom-pom on board the gun-boat twice silenced this pill-box, but only for short periods. And meanwhile the gun-boat itself, lying only about 100 yards off shore, was subjected to continual fire from enemy guns on the waterfront, in pill-boxes and on the roofs of houses. It could not return to the Old Entrance, for the German guns were keeping up an almost continuous crossfire across the inlet by which it had to be approached, and it could not lay alongside the Mole. German troops had now boarded *Campbeltown* and were firing from it with one of the Oerlikons. The gun-boat was crowded with survivors from the raiding parties, about forty in all, many of them seriously wounded. No other craft remained in sight—nothing but blazing wrecks. A hasty consultation was held. It was unlikely, in view of the weight of fire that was now being concentrated against her, that M.G.B. 314 could survive for another five minutes, and it was clear that nothing further could be done to aid the troops on shore. Reluctantly Commander Ryder decided that the time for withdrawal had arrived. At 2.50 a.m. he gave the order that the gun-boat should move off downstream and make for the open sea with all speed possible. It was the only decision that could have been taken under the circumstances.

The M.G.B. had been fortunate to an extent which was almost miraculous while she lay close up to the quays, and even now her hazards were not at an end. She was straddled with fire from enemy shore batteries, and even after she had passed out of range of these she nearly met with disaster, coming close to a German patrol vessel which opened fire on her at short range and scored yet another hit. A little later the gun-boat sighted one of the M.Ls. which had dropped out of the fight owing to a breakdown in her steering gear. She proved able to maintain a speed of 15 knots, and the two ships moved out to sea together.

Just after daybreak the two destroyers, *Tynedale* and *Atherstone*, which had been patrolling throughout the night some distance off the mouth of the river, were sighted, and Ryder ran the M.G.B. alongside *Atherstone* in order to transfer a number of the wounded from his heavily laden and limping craft. The destroyers had only a little earlier made contact with the five German torpedo-boats whose presence in the river, detected by the most recent aerial photographs, had caused such justifiable concern. The *Atherstone* and *Tynedale* engaged them with gunfire at the extreme range of seven miles, whereupon the enemy vessels altered course and vanished under a smoke screen.

Two further M.Ls. (Nos. 5 and 15) had made their escape from the river and joined up with the destroyers soon after this engagement, and together they proceeded on a south-westerly course until shortly after 9 a.m. when they were joined by H.M. ships *Cleveland* and *Brocklesby*, which had been despatched by the Admiralty to reinforce the escort on the return passage when news was received of the presence of the five German torpedo-boats in the neighbourhood. Commander G. B. Sayer, commanding *Cleveland*, now took over as senior naval officer.

As more than one air attack had occurred since dawn and others were to be expected, it was necessary to speed up the convoy which, owing to the damage suffered by the M.Ls. was down to a rate of only ten knots. The weather was now worsening, making it doubtful whether even this speed could be maintained. Accordingly Commander Sayer decided in the interests of the force as a whole to transfer the personnel of the gun-boat and the launches to the destroyers and then to sink the former craft with gunfire. It is difficult to see what other decision was possible. The motor launches had always been regarded as expendable craft and the immediate necessity was to make as good speed as possible back to port, particularly in view of the number of wounded—many of them serious cases—who were involved.

And so the troops and wounded were trans-shipped, and the M.Ls. were sent to the bottom, as was the M.G.B. which had played so distinguished a rôle as Headquarters Ship throughout the operation. Thereafter, the four destroyers maintained the good speed of twenty-five knots and made Plymouth an hour after midnight, March 28th–29th, without further mishap.

Three other M.L's. (Nos. 12 and 13 from the port column and No. 8, which after being in the thick of the fighting had rescued the crew of one of the damaged launches) successfully extricated themselves from the river during the course of the night. After 'stooging around' for some time at the rendezvous and failing to make contact with the destroyers, to which they had hoped to transfer their wounded, they moved out to sea and though attacked sporadically from the air during the course of the afternoon sailed on through the night and reached Falmouth on the following morning when down to almost their last gallon of fuel—a highly meritorious performance.

And so we must return, for the last time, to H.M.S. *Campbeltown*, which we left firmly wedged in the entrance to the Forme Ecluse at 1.30 a.m. on the morning of March 28th when the assault troops swarmed ashore. The depth charges, which had been built into the body of the ship were timed to detonate after a delay of two and a half hours, i.e. before it would be light enough for the Germans to go aboard and examine the ship thoroughly, even assuming that they had cleared our troops from the quayside by this time. Accordingly when shortly after 4 a.m. an orange flash, clearly visible from the deck of M.G.B. 314 nearly twenty miles away, flickered across the horizon above St. Nazaire, it was assumed with some reason that the charges had detonated. Actually this was not the case, and when morning came *Campbeltown* was still in position in the lock gate. In the course of the morning an inspection party went on board. It included a number of senior officers, and when all seemed well and no indication was found of any booby-traps it appears that a number of sightseers also swarmed on to the derelict ship, seeking to satisfy the immemorial urge to 'go and view the Doric camp'.

Their curiosity was gratified—overwhelmingly. For at about 11 a.m. with an immense explosion *Campbeltown* blew up. Her decks were crowded at the time and every man on board or on the neighbouring quays lost his life. It has since been established that the number amounted to some 60 officers and 320 men. Nor was that the end.

For two days the whole dock area was closed to French civilians while German propaganda sought either to nullify the effects of the affair or else to assert that it was an attempt at an invasion which had been beaten off with heavy loss to the attackers. Then on Monday March 30th, since all seemed clear, French dockyard workers were allowed back into the vicinity of the harbour. They found the quayside littered with human remains which small German working parties were endeavouring to shovel away or cover with sand.

While this funereal task was still in progress in mid-afternoon there was a further heavy explosion. One of the delayed action torpedoes lodged in the Old Entrance by M.T.B. 74, had exploded two and a half days instead of two and a half hours after its discharge. An hour later a further explosion shattered what remained of the entrance.

Then pandemonium broke loose. The French workers in the port, convinced either that *Campbeltown* was a veritable Trojan Horse by means of which British liberation forces would burst into their town, or that these later explosions would be attributed to the efforts of French saboteurs, began to attack the sentries. Having no arms they were for the most part mown down by the thoroughly rattled German troops who now began to loose off in all directions. As the firing increased in volume more and more French began to be convinced that a British counter-invasion had indeed begun. Producing such arms as they had concealed in preparation for such a day as this, they began to move into sheltered positions from which they could snipe at the Germans.

These latter were now in a state of near-chaos. Since Commando troops had been at large in St. Nazaire throughout most of Saturday, it seemed quite reasonable to suppose that there were numbers, not yet rounded up, who were responsible for these later explosions. Indiscriminate firing broke out on all sides. The German troops, shooting at anything in khaki, succeeded in massacring a number of their fellow-countrymen, workers in the Todt Organisation who wore a uniform not unlike a British battle-dress.

And so the mill went on, and not until Tuesday evening was order finally restored. The losses among the French civilians—these early spontaneous *Maquis*—were unfortunately high, since they were of course only lightly armed, and the Germans were fighting in the manner of badly shaken men and behaving as though they believed every workman's blouse to conceal a British soldier with a tommy-gun. It seems that about 400 Frenchmen lost their lives during these days. German losses were inevitably a good deal less, but were not inconsiderable.

The cost of the raid upon St. Nazaire was not light. Out of a total of 353 naval officers and ratings who sailed from England (exclusive of the men in the supporting ships which did not actually enter the river) 85 were killed and a further 106 were taken prisoner. Commando losses, as might be expected, were still higher. Of the 277 officers and men who took part in the assault, 59 were afterwards learned to have been killed and 153 passed into captivity, apart from a few who succeeded by devious routes in making their way home again. In other words, out of 630 men committed, 403 failed to return from the action.

Of the eighteen coastal craft that entered the river, in addition to the foredoomed *Campbeltown*, ten were sunk by enemy fire, four scuttled by our own forces, and the remainder reached England.

But at the cost of these losses, proportionately higher than those incurred in the Zeebrugge raid of the previous war,[1] the main object of the operation was brilliantly achieved. The Forme Ecluse, the great dry dock which alone on this coast could have carried the *Tirpitz*, was effectively and completely wrecked until the end of the war. The outer caisson had been destroyed by H.M.S. *Campbeltown*, the inner caisson seriously damaged, the pumping station and operating machinery completely wrecked. It is the more satisfactory that the Germans, reluctant to realise the extent of the damage, made strenuous, costly, and quite unsuccessful attempts during the course of the next eighteen months to repair the damage and only abandoned these efforts when the prospective imminence of invasion across the Channel compelled labour to be withdrawn for works of more immediate need.

The outer lock at the Old Entrance was also destroyed as the result of the delayed action torpedoes of M.T.B. 74.

Less successful was the attempt to impair the operation of U-boats from this port by demolitions aimed at rendering the basins tidal. This failed through the destruction or driving off of the motor launches on the port side and the consequent failure to secure the Mole as a base for operating against the South Entrance. This, like the destruction of the fuel storage tanks close to the Forme Ecluse, which also failed to materialise, was essentially a subsidiary object of the raid.

Unfortunately the air attack by the seventy bombers, did not fulfil its purpose. It had been hoped that this would both distract the attention of the enemy from the sea-borne approach and also that the chaos caused by the effects of the bombing would enable the Commando troops to get ashore and re-embark without unduly heavy losses. In effect, therefore, the sea-borne landing was tied to the air plan, and the air plan was of necessity tied to the weather. And the weather turned against us on the night of March 27th–28th. The bombers arriving over the target found it obscured by thick cloud. Since the danger to our own forces, who would be landing almost simultaneously close to the target area, had to be considered as well as the general directive which prevailed at this stage of the war against indiscriminate bombing of French towns, the force turned back. Their presence had been detected, however, by German radar, with the result that the enemy were on the alert when the sea-borne force

[1] In the Zeebrugge operation out of 1,780 men committed 195 were killed.

*Photo: Imperial War Museum*

THE DOCK AT ST. NAZAIRE: OUT OF ACTION TEN MONTHS AFTER THE RAID

THE DIEPPE RAID : LANDING CRAFT GO IN

*Photo: Imperial War Museum*

THE DIEPPE RAID: ABANDONED TANKS ON THE BEACH

*Photo: Associated Press*

THE DIEPPE RAID : RETURN TO NEWHAVEN

*Photo: Imperial War Museum*

approached. It required only some seconds to depress the barrels of the dual-purpose guns, which were sited so as to defend the waterfront, and turn against the unfortunate M.L's. a storm of fire, with the melancholy results which we have seen.

To land troops at one point with instructions to withdraw from another was probably an error. Since it was certain that a period of general confusion would follow the disembarkation of the assault parties, the best chance for withdrawal would be provided by each party being given instructions to re-embark from the point where it had landed. As it happened the Mole, which had been selected as the point for general re-embarkation was the one where fewest troops got ashore and where the holding of a bridge-head for any length of time would have been most difficult.

The vulnerability of the M.Ls. calls in question their value for an operation of this nature. But it was really Hobson's Choice. Light vessels of a low silhouette and shallow draught were an essential and none others were so well fitted to perform the particular function for which they were called upon. In the opinion of Colonel Newman the extra petrol containers which they were compelled to carry were responsible for the majority of the sinkings. They were too exposed, and when hit the ships promptly blew up. Yet without the extra tanks the M.Ls. could not have made the double journey, and there could be no certainty that they would encounter the escorting destroyers in the course of their return voyage. Three of them in fact did not.

St. Nazaire, though far from being the turning-point of the war, at least indicated a trend that grew more marked as the passing months began to bring defeat instead of victory to Germany on land, on sea, and in the air. It was a flip under the nose of a sort to which the Germans found no effective reply. It might have done no more than singe the moustache of the Lord of Berchtesgaden (it did in fact achieve much more than that, in terms of the Battle of the Atlantic) but it would still have been worth while for the defensive trend which it helped to impose upon the German Command in the west. The words of Commander Ryder, who, with Lieut.-Commander S. H. Beattie, Lieut.-Colonel A. C. Newman, and (posthumously) Able Seaman W. A. Savage and Sergeant T. Durrant, won the Victoria Cross for his share in this operation, may fitly here be quoted:

'The mighty army that had turned the Maginot Line, invested its future security increasingly in concrete and hung its hopes to a growing extent on beach obstacles and mine-fields. The St. Nazaire raid disclosed the beginning of this defensive outlook.'[1]

[1] Commander Ryder, *The Raid on St. Nazaire*, p. 96.

# THE RAID ON DIEPPE

# The Raid on Dieppe

## 1

### *Plans and Preparations*

THE raids on the coasts of North-West Europe that have been hitherto described were no more than limited operations with quite specific *ad hoc* objectives. They had tactical significance, particularly as regards the employment of all three Services in combined operations; but they could not, and did not attempt to, exercise any influence upon the general strategy of the war. The most that can be said of them in this connection is that they contributed to keeping the German defenders along the immense western coast-line from Narvik to Bayonne continually on the *qui vive*. Admiral Canaris's Intelligence Service had made so many elementary mistakes in the early part of the war that by 1942 there was a marked tendency on the part of the General Staff both O.K.H. and O.K.W. to ignore its findings, even perhaps to invert them. Consequently, though the Intelligence Service reported to the contrary, there was a general belief, which was shared by General Keitel, Chief of Staff at Hitler's own personal G.H.Q., that an Anglo-American invasion from the west was a practical possibility in the summer of 1942, despite the serious situation of our forces both in the Middle East and Far East and the very great commitments of manpower and material that would be necessary to stabilise the situation and then resume the offensive in either theatre.

The raid with which we shall now deal differed altogether in character from a Commando raid, for land, sea, and air forces, were to combine in an operation far more ambitious than anything that had yet been attempted. It involved not only Commando troops, but no less than six trained infantry battalions and one tank regiment of the Canadian Army which, apart from the contingent which shared in the defence of Hong Kong, was thus to participate in the land fighting for the first time.

Some such enterprise as the attack upon Dieppe was regarded as an indispensable preliminary to the planning of a full-scale invasion of France. It was deemed necessary to test the possibilities of the assault and seizure of a port; to practise in action the handling of an assault fleet; and to try out the new types of assault craft and equipment which had become available. The raid was first considered by the Planning Staff at Combined Operations Headquarters early in April 1942. The objectives were named as the destruction of the Dieppe defences, the capture of the invasion barges reported to be in the harbour; the destruction of the neighbouring radar (R.D.F.) station, and of the installations at St. Aubin aerodrome three miles inland; the raiding of the German divisional headquarters at Arques-la-Bataille; and the capture of prisoners.

It is known that the Planning Staff had under consideration two plans. The one involved the landing of two battalions at Puits, about a mile and a half east of Dieppe, two battalions at Pourville, two and a half miles to the west of the town, another battalion at Varengeville, about three miles further on, while two more were held as a floating reserve to exploit any success that might be achieved.

The alternative plan included the landings at Puits (locally known as Puys) and at Pourville on either flank of the port, landings at Varengeville and Berneval by parachute troops to destroy or neutralise the coastal batteries at these points, and—the characteristic feature of the whole operation—a direct attack in strength by infantry and tanks against the beaches of Dieppe itself.

Because the approach to Dieppe from the flanks was considered as likely to be too slow in its development; because tanks landed at Quiberville (the nearest practicable beach) would be committed to the passage of the two rivers, the Saane and the Scie; because the Dieppe area was believed to be only weakly held by one low-category division, of which only about 1,400 men were thought to be posted in and around Dieppe itself; and because it was calculated that the rate of German reinforcement would necessarily be slow, only about 2,500 additional troops being able to arrive on the scene of action during the first eight hours; the second plan was adopted at a meeting on April 25th. It was sent by Lord Louis Mountbatten, Chief of Combined Operations, to the Chiefs of Staff Committee on May 11th and approved by them two days later.

Lieut.-General B. L. Montgomery, G.O.C.-in.-C. South-Eastern Command, had acted as chief representative of the Army at some of the preliminary discussions. It was his influence which made the raid on Dieppe so largely a Canadian affair. At the end of April he had confided the outline of the plan to Lieut.-General A. G. L. McNaughton, commanding the Canadian Army in England. The 1st Canadian Corps was in the South-Eastern Command and its commander, Lieut.-General H. D. G. Crerar selected the 2nd Canadian Division to provide the troops. The points of attack—the four flank landings and the frontal assault by tanks and infantry upon Dieppe—were already settled: henceforward Canadian commanders and staffs bore their full share in hammering out the details of the plan.

North-eastern France offers no very inviting prospect to the would-be invader. For the most part the coastline is formed of high unscalable chalk cliffs, broken in only relatively few places by narrow clefts or by the gaps formed by river-mouths. One of the principal of these rivers is the Arques, at the mouth of which the town and port of Dieppe are situated. Here there is a mile-long beach, about fifty yards in depth at high water, bounded on the landward side by a sea-wall. Behind this sea-wall is a stretch about 150 yards deep of lawns and flower beds, and beyond this natural field of fire is the line of hotels and other buildings facing the sea which forms the Boulevard de Verdun. Directly in front of the beach at the western end of the plage stood the Casino, a large and imposing building. On either side the town and beaches are dominated by a headland, the one overlooking Dieppe harbour, the other rising up almost immediately behind and above the Casino.

To the natural obstacles of such a coast were added the defences created by the Germans during their two years of occupation. On the headlands were mounted French '75s' and anti-aircraft guns. At Berneval, away to the east, was a coastal battery (three 17-cm. and four 105-mm. guns) and another over on the west at Varengeville (six 15-cm. guns), whilst a third (four 15-cm. howitzers) was near Arques-la-Bataille. The artillery battalion (sixteen 10-cm. field howitzers) of the 302nd Division was disposed in four battery positions, two east and two west of Dieppe which was enclosed on the landward side by barbed wire defences embracing Pourville and Puits. In many respects the German defences appear to have been at least as strong as those which the Anglo-Canadian-American forces assaulted two summers later; while the lofty cliff wall is in marked contrast to the low coastline from the mouth of the Arne past Arromanches to the Cherbourg Peninsula. It was, if not the strongest, at any rate an extremely strong position against which the Canadian forces would be launched to receive their baptism of fire in the West.

The German force stationed in the Dieppe area consisted of one infantry division which at this time was responsible for the entire coast-line from St. Valéry-sur-Somme in the north to St. Valéry-en-Caux well to the west of Dieppe. Some weeks before the raid this sector was shortened on both flanks; but even then it extended for some forty miles, a wide front for a single division to defend. It was believed, prior to the raid, that the 110th Division, a formation with a good fighting record, was present; but we were to discover that this part of the coast was held by the low-category 302nd Division, with the 571st Regiment in the immediate neighbourhood of Dieppe itself, one battalion being in reserve at Ouville-la-Rivière five miles to the south-west. Whatever the weakness of the enemy in the quality of his troops or in the actual manpower at the assault points, it was more than counterbalanced by the natural and artificial strength of his defences.

As regards air defence the Germans disposed of about 260 fighters ranging over the whole area from the Texel to Brest. About 40 of these were estimated to be based upon Holland, 125 in the Pas de Calais, 95 in Normandy and Brittany. There were also about 120 bombers based on Holland and 100 over the whole of northern France. The process of bringing up planes to the combat area over Dieppe, would not, however, be by any means instantaneous and it was estimated that the available German aircraft in the early stages of the battle would not amount to more than 120 and that reinforcement later in the day was unlikely to exceed 75. This estimate proved to be tolerably accurate.

Once the plan had been adopted in principle, training went ahead with a view to delivering our attack upon Dieppe around midsummer, at one of the recurring periods when both tide and moon would be appropriate for the enterprise. A full moon and a high tide were judged requisite conditions for the assault, which was to be launched at dawn.

The provisional date fixed for the raid had been the night of June 20th–21st, the earliest occasion when the necessary conditions would prevail. When, however, a 'dress rehearsal' was held on the Dorset coast on June 11th–12th many deficiencies were revealed: units were landed far from their designated beaches and the tank landing craft arrived late. Lord Louis Mountbatten therefore decided that the operation must be postponed in order to give time for further rehearsal. The troops remained concentrated in the Isle of Wight and another exercise was carried out near Bridport on June 22nd–24th, when the whole procedure of assembly and assault was carried through in much better style. The raid was now fixed for July 4th, and on the 2nd, the troops were embarked and fully briefed. Then the weather broke, causing further postponement, and the Navy eventually decided that conditions were too bad for the raid to be attempted on July 8th, the last day for some time when moon and tide would be favourable. As a result the enterprise was cancelled, for the preparations and intention could hardly now remain secret, and the disappointed Canadian battalions were landed and dispersed to their normal stations. Yet their opportunity was not to be long delayed.

Before the cancellation certain important modifications had been made in the plan. It was decided that instead of a re-embarkation starting about 2.30 in the afternoon on a rising tide, the whole operation would be compressed to the extent that evacuation of the infantry would begin about 11 a.m., and of the tanks possibly an hour earlier still. The intention to employ airborne troops for the outer flank assaults was abandoned. The reason for this lay in the fact that weather conditions suitable for the sea-borne attack were not necessarily those which would be ideal for airborne troops, and since the destruction or neutralisation of the two formidable flanking batteries was an essential part of the general plan, no chances could be taken. Therefore it was decided to substitute Commandos for the airborne troops originally allocated to this part of the operation. As it happened, this proved a wise decision.

Another change of material importance was made before the operation was cancelled. It had been the original intention that the assault should be preceded by a heavy air bombing attack. But weighty arguments were advanced against this method. It was realised that it would serve to forewarn the enemy; it would inflict, in all probability, severe loss of life upon French civilians, which was entirely contrary to the principle governing our raiding policy; above all—and this was the deciding factor—there could be no guarantee of accuracy in a high-level night bombardment, and it was feared that the damage done in blocking the streets would delay the progress of our tanks through the town.

These arguments were sound; but the elimination of air bombardment removed the one element of heavy fire-support contained in the plan. We were now staking everything on surprise rather than on weight of striking power.

Only a week after the raid had been cancelled Combined Operations Headquarters proposed to revive it and the approval of the

Chiefs of Staff Committee was secured on July 20th. Certainly the value of a combined operation of this nature had not diminished; and, as the whole force was now well-trained and organised, secrecy might be preserved by quickly embarking the troops at their nearest ports, thereby avoiding a large concentration of shipping liable to be detected before it sailed. Thus the whole expedition was quickly assembled and, without delay, left for its objective on the evening of August 18th.

The troops were under the command of Major-General J. H. Roberts, Commander of the 2nd Canadian Division. They included the 4th Canadian Brigade (Brigadier S. Lett), (Royal Regiment of Canada, Royal Hamilton Light Infantry and Essex Scottish); the 6th Canadian Brigade (Brigadier W. W. Southam), (South Saskatchewan Regiment, Queen's Own Cameron Highlanders of Canada and Fusiliers Mont-Royal); the 14th Canadian Army Tank Regiment (The Calgary Regiment); No. 3 Commando, No. 4 Commando and Royal Marine 'A' Commando. With the Commandos were small detachments from the Inter-Allied Commando, which included a number of Fighting French, and from the American Rangers.

The total force, including engineer detachments from the 2nd Canadian Division, numbered about 6,100 of all ranks: of these 4,963 were Canadians.

The naval component, under Captain J. Hughes-Hallett, R.N., had the task of carrying and escorting the troops to the shores of France, of providing covering fire during the period of their landing and such time as they remained on shore, and subsequently of withdrawing them. It consisted of 252 ships and landing-craft, apart from the two flotillas of mine-sweepers which would be employed upon the preliminary and highly necessary task of clearing a channel. Included in this force were eight destroyers, H.M. ships *Calpe* (the Headquarters ship), *Fernie*, *Brocklesby*, *Garth*, *Albrighton*, *Bleasdale*, *Berkeley*, and the Polish destroyer *Slazak*, and one gun-boat, H.M.S. *Locust*. It was not considered safe to venture larger vessels in these narrow seas. After the operation was over, however, the Naval Officer Commanding expressed the view that under the circumstances the risk might justifiably have been taken. Certainly the additional fire-power of the guns of one of our battleships would have provided just that quality of support that was sorely needed by the troops on shore; but at this time we had no battleship to spare from other, essential, duties.

The air-force allotted to the operation was under the command of Air Vice-Marshal T. L. Leigh Mallory, afterwards destined to hold the air command for the great 'Second Front' operation against Normandy in 1944. On the day of the raid there were sixty-nine squadrons—eight of them belonging to the Royal Canadian Air Force—employed on various missions: they included four Army co-operation squadrons for tactical reconnaissance, and three for operating smoke to mask the enemy's guns and to cover both the attacks and the withdrawals of our men.

Two brigades of infantry with a tank regiment in support, 250 ships, 69 air squadrons: this seemed a powerful force to commit to action. There could be no doubt that these eager and highly trained men would give an excellent account of themselves and would, if they could not command success, at least deserve it. In the skies over Dieppe, as at the actual points of assault on land, we had every prospect of obtaining and even maintaining numerical superiority.

While the troops were busily engaged upon exercises—practising landings, climbing up steep banks with assault equipment, negotiaing wire, attacking pillboxes, street fighting, crossing rivers, co-operating with tanks, handling weapons of all kinds—an elaborate plan of attack had been worked out.

It involved assault landings on eight separate beaches. There were to be two outer flank attacks against the batteries at Berneval and Varengeville, two inner flank attacks at Puits and Pourville, and a landing in strength at Dieppe itself.

On the east No. 3 Commando (Lieut.-Colonel J. F. Durnford-Slater) would land below the village of Petit Berneval (Yellow Beach I) and opposite a narrow defile near the village of Belleville (Yellow Beach II) with the object of attacking and destroying the battery near the former village. The other outer flank attack would be made by No. 4 Commando (Lieut.-Colonel Lord Lovat), landing one detachment at Varengeville (Orange Beach I) and the other nearly a couple of miles further west close to the mouth of the Saane (Orange Beach II) to carry out a similar mission against a six-gun battery of 5·9s in the wooded country behind Varengeville cliffs.

The inner flank attack would be carried out on the east by the Royal Regiment of Canada (Lieut.-Colonel D. E. Catto) which would land at Puits (Blue Beach), storm the light and heavy A.A. batteries on the cliff, a heavier battery inland, detach a party of engineers to blow up the gasworks south-east of Dieppe, and join forces with the Essex Scottish who, it was hoped, would by that time have penetrated through Dieppe.

On the west of Dieppe the South Saskatchewan Regiment (Lieut.-Colonel C. C. I. Merritt) would disembark on the beach of Pourville (Green Beach), seize the village and the headland between it and

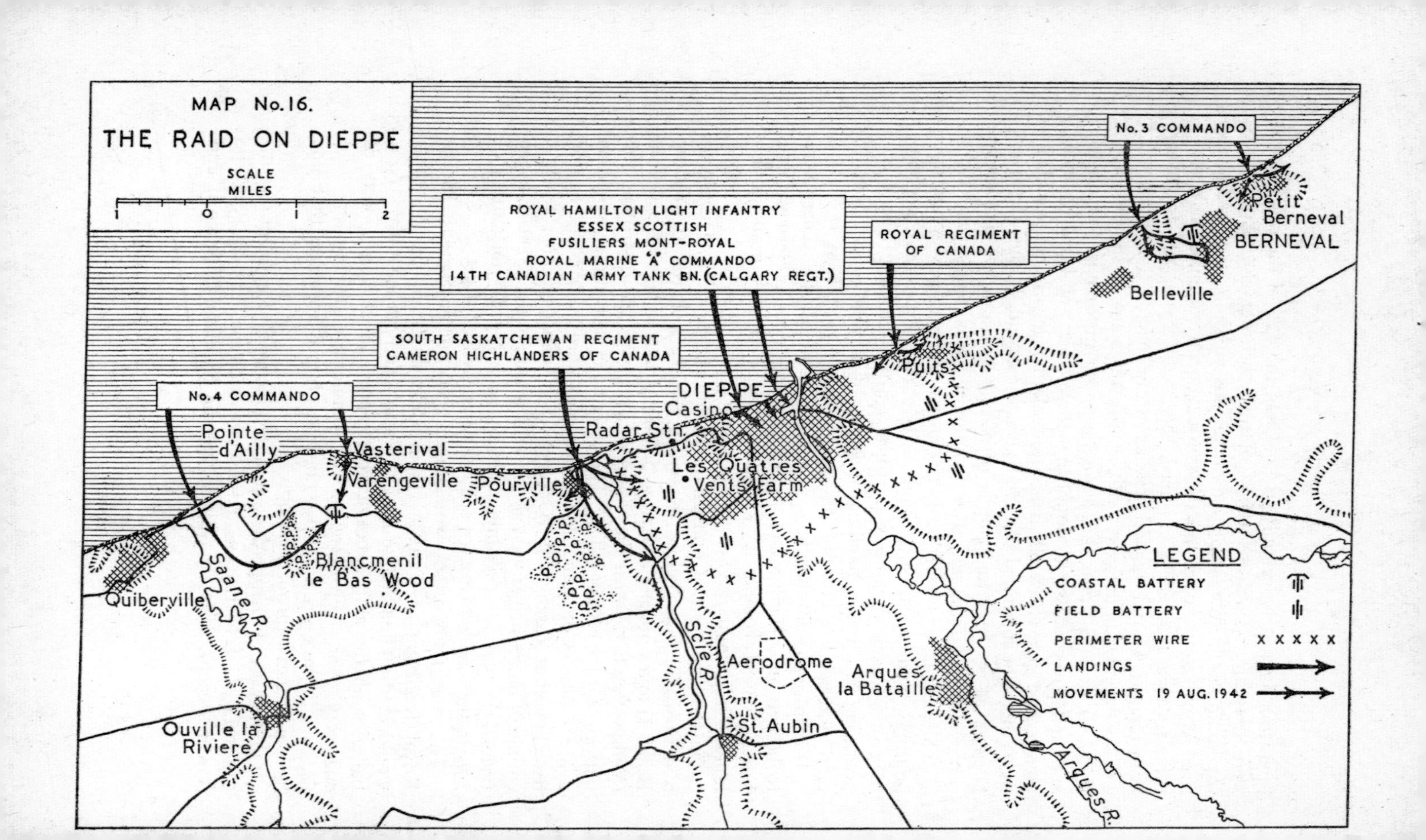
MAP No. 16.
THE RAID ON DIEPPE
SCALE
MILES
1
0
1
2
No. 3 COMMANDO
Petit Berneval
BERNEVAL
Belleville
ROYAL HAMILTON LIGHT INFANTRY
ESSEX SCOTTISH
FUSILIERS MONT-ROYAL
ROYAL MARINE 'A' COMMANDO
14TH CANADIAN ARMY TANK BN. (CALGARY REGT.)
ROYAL REGIMENT OF CANADA
Puits
SOUTH SASKATCHEWAN REGIMENT
CAMERON HIGHLANDERS OF CANADA
DIEPPE
Casino
Radar Stn.
Les Quatres Vents Farm
No. 4 COMMANDO
Pointe d'Ailly
Vasterival
Varengeville
Pourville
Blancmenil le Bas Wood
Quiberville
Saane R.
Scie R.
Aerodrome
Arques la Bataille
St. Aubin
Ouville la Riviere
Arques R.
LEGEND
COASTAL BATTERY
FIELD BATTERY
PERIMETER WIRE
X X X X X
LANDINGS
MOVEMENTS 19 AUG. 1942

Dieppe, where was situated a radar station and light A.A. guns, and the fortified farm, on a crest three-quarters of a mile back from the cliffs, known as Les Quatre Vents. It was intended that they also should make contact with troops from the Dieppe beaches, the Royal Hamilton Light Infantry in this case. Half an hour after the initial landing at Pourville the Queen's Own Cameron Highlanders of Canada (Lieut.-Colonel A. C. Gostling) would be put ashore, would pass through the South Saskatchewan and continue straight up the eastern side of the Scie river to the aerodrome at St. Aubin, about four miles inland. This was to be taken by the joint assault of the Camerons and the tanks of the Calgary Regiment, which were to penetrate through Dieppe town and rendezvous with the Camerons at this point. Thereafter, the united force would assault and seize German divisional headquarters, believed to be situated at Arques, laying hands on all available documents and causing the maximum operational chaos to the enemy.

All these four flank landings (with the exception of the follow-up by the Camerons) would be made simultaneously at 4.50 a.m., the beginning of nautical twilight.

The main landings against the town of Dieppe itself would take place half an hour later. It may be asked why the main and flank objectives were not to be assailed simultaneously which seems the only plan by which complete surprise might have been achieved. There were two reasons. First, if the whole force were to arrive together off the French coast the slow-moving tank landing craft would have to make such an early start that they could hardly hope to escape detection by enemy air reconnaissance on the evening of the 18th August. Secondly, in naval opinion, there was insufficient sea-room for the whole expedition, comprising some 250 vessels of varying speeds and handiness, to close the stretch of selected coast-line at precisely the same hour.

At Dieppe the Essex Scottish (Lieut.-Colonel F. K. Jasperson) would go ashore on Red Beach, the eastern half of the mile-long stretch of shingle; the Royal Hamilton Light Infantry (Lieut.-Colonel R. R. Labatt) on White Beach, the western half. These beaches were to be seized and securely held to enable the tanks, which would be landed immediately after, to go through. Infantry and tanks would then clear the town and port, and while the infantry made contact with the flanking battalions, the latter moving inwards from Puits and Pourville, the tanks would go through to the attack on the aerodrome and the German divisional headquarters presumed to be located at Arques-la-Bataille.

As soon as the harbour was clear Royal Marine 'A' Commando (Lieut.-Colonel J. P. Phillipps), carried in light craft manned by the Fighting French, would sail in and capture or destroy the German shipping lying there.

The Fusiliers Mont-Royal (Lieut.-Colonel D. Ménard) would be retained at sea as a floating reserve.

The Dieppe beach landings would be preceded by a five-minute intense bombardment of the buildings along the sea-front (actually these were a full 300 yards short of the sea itself at high-water level), after which the ships would shift their targets to the flanks and the cannon-firing Hurricanes would sweep in with low-level attacks upon the main German defences just as the first landing-craft touched down. Meanwhile the eastern headland, from which the main counter-fire was expected, would be masked by smoke.

That was the plan. It assumed, and indeed attained, a measure of surprise. It assumed also a careful synchronisation of land, sea, and air movements, less easy to achieve. The success of the main assault, against Dieppe itself, was dependent upon the capture or neutralisation of the headlands immediately above Dieppe on either flank. If the two headlands were not effectively controlled, not only would the troops on the main beaches remain under direct observation and fire and find it well-nigh impossible to get forward, but it was likely to prove extremely difficult to withdraw them.

After dark on the evening of Tuesday, August 18th, the force put to sea from the ports of Southampton and Portsmouth, Shoreham and Newhaven. It was a varied collection of shipping. The low silhouettes of destroyers and gunboats were interspersed with the infantry landing-ships filled with armed men, while astern steamed the blunt-nosed vessels that were carrying the new and as yet unblooded Churchill tanks. The weather reports received by the Air Ministry were only moderately reassuring, though in the event the conditions, while deteriorating as the day lengthened, fulfilled our needs.

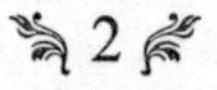

## *Berneval*

The minesweepers had been out since noon and had cleared a path through a suspected enemy minefield, with the result that the passage across the Channel was accomplished without a single vessel being lost or damaged by mining. The assault fleet was drawing near to the French coast with every prospect of obtaining complete surprise when at 3.47 a.m., some seven miles short of the coast, a star shell illuminated the group of landing-craft which was conveying No. 3 Commando, destined for the Berneval assault on the extreme eastern flank.

By sheer bad luck they had run into a small German convoy proceeding down the Channel. It was only lightly escorted by a few armed trawlers, and its presence, moving casually across the line of our approach, was sufficient evidence that our assault came as a complete surprise to the Germans.

Two of our destroyers were covering the eastern flank of the expedition during its passage, and this convoy should have become their prey. The presence of the Germans had been detected by our shore-based radar; it was unfortunate that neither of the warning signals sent out by the Commander-in-Chief Portsmouth were received by these destroyers.

The enemy trawlers opened a heavy fire which was answered by our gun-boats. Commander D. B. Wyburd, who was in charge of the Group, held grimly on his course in an endeavour to fight a way through for his landing-craft, but in the course of the action his gun-boat (S.G.B. 5) was badly hit and disabled. We gave at least as good as we got in the process of the engagement, for one of the German trawlers was certainly, and another probably, sunk. But, as the result of this encounter, the landing-craft carrying the officers and men of No. 3 Commando were most unfortunately scattered, and as daybreak was now approaching it seemed that the chance of surprise had been lost. Only seven of the twenty-three vessels in the Group actually succeeded in touching down and landing their troops.

Five of these arrived off Yellow I Beach (Berneval) at 5.15 a.m.—which was twenty-five minutes late on their zero hour; a sixth followed a little later. The troops scrambled ashore, and Captain R. L. Wills, the senior officer present, took command. By now it was broad daylight and the defenders were roused and ready. The men of the Commando endeavoured to storm their way up into Berneval. Captain Wills soon fell badly wounded. Lieut. E. D. Loustalot of the United States Rangers then took over. But the Germans were fighting back from the adequate cover of a dominating ridge and houses, and the few score men of the Commando were soon scattered. In an overhung lane parallel with the beach, Lieut. Loustalot was killed with several of his men. He was the first American soldier to die in the land fighting against Germany in the Second World War. Scattered and overwhelmed, the men of No. 3 Commando attempted a withdrawal about seven o'clock. But the enemy was now firing directly down on the beach, where three of the landing-craft had been grounded. Only one of these succeeded in extricating itself, carrying the naval beachmaster and the beach signals party. The rest of the troops landed at Berneval kept up the fight throughout the morning. A number of them were concealed by villagers of Petit Berneval in their houses and cellars for some hours until rounded up on the evidence of an Alsatian. No. 3 Commando lost 120 men in that tragic day's fighting. About 80 of these, many of them wounded, were captured.

Though the attack on Yellow I ended in such a fiasco a larger measure of success was achieved by the mere handful of men who succeeded in landing over at Yellow II near Belleville. Following the encounter with the German trawlers, a single landing-craft under the command of Lieut. H. T. Buckee, R.N.V.R., maintaining a steady course, kept straight on towards the beach without being spotted by the enemy. This craft carried Major Peter Young, with two officers and seventeen men forming the Headquarters party of the attacking force. In the shadowy twilight they were able to discern the gap in the cliffs ahead which was their goal. By this time the landing-craft was alone, clear of the enemy and out of touch with the remainder of the Group.

Indicating the beach, Lieut. Buckee inquired, 'What do we do now, cock?'

'My orders,' said Major Young, 'are to land and demolish the battery.'

'Right! In we go!' was the reply, and the craft was headed straight for the beach.

At five minutes before zero hour Major Young and his nineteen followers sprang ashore. They had between them ten rifles, a Bren gun, six tommy-guns, three pistols, and two mortars, these latter having only a few shells. With this armament they set out to attack a battery defended by some 200 Germans by now fully on the *qui vive*. The point where they had landed was a mere sword-cleft in the steep cliffs, up which ran a flight of steps just wide enough for two men to go abreast. This soon gave place to a narrow gulley choked with brambles and undergrowth to a height of fully six feet and, as though this were not sufficient, with thick wire.

The party possessed no Bangalore torpedoes or wire-cutters to blast or hew a way through. Lacking these they made use of the wire, strands of which were stretched taut along the side of the gulley to pull themselves up to the top. It was a distance of not more than half a mile, but it took them three-quarters of an hour to complete the climb.

They emerged on the open downland and swung east towards Berneval. At the approach to the village they encountered a French boy on a bicycle who confirmed their information that 200 Germans held the battery on the further side between the village and the cliffs. The party moved into a small copse which fringed Berneval on the west and broke into the village just as our cannon-firing Hurricanes delivered a low-flying attack on the battery. This was encouraging, and Major Young set himself with his nineteen men (it challenges comparison with John Brown's nineteen who stormed Harper's Ferry) to stalk the battery, snipe the gunners and if possible neutralise the guns.

Outnumbered by ten to one, they could not hope to rush the battery; but they could and did give the gunners an extremely unnerving time. They raced through the village and reached the church at the northern end. Here Major Young endeavoured without success to establish an observation post in the belfry, which however proved to be unscalable. Meanwhile they continued to harass the gunners. Every time a gun was reloaded or a man was seen to move they opened up with all they had. They were within 200 yards of the battery and their tactics proved successful in minimising its fire by their sniping. It is fairly certain that not one of the guns succeeded in firing out to sea during this period.

After a time the Germans, who can have had no idea of the smallness of the force opposing them, for they made only tentative efforts to counter-attack, became exasperated by this constant harassing fire. They began to swivel one of the guns round and turned it upon the attackers; but it proved impossible to obtain sufficient depression of its muzzle against men who were lying up so close, and the shells burst harmlessly over their heads inland.

And so it went on for over an hour and a half, with all the points for enterprise and the offensive spirit going to Major Young and his nineteen men. By the end of this time, however, ammunition was running low and Young had to take thought for his disengagement and return. An arrangement had been made that the landing-craft should remain off-shore unless excessively heavy fire were directed against it, in which case it would pull out and Major Young's party would endeavour to make their way overland into Dieppe town and leave with the Canadian troops from Red or White Beach. Accordingly an officer was sent back to form a one-man bridge-head at the beach and to fire three white Very shots from his pistol if the landing-craft were still there.

Back at the beach, Lieut. Buckee had lain all this time under fire but had refrained from withdrawing his craft. In due time Major Young saw the signal fired which meant that the boat was still available for his party. Keeping his men closely in hand he began a withdrawal by stages across half a mile of open country to the gulley and the beach. The enemy followed up but at a respectful distance, and the British party regained the beach and re-embarked at 8.10 a.m. For over two hours they had diverted and pinned down forces ten times their number and greatly interfered with the effectiveness of the German battery, thereby averting, in the words of Captain Hughes-Hallett's official despatch 'the exceedingly serious consequences which might have resulted from the failure of the Yellow Beach landings. In my judgement this was perhaps the most outstanding incident of the operation.'

The degree of success that was achieved was primarily due to the courage, enterprise and sense of leadership displayed by Major Young and also to the resolution with which Lieut. Buckee brought the troops to shore and remained under heavy fire to take them off more than three hours later. For their share in this operation both officers received the D.S.O.

## *Varengeville*

Over on the western flank No. 4 Commando, 250 strong, under Lord Lovat, was moving in towards a similar objective, the coastal defence battery between the high road and the sea at Varengeville. Like the battery at Berneval, it was to be the object of a double assault. The smaller part of the Commando, consisting of one and a half troops under Major Mills-Roberts, would land as nearly as possible directly below it and would keep the gunners pinned down while the remainder, led by Lord Lovat in person, would execute a wide flanking movement from a landing-beach near Quiberville and would come in upon it from the rear.

No mishap interfered with the smooth passage of these troops across the Channel towards their objective. In the distance, to the north-east, they saw the gun flashes that marked the brush between the ships carrying No. 3 Commando and the German trawlers. Ahead there loomed up the darkened hulls of three German ships moving up the Channel. The British flotilla altered its course to starboard and the three ships passed on in the direction of the action towards Berneval.

Guided by the outline of the lighthouse on Pointe d'Ailly, the ships approached the beaches. We may first follow the fate of the party that was to land under the command of Major Mills-Roberts.

The landing-craft ground on to the shingle at 4.53 a.m., just three minutes after zero hour. It was high tide, and only a few paces ahead the chalk-white cliff a full hundred feet high appeared to present a formidable and impenetrable barrier. The landing-point, known as Vasterival, was really no more than a shallow beach and an outcrop of villas and chalets running down towards the sea from the straggling holiday resort of Varengeville. Directly inland, only half a mile distant, was the battery which was to be silenced.

It had been almost, but not quite, an unopposed landing. For as the assault troops stumbled, bending low, across the shingle to the cliff foot one German machine-gun began to stutter out from the cliff top above.

Wasting no time, Major Mills-Roberts's detachment made for the two clefts in the cliff face which had been indicated on the large-scale models, so carefully studied during the preceding days, as the places for their ascent. The left-hand gulley was so crammed with barbed wire that any attempt to force it had to be ruled out. But the cleft a hundred yards or so to the west looked more promising. It, too, was wired; but it did not seem impassable. The cliff was ascended by an almost vertical beach staircase constructed for holiday bathers and fishermen, and beyond that a gulley, just as narrow at the start, climbed towards the fields and woods, flanked by occasional villas and one or two châlet-like hotels.

It was an approach very similar to that which Major Young and his party were tackling at that precise moment over on the eastern flank, but the gulley beyond the beach steps was clear of any sort of undergrowth, and once the landing-party were through the wire at the bottom they could make good speed up the lane towards the battery.

A pioneer section got rapidly to work. They raced up the steps and placed their Bangalore torpedoes in position, exploding them against the wire at the bottom of the gulley. To the men below it seemed that the explosion must bring the defenders down upon them, but most happily it coincided almost exactly with the cannon-firing attack by our fighters upon the battery above, and the defenders during the next critical minute or two had plenty to think about. And while the cliffs reverberated with the explosion the spearhead of the Commando scrambled up the steps over the chalk rubble, across the smashed concrete and flattened wire and into the leafy branch-hung lane above.

The German guns above were firing now—dull, hollow, booming sounds like an explosion in a quarry. But the shells were bursting quite harmlessly out to sea, and meanwhile the men below were working forward into position. Major Mills-Roberts was deploying his small force to the best advantage. Having to guard against the possibility of counter-attack by German infantry he pushed out half a troop under Captain Dowson to the right and another half troop under Lieut. Style, who had led the advance up the gulley and lane, some distance along the top of the cliff to the left. Meanwhile a mortar section under Lieut. Ennis had worked its way forward up the lane into the wood at the summit and so close to the battery that they could hear the words of command of the German gunners.

All this had taken time—much longer than seemed possible to the deeply pre-occupied men nibbling their way forward towards the battery. The plan was for the mortars to range on the battery, keep the gun-crews pinned down and prevent them firing while Lord Lovat's flanking party worked their way round from the landing-beach near Quiberville and got into position to deliver an attack from the rear. But it was ten minutes to six, an hour after the landing-craft had touched down, before our mortars began to open fire. Almost immediately there was a deafening explosion, described by an eye-witness as 'the father and mother of all explosions'; for the third shot from one of the 2-inch mortars had landed a shell slap in the middle of a German ammunition dump.[1]

Then started a mighty conflagration, and the battery did not fire again. The German gunners, struggling to quench the flames, found themselves exposed to the attention of our snipers. In particular, Lance-Corporal Mann, with his hands and face painted green, lay concealed in the bushes barely 150 yards from the nearest gun and did repeated execution. For half an hour, with mortar and small-arms fire at close range, our men pinned down the German gunners. Suddenly at 6.20 a cluster of white Very lights broke in the sky behind the battery. It was the signal that Lord Lovat was in position and was about to launch his attack upon the battery from the rear.

This force, which formed the larger part of No. 4 Commando, had landed dead on zero hour on Orange II Beach, immediately to the east of the mouth of the river Saane. The cliff drops down here to the river mouth on the east side and is open on the west towards the sea-side village of Quiberville. No necessity for scaling any natural defences therefore arose. The men of the Commando promptly

[1] According to German records, however, the explosion took place earlier and was the result of machine-gun and cannon fire from our aircraft.

subdued two pillboxes between the river-mouth and the cliff and then, after cutting the telephone and telegraph wires, moved off inland at the double along the east bank of the Saane. Having proceeded for a mile in this direction, sheltered from observation by a low ridge overlooking the river, they swung sharp to the east, and pushed on unopposed in the full morning light until they entered Blancmenil le Bas wood immediately to the rear of the battery. From this point they could hear the rattle of the machine-guns and the bursting of the mortar bombs from the Mills-Roberts detachment not more than half a mile distant on the further, or shoreward, side of the battery. Two scouts, pushed forward from the wood, reported a force of about thirty-five German assault troops forming up for a counter-attack against Mills-Roberts. They were rapidly mown down with tommy-gun fire. And while the main body of the Commando moved into position to deliver the attack from the rear, a number of snipers, infiltrating into farm buildings, began to harass the enemy. Some of these snipers were American Rangers.

'We got to a little farm built round a yard,' said Corporal Koons, probably the first soldier of the United States Army to kill a German in this war. 'We found a small stable into which we put the wounded . . . and there I found a splendid spot for sniping. It was over a manger, and I fired through a slit in the brick wall. I had not been there long when I saw the battery receive a tremendous plastering by bombs from the mortars.' Then the cannon-firing fighters of No. 129 Squadron swept into a further low-level attack, heedless of the attempt of a number of Focke-Wulf 190's to intercept them. And as the air attack was pressed home, Lord Lovat's men went in with the bayonet.

They had to cross 250 yards of open ground to reach the approaches to the battery, and before this danger belt was passed two leading officers of the Commando had fallen. Captain Porteous, who had been acting as liaison officer between the two parts of the Commando now raced up to take the lead at the wire which surrounded and protected the German battery. He had already been wounded in the hand but had closed with his assailant and killed him with his own bayonet. Now he broke in with his men close beside him, grenading, bayoneting, and shooting their way through to the guns, where their leader fell unconscious from two further wounds. He was subsequently to receive the Victoria Cross.

It was a sharp but short fight. The Germans were already rattled by the effect of fire from both front and rear, and could not resist for long. Out of about one hundred of all ranks 30 were killed and 30 wounded; four were made prisoner and brought to England. While one troop of the Commando cleaned up the last remnants of opposition, the other systematically demolished each of the six guns. The battery would never fire again.

For the loss of 5 officers and 41 other ranks (12 of these were fatal casualties and 13 were missing) No. 4 Commando had carried out its task. It was the one entirely satisfactory and perfectly rounded action of that tragic day. Luck had been with the Commando, but dash and skill under the inspiring leadership of Lord Lovat and Major Mills-Roberts reaped their deserved reward.

When the guns were demolished the Union Jack was run up over the British dead and the Commando withdrew down the steps of Vasterival beach. All the guns had been destroyed and the action completed by 6.55. By 7.30 the re-embarkation was already under way, the troops carrying their wounded and wading out to the landing-craft, now lying further out to sea on the ebbing tide.

Such was the outcome of the outer flank attacks. One had been completely successful—a model of its kind; the other, despite the clash with the German convoy, had prevented the enemy from making effective use of his eastern flank battery during the most crucial period of the raid.

Very different was the fate of the attackers at the other four beaches.

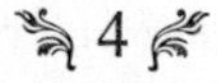

## *Puits*

The inner flank landings were to be made at two small holiday resorts, Puits and Pourville, each about a mile and a half or two miles distant from Dieppe to east and west respectively.

The operation against Puits was ill-fated from the first. The beach is fairly broad but overlooked by cliffs on either flank and is bounded on the landward side by a lofty sea-wall, ten to twelve feet high and more than one hundred yards long. From here a road, wider and less steep than the lane at Vasterival, runs inland towards the various objectives assigned to the Royal Regiment of Canada.

It will be clear from this description that success depended, here perhaps more than at any other beach, upon the achievement of surprise. Otherwise the sheer sea-wall was likely to prove a death-trap to men exposed to cross-fire from the cliff above.

And just where no delay could be afforded there was delay—of seventeen precious minutes in the growing light. Although the flotilla under the leadership of Lieut.-Commander H. W. Goulding, moved without disturbance, the landing-craft became disorganised and scattered during the run-in. As they approached they were easily visible, and, as they touched down, jets of fire began to pour from the pill-boxes straight into the ships.

The assault wave of the Royal Regiment sprang ashore. Many died in those few seconds of withering fire, and within a few minutes almost every officer was a casualty and the few men who survived raced for the shelter of the sea-wall.

But this afforded little protection, for the Germans on top of the cliff were able to bring enfilade fire to bear upon the exposed left flank of the Royals. Casualties began to mount rapidly even among the second wave who had landed only a few minutes after the first. It was desperately important to secure an exit from the beach, otherwise the attackers would be enclosed like bears in a pit and wiped out by the fire from above.

Three officers rushed forward in an attempt to blow the wire off the top of the wall with Bangalore torpedoes. One of them did succeed in making a gap, and through it a single man, Corporal Ellis, passed unscathed and, clambering up under the shelter of bushes, reached the top of the cliff. Here he took cover in a deserted slit-trench and engaged the enemy with rifle fire, but finding himself completely isolated, he eventually withdrew and climbed safely back to the beach.

Following the virtual elimination of the first two waves, C and D Companies had landed under the battalion commander, Lieut.-Colonel Catto, at the extreme western end of the beach. Though met by heavy fire, Colonel Catto and sixteen of his men succeeded soon after 6 a.m. in cutting a way through the wire beyond the end of the sea-wall and scaling the cliff. The Germans, engaged upon easy target practice against the men on the beach, appear to have paid little attention to this detachment, which now found itself isolated on the summit of the cliff, for the enemy had rapidly got a machine-gun trained on to the gap by which they had ascended and no further troops could follow them.

Colonel Catto decided to try and move west along the cliff top in the hope of making contact—according to plan—with the Essex Scottish, which by now should have penetrated into and through Dieppe. At first bushes and houses provided cover, and his party found its way into a small wood overlooking the road into Dieppe.

As the country was open beyond this point they could not penetrate further but they had the satisfaction of watching and hearing a succession of low-level attacks by R.A.F. fighter-bombers upon a battery nearby and the chagrin of noting the regularity and promptitude with which it re-opened fire after each attack. In their isolated position they had no chance either of escape or of taking any effective part in the battle, and after two reconnaissances to the edge of the cliff had failed to reveal the presence of any landing-craft below, they surrendered at 4.20 in the afternoon.

Below them Blue Beach was being turned to a shambles of dead and dying. In the words of Captain G. A. Browne, the Forward Observation Officer, who had vainly endeavoured to indicate targets to H.M.S. *Garth* at sea:

'Owing to the heavy and accurate fire of the enemy, the Royal Regiment of Canada was changed in five minutes from an assault battalion on the offensive to something less than two companies on the defensive, pinned down by fire from positions they could not discover.'

These are grim words, but they constitute no more than the truth. The men of the Royals had lost heavily as they landed, and were now being pinned against the near side of the sea-wall and gradually annihilated. The landing had failed, as apart from Colonel Catto's tiny detachment, isolated and impotent on the cliff-top, the Royals had not been able to approach a single one of the objectives marked out for them. At 7 a.m. a message was picked up by the Naval Force Commander asking that all available landing-craft should return to Blue Beach for the evacuation of the troops. The origin of this signal was never satisfactorily cleared up; had it been acted upon very many of our craft might have approached the shell-swept beach and met destruction there. Only two of the landing-craft picked up the message. Both moved in to re-embark what troops they could; and one, loaded with men, received a direct hit and capsized. A number of the Royals clinging to this craft, managed to hang on for some hours until they were rescued by light naval units later in the morning.

This was not the end of the efforts to relieve the men on Blue Beach. Around nine o'clock that morning Lieut.-Commander Goulding received instructions to take in four assault landing-craft to Blue Beach to withdraw whatever troops still remained alive and uncaptured. This officer did his best to carry out his mission, but heavy fire prevented him from closing into the shore; moreover, from what could be seen no troops remained alive on Blue Beach.

In the space of two or three hours the Royal Regiment of Canada had been practically exterminated. Of 26 officers and 528 other ranks who had embarked for the operation on the previous night, all the officers and 496 other ranks became casualties. Two officers and 65 others, half of whom were wounded, were brought away; no less than eight officers and 199 others were killed; 16 officers and 264 others, wounded and unwounded, fell into German hands and of these, two officers and 16 others died while prisoners of war.

## 5

### *Pourville*

A somewhat better fate had attended the western inner flank landing at the little watering place of Pourville on the further side of Dieppe. The South Saskatchewan Regiment had a task in many ways similar to that of the Royals at Puits. A beach had to be carried by assault and a number of objectives inland seized and held. But they enjoyed three advantages which the Royals did not—an undelayed approach, an easier preliminary objective, and the prospective support of a follow-up battalion half an hour after their landing.

Trans-shipping on to their landing-craft at much the same time as the Commandos and the Royals, the South Saskatchewan moved shoreward and at 4.55 a.m., only five minutes after zero hour, they touched down along Pourville's half-mile stretch of beach. It was both a larger and more open beach than at Puits, and the village, instead of straggling back up the lanes inland, stood four-square with the sea-shore—a single plage and a single street behind it. That meant that, given a measure of surprise, it might be possible to rush the entire German coastal position in a few minutes instead of having to fight a way inland up steep and narrow defiles.

Almost total surprise was achieved, yet the South Saskatchewan were, to a great extent, robbed of this advantage owing to an unfortunate loss of direction by many of their landing-craft. The intention was to land the battalion astride the mouth of the river Scie, in the centre of the beach. Actually only one company was put ashore on the eastern side; the others all landed on the western bank so that the river lay between them and their objectives. This caused delay and delay proved fatal to success.

The Canadians rushed ashore, crossed the beach, and cleared the houses facing the sea under a mere spatter of machine-gun fire. A

Company, which was on the correct (eastern) side of the river, scaled the sea-wall with ladders and, after disposing of a couple of pill-boxes, moved towards the radar station, an A.A. battery and the farm known as Les Quatre Vents standing on the high ground to the east. A patch of swamp and subsequently a road-block delayed them until about six o'clock, when they began to develop their attack against the Farm of the Four Winds, which was surrounded by pill-boxes commanding a fine field of fire in all directions.

C Company had little difficulty in killing or capturing all the Germans in Pourville. Taking over the large white house which had been their headquarters it pushed a platoon on to the sharply defined spur immediately to the west, overlooking the beach. So long as this could be held, the village and beach were covered from direct fire, and it would be possible to re-embark the troops, when the time came, without serious losses.

In the centre B and D Company went straight through the village and swung east to join in the attack upon Four Winds Farm, and also to widen the beach-head to permit the Camerons to come through. The pressing task was to accomplish the passage of the river.

The bridge which carries the main road across the Scie was under heavy machine-gun and mortar fire from the Germans on the down-land to the east around Four Winds Farm, and casualties were beginning to mount, when Lieut.-Colonel Merritt, commanding the battalion, rallied his men. In the manner of a man born to win the V.C., he walked gaily up to the bridge and over it, taking off his steel helmet and swinging it carelessly in his hand.

'See!' he exclaimed, 'there is no danger here!'

It was a gesture worthy of a Bayard or a Cyrano, and four times it was repeated as Colonel Merritt returned to lead fresh waves across to the assault. Stirred by his example the men of B and C Companies swarmed forward to the attack. Some crossed the river by the bridge, others by swimming or by means of a raft, and in increasing strength they moved against the pill-boxes on the open downland above them.

By this time the support battalion, the Queen's Own Cameron Highlanders of Canada, was arriving on Pourville beach. They landed in broad daylight at 5.30 a.m., while a piper, playing 'A Hundred Pipers' stood erect as bullets whined around him. A shot from an uncleared pill-box at the eastern end of the beach struck and killed the battalion commander, Lieut.-Colonel Gostling, just as he stepped ashore. Major A. T. Law took over, and the Camerons moved briskly forward through the village. One Company was detached to reinforce the attack up the slope to the east, while the remainder continued directly inland towards their objective which was the aerodrome of St. Aubin, more than three miles beyond. Here they were to be joined by the tanks which would by this time, it was estimated, have penetrated through Dieppe.

Owing to the fire still coming from Four Winds Farm, Major Law decided to lead his men up the western bank of the river, i.e. the side more remote from the farm. This decision certainly had the advantage of avoiding casualties during the first stage of the advance, but it meant that the river must ultimately be crossed higher up and nearer to the airfield.

Moving in good order the Camerons covered about two miles inland and reached a wood opposite another bridge over the river. Here they lay up and waited for the first sign of the tanks. But no tanks appeared. As we shall see, they were having their own difficulties on the sea-front of Dieppe. It was evident that the Germans were holding this passage over the Scie in some force—actually the reserve battalion of the 571st Regiment had arrived from Ouville—and Major Law had already decided to withdraw to Pourville when he received a wireless signal ordering him to do so.

The reason for the abandonment of the operation against the aerodrome lay partly in the failure of the main attack at Dieppe, partly also in the increasingly precarious situation of the two battalions which had been landed at Pourville. The enemy fire at first had been weak and intermittent, and the progress made by the attackers had been most encouraging. But as the morning wore on the fire from the defence steadily increased in volume. The Saskatchewan had gradually reduced the pill-boxes around Four Winds Farm, great gallantry being shown in these attacks. But they could not reduce the farm itself nor the radar station nor yet the A.A. battery on the cliff. This was mainly due to the lack of supporting artillery; moreover, in the mortar duels, the German heavy mortars outranged our own by as much as 600 or 700 yards. No gallantry could avail against this disadvantage.

Things became worse when the enemy recaptured the spur on the further side of Pourville and thereby obtained direct observation on to the beach. By this time all hope of a successful attack upon the aerodrome was at an end, and it was clear that there would even be difficulty in extricating the two battalions from Pourville. Accordingly, orders went out for the withdrawal of the Camerons. Major Law conducted a fighting retreat and regained the beach at Pourville just before ten o'clock with eighty per cent of his battalion still intact and in hand.

It had been intended that embarkation should begin immediately, but it was now learned that no landing-craft would be available before eleven o'clock, and consequently the troops would have the prospect of maintaining a beach-head for a further hour in the face of intensifying enemy fire from dominating positions. The wounded were carried down and laid under the shelter of the sea-wall in preparation for the arrival of the first boats, and Colonel Merritt organised a perimeter defence. The tide was now falling, and the beach being wider it was impossible for the landing-craft to come in so close. The troops had to withdraw first of all over open ground and then through about 150 yards of shallow water to reach the extremely relative security of the craft when they began to arrive a little before eleven. Many casualties were incurred during this stage of the operation, but the destroyer *Brocklesby* gave what proved to be extremely effective covering fire with her guns, and by noon most of the men of the two battalions had been taken off.

Colonel Merritt was not among them. Though wounded, he had remained with the rearguard, consisting of about a hundred men which covered the withdrawal, and no shipping was available to take them off. They held out successfully until their ammunition was exhausted and then were compelled to surrender about 1.30 p.m. It was in recognition of his exceptional valour throughout the day that Colonel Merritt was awarded the Victoria Cross.

Such had been the fate of the two inner flank landings. Unrelieved disaster at Puits; success in the opening phases, but no important advantage gained, at Pourville. The Canadians had not succeeded in destroying the radar station or the A.A. battery, they had approached but not attacked the aerodrome. Their other objective lay beyond their grasp in any case, for the German divisional headquarters had been moved from Arques to Envermeu, six miles away, in April. On the other hand, a successful disembarkation had been made, losses had been inflicted on the enemy, a number of pill-boxes destroyed, and the bulk of the troops re-embarked. The lack of success was due to no lack of resolution on the part of the attacking troops but rather to the grave failure of the main assault in the centre against Dieppe. For it had not proved possible for the tanks or infantry from Dieppe to keep their rendezvous at the aerodrome or at Four Winds Farm; and for that reason the achievements of the South Saskatchewan Regiment and the Camerons had proved largely sterile.

## 6

### *The Seafront of Dieppe*

Varengeville and Berneval had been in relation to the main assault, sideshows, 'daring cavalry charges on the enemy's flank'.[1] Puits and Pourville had been to a certain extent subsidiary in the general scheme to the direct assault upon Dieppe itself, an assault that was to be made by two battalions with tank support and followed up by the floating reserve.

The time chosen for the assault landing was 5.20 a.m., half an hour after the four flanking attacks had gone in. It was hoped to compensate for the inevitable loss of surprise by the effect of the preliminary naval and air bombardment.

Despite the courage and determination with which it was delivered, the scale and intensity of this bombardment was quite inadequate to balance the loss of tactical surprise. This was perhaps the supreme lesson of that costly day. As a result, when the troops went in they found themselves launched against defenders already put on the alert by the reports of fighting on their right and left flanks and commanding a magnificent field of fire against a force approaching from the sea.

The plan was for the Royal Hamilton Light Infantry to attack against the western half of the beach (White Beach), which was overlooked by the Casino, standing well forward, level with the sea-wall, and the only building breaking the broad lawn-covered expanse of the plage between the sea-wall and the Boulevard de Verdun. Simultaneously the Essex Scottish were to assault the eastern half of the beach (Red Beach) as far as the entrance to the port. Each battalion would thus be attacking upon a front of approximately half a mile.

The two battalions would clear the beaches in order that the tanks, the first wave of which would be landed with the assault troops, might exploit the success by penetrating into the town. The tanks would continue on towards the aerodrome and the presumed divisional headquarters at Arques, sending off a detachment to co-operate in the attack against Four Winds Farm. The infantry meanwhile would mop up the remaining posts of resistance in the town and maintain the momentum of the attack; the R.H.L.I. bearing round to the west and joining in the attack against the batteries and Four Winds Farm which were the objectives of the South Saskatchewan Regiment from Pourville; the Essex Scottish clearing the harbour,

[1] Austin, *We Landed at Dawn*, p. 98.

one company to assist Royal Marine 'A' Commando to seize the shipping, and swinging east to make contact with the Royal Regiment of Canada who had landed at Puits.

That was the plan. It required that much should be done in a short time, for the troops landing at Dieppe would not go ashore before 5.20 a.m., while re-embarkation was timed to start at 11 a.m. that same morning.

The two battalions, R.H.L.I. and Essex Scottish went in together as dawn was breaking. Their approach in the landing-craft was accompanied by a five-minute bombardment from the guns of the destroyers, against the buildings of the Boulevard de Verdun facing the beach across the open width of the plage, and, as the ships' fire was lifted from this target to concentrate against the headland defences on either flank, the cannon-firing Hurricanes swept down in a low-flying attack upon these same sea-front buildings.

Colonel Labatt has preserved a graphic account of the whole course of the attack of his battalion upon White Beach. The landing-craft had been moving in towards the shore where all was still quiet, despite the firing that had broken out at sea some time before and upon either flank. They were still 500 yards short of the beaches when the fighter-planes swept in overhead. The attack lasted only a matter of seconds, and to the men on the landing-craft there was a certain sense of disappointment and even of concern, for they had expected a longer and more intensive bombardment.

Five hundred yards . . . four hundred yards . . . three hundred yards . . . and then a sudden outburst of fire from the shore. Machine-guns, mortars, anti-tank guns, infantry guns. Men were firing from well-concealed pill-boxes, they were firing from the houses, they were visible firing from the upper windows of the Casino, they were firing from the cliffs on either flank. As one Canadian tersely phrased it 'the natives appeared to be hostile'.

The first craft slid to land and touched down, almost exactly on time. Several men have recorded that there seemed to be a temporary slackening of fire just as they sprang ashore. If it were so—and it was scarcely more than an impression formed in the heat of action—it was only of momentary duration. Almost in a matter of seconds the fire opened up with redoubled vigour. It was clear that the preliminary bombardment from sea and air had been inadequate to silence the defence, and in particular the cannon of the fighters had been quite ineffective against the concrete of the German pill-boxes.

Under this withering fire the men of the Royal Hamilton Light Infantry and the Essex Scottish rushed forward to gain the sea-wall nearly 200 yards from the water's edge. Caught in the open and enfiladed by concealed batteries in the cliff face the assault troops soon began to suffer heavy losses.

We will first follow the experience of the R.H.L.I. on White Beach. Caught in a storm of fire they made a determined attempt to rush the sea-wall and cut passages through the wire that surmounted it.

'When we landed [said a private in this battalion] we were confused for some time, but finally we got down and began to return some of the fire. We encountered barbed wire and began cutting it. We found it could be crossed without cutting . . .

'I think the German sniper is a real specialist. They are wonderful shots and go for the officers and N.C.Os. We found that they are mostly all planted on roofs or in very high buildings. At any rate, their snipers should not be underrated. The Germans seemed to be able to lay down mortar bombs where they damn well pleased. The beach was very well covered by fire from light machine-guns from the buildings and by heavy or medium machine-guns from our flanks.'

There was one immediate objective for the R.H.L.I. and that was the Casino standing out in splendid isolation, its front four-square with the sea-wall. In view of its exposed position the Germans had not attempted to treat it as part of their main defences. So conspicuous a mark could easily be destroyed by concentrated naval gunfire. Accordingly the building though defended by wire had not been treated as a strong point. Its windows were neither sandbagged nor bricked up. Nevertheless it had been used, rather incautiously, to provide sleeping quarters for a number of German troops.

It was Colonel Labatt's plan to carry the Casino by storm and then to employ it as cover through which his battalion could be 'siphoned' into the town. The Germans continued to fire from the windows and from the tower, but the Canadians broke into the building and after some 'hide and seek' fighting among the rooms and passages cleared the place, taking twenty-three Germans prisoner in the process. Subsequently these were mostly killed by the guns of their own side during the final part of the operation when the beach remained under very heavy fire from the enemy.

The fighting for the Casino lasted, according to one of the combatants, nearly an hour and was not finally concluded until Sergeant G. A. Hickson, who greatly distinguished himself throughout the operation, blew up a 4-inch gun sited there, while others of the infantry destroyed pillboxes in the neighbourhood with Bangalore torpedoes. At 7.12 a.m. H.M.S. *Calpe*, the Headquarters ship, received a signal that the Casino had been captured.

It was now possible for small parties to begin to infiltrate into the town. Two such groups, each consisting of about eight or ten men, made their way some little distance into Dieppe. Captain A. C. Hill with one of these fought his way into a cinema just behind the western end of the Boulevard de Verdun and thence to the church of St. Remi, designated as Headquarters for the 6th Canadian Brigade and the tank battalion, and even a little deeper into the town. Meeting with no support they eventually fought their way back to the cinema and thence to the Casino and the sea-front which they regained at about 10 a.m. Sergeant Hickson took another party by a somewhat similar route, but finding that civilians, or persons in civilian clothing, were apparently signalling their position to the German posts (the only recorded instance of assistance being given to the enemy by the French population) they took cover and kept up a brisk fire until, their ammunition being expended, they were likewise compelled to withdraw to the beach. After the liberation the French placed a tablet in the wall of St. Remi church above the spot where two Canadian soldiers were killed.

Further along the beach to the east the Essex Scottish were suffering an even greater ordeal than the R.H.L.I. Here there was no feature corresponding to the Casino to mask infiltration into the town, and the battalion was committed to a frontal assault over open ground against a fully prepared enemy. It appears to have made its landing somewhat earlier than the R.H.L.I., for Captain (afterwards Colonel) D. F. MacRae, the only officer of this battalion to return from landing, has stated that the cannon-fighters were still in the process of delivering 'a very heavy and audacious attack' when the landing-craft touched down and the troops rushed ashore. In consequence they actually gained the first beach obstacle, he states, with only a single casualty. But this respite was not of long duration. The combination of fire from the buildings in front with the deadly enfilade by the guns firing from caves in the eastern cliff began to take an appalling toll of the battalion. Within twenty-five minutes of landing it was estimated that they had lost between thirty and forty per cent of their strength. Three-quarters of an hour later the estimate had almost doubled. The men sought what shelter they could against the sea-wall, but it was very much lower than at Puits, being generally only about three feet above the level of the shingle. At some points the men succeeded in blasting a way through the wire at the top; at others they threw themselves upon it to enable their comrades to cross.

Three separate attempts were made to break into the town. The most successful was that of C.S.M. Stapleton who, under heavy fire, cut gaps in the wire at the sea-wall and led a dozen men in a dash across the bullet and shell-swept lawns of the esplanade. They reached the houses beyond and worked towards the harbour, accounting for German snipers and machine-gun posts on the way. Then, after engaging with deadly effect the crew of a ship by the dock-side, Stapleton was obliged to bring back the survivors of his party. His gallant leadership and fine fighting spirit won him the Distinguished Conduct Medal.

Meanwhile what of the tanks, Churchill tanks, carrying a six-pounder gun, in action for the first time? Their employment was one of the chief tactical features of the Dieppe operation, and much depended upon their ability to gain the town, clear their way through the streets, and break through into the open country beyond.

It had been intended that the first wave of nine tanks should land with the assault infantry so as to provide them with much-needed covering fire during the first few vital minutes. Unfortunately the L.C.Ts. carrying the first wave were delayed, with the result that the tanks did not reach shore until 5.35 a.m., twelve to fifteen minutes later than the infantry. But the next wave of nine tanks followed hard upon the first and the third and last wave, numbering twelve, touched down about 0605 hours, its appointed time.

Again there was an impression that the German fire slackened somewhat as the first tanks gained the beach: again this slackening, if indeed it occurred, was only momentary. Some of the first tanks to land were hit, but many went into action at once as they moved forward up the shingle. Fortunately the beach had not been mined. Of a total of thirty tanks, twenty-nine left their landing craft and twenty-seven landed, the other two being 'drowned' in deep water when the ramp-chains of the L.C.T. were cut by enemy fire and caused the ramp to fall prematurely. In one of these tanks was Lieut.-Colonel Andrews commanding the Calgary Regiment. A little later he was killed as he gained the beach. Brigadier Lett, commanding the 4th Canadian Brigade, intended to land with the regiment, but was wounded on his L.C.T.

The sea-wall beyond the beach was regarded as a formidable obstacle as indeed it was in the centre; but towards its eastern and western extremities it was low enough for tanks to negotiate which a number of them did, some using a track-laying device of timber palings made by the sappers for this purpose. Fifteen tanks thus gained the esplanade, but here they were exposed to anti-tank gunfire to which they had no adequate reply. Strong road-blocks barred the entrances to the town and not all the Canadian demolition parties had succeeded in landing. In spite of considerable loss of equipment some of the sappers went forward to their tasks under heavy fire, but all to no avail. Gradually these tanks began to return to the beach where the men of the Calgary Regiment whose Churchills were still fit for action sought hull-down positions in which to maintain the fight. Despite contemporary reports to the contrary, no tank actually penetrated into the town.

## 7

### *The Last Effort*

Already by 6.30 a.m. it was becoming clear that the main attack was by no means proceeding according to plan, and at a conference held on board H.M.S. *Calpe* between Captain Hughes-Hallett, Commander R. E. D. Ryder, V.C. and Major-General Roberts it was decided that in view of the failure of the Blue Beach landing at Puits, and of the consequent failure to carry the east cliff, it was out of the question for H.M.S. *Locust* and the light craft manned by the Fighting French to enter the harbour and seize or destroy the shipping.

Other messages received by General Roberts were inaccurate and misleading in the extreme. It was reported that the Royal Regiment of Canada had been unable to land at Puits, but that the Essex Scottish at Dieppe had penetrated into the town. Rapid decisions were called for. Orders were issued for the Royal Regiment to land at Red Beach and support the Essex Scottish; but, as we know, the battalion was already committed at Puits. The Fusiliers Mont-Royal still under the commander's hand, was ordered to land at Red and White Beaches. Acting on the information which had reached him, General Roberts was intent upon using his reserve to exploit success: he could not know that he was reinforcing failure.

So the Fusiliers went in, landing just after 7 a.m. It had been intended that they should go ashore evenly between Red and White Beaches, but the landing-craft were carried some distance down to the west, and a large proportion of the battalion (apparently as many as 300 men) came ashore well beyond the R.H.L.I. right flank and immediately under the west cliff, where they had little opportunity for movement or manoeuvre.

From the start the whole battalion came under heavy fire, and casualties soon began to mount. The battalion commander, Lieut.-Colonel Ménard was among the first to be hit, and the majority of the men found that there was no opportunity for them to take offensive action save by crouching in the fold of the shingle half way up the beach or behind the hulls of wrecked tanks and firing from the cover which these provided. Followed by a number of men, Sergeant Dubuc broke into the town by much the same route as that taken by the parties of R.H.L.I. earlier in the morning. Turning east, the party moved through the streets and eventually are said to have approached the docks. They engaged numbers of Germans and fought until their ammunition was exhausted when they were compelled to surrender.

The Germans were taking no chances with these adventurous men. They ordered them to strip off their battle-dress and then lined them up in their underclothing facing a wall. Only a single German sentry was left in charge of them. It seemed sufficient under the circumstances. But no sooner was the sentry alone than Sergeant Dubuc asked him for a drink of water. The man's attention was momentarily distracted and the Fusiliers fell on him as one man. He was overwhelmed and killed, and the little party made off through the streets in the direction of the beach. They must have presented an odd spectacle that morning, Aldwych farce superimposed on the Jacobean tragedy of the scene at the beaches. It is just possible, however, that the very absence of uniform may have saved many of them from being shot down in the streets. Some seem to have got lost on the way back, but Sergeant Dubuc himself regained the beach where he found the evacuation already in progress and his own commanding officer lying badly wounded on the shingle. Disobeying his orders to leave him where he was, Sergeant Dubuc got Colonel Ménard on board one of the landing-craft and himself succeeded subsequently in boarding another and returning to England.

For his behaviour in action this day Sergeant Dubuc received the Military Medal.

Viewing the situation about eight o'clock, General Roberts still had reason to feel that despite the many unfavourable developments there was a chance of achieving some at least of the objects of the raid. He had received information of the capture of the Casino, and about 7.30, that the sea-wall had been breached and that the tanks had been ordered through. This implied something in the nature of a real break in the crust of the defence, which was very far from being the case, but there seemed a chance that the west headland might be carried by a combined assault from the town and from the South Saskatchewan who had landed at Pourville. He had still the Royal Marine Commando available as a general reserve, and he was faced with the choice of throwing them in either on the Dieppe beach or at Pourville, where also a measure of success had been gained. But Pourville seemed too remote from the main scene of action, and the decision was taken to commit the Marines to Dieppe itself. This was strengthened by the information received to the effect that White Beach was now clear and under control. The capture of the west cliff, believed to be already partially in our hands, would be completed, after which the troops might be passed right round the back of the town to attack the east cliff from the rear.

And so the last of the floating reserve was thrown into an action that was already lost, though this could scarcely be appreciated on the Headquarters ship at that stage in view of the paucity of reliable reports from the shore. Under cover of one of the many smoke-screens laid down—and very effective most of them were—the Royal Marine Commando was transferred from the light *chasseurs* of the Fighting French to landing-craft detailed from the Boat Pool which had been established some distance out to sea; and at 8.30 a.m., Commander Ryder giving covering fire from H.M.S. *Locust*, they began to move forward through the smoke.

But as the craft emerged from this welcome and greatly needed screen they were met with a murderous wave of fire. The Marines kept on their course. From the decks of the landing-craft they kept up a return fire from positions quite devoid of cover. But the assault never had a chance from the first. The enemy fire was now heavier than at any time previous and was directed straight into the landing-craft. To a Fighting Frenchman who witnessed it from close quarters the whole affair appeared as a naval repetition of the Charge of the Light Brigade.

To the Royal Marine commander, Lieut.-Colonel J. P. Phillipps, the true situation became apparent directly his landing-craft emerged from the cover of smoke. Realising that the position on the beaches was very different from that which the Military Force commander, back on H.M.S. *Calpe*, had envisaged, he determined to take the responsibility for stopping the landing if he could. He leapt to a conspicuous position on the forward deck and with complete disregard for his own personal safety began signalling with his hands to the other craft to put about and return within the cover of the smoke-screen. Some of them caught the signal and understood his meaning. They began to withdraw. Colonel Phillipps himself fell mortally wounded. A witness who was close by at the time has stated that he remembers having seen the colonel standing alone and erect still signalling when everyone else on his craft had been killed.

Some Marines had already landed and were taking shelter as best they could behind the hulls of tanks, but Colonel Phillipps saved the greater part of his Commando from certain destruction.

At nine o'clock General Roberts reviewed the situation. On his two outer flanks all was over by this time. Lord Lovat's Commando had fulfilled their task at Varengeville and were now on their way back, as was Major Young's detachment who had performed so useful a delaying role on the other flank at Berneval. There was no news of the men still fighting a hopeless battle in the lanes of Petit Berneval, nor was it even realised at this time that they had landed. At Pourville good progress had been made, with the South Saskatchewan attacking Four Winds Farm and the Camerons a good two miles inland preparing to attack across the defended Scie river towards the aerodrome. But at Puits those who were not already dead were pinned down against the sea-wall and quite helpless, while the situation was little better on the main Dieppe beaches where heavy losses had been suffered by every unit that had landed. All the troops available had now been committed to the attack, and with the enemy fire increasing in power it was now clear that further success was beyond our capacity, since the fire from the ships' guns was quite inadequate to ensure the men ashore cover and freedom of movement. This fire was further hampered by the difficulty of getting forward observation officers into positions of vantage.

At the same time Captain Hughes-Hallett advised that, from the naval point of view, withdrawal should take place as soon as possible, since it was becoming increasingly difficult for ships and landing-craft to close into the beaches. The earliest practicable time for the embarkation to begin, however, would be 10.30 a.m. which meant another hour and a half for the men on the beaches under the ordeal of intensifying enemy fire. The hour of embarkation was provisionally fixed, but was later altered to eleven o'clock.

Meanwhile overhead a great battle was in progress between planes of the R.A.F. and the Luftwaffe. The task of the former had been fourfold:

1. To provide general air cover for the operation, including protection for the troops and shipping.
2. To deliver attacks upon the five coastal batteries at Berneval, Puits, on either side of Dieppe, and at Varengeville—also other targets to be indicated by the troops.
3. To attack and mask with smoke the east and west headlands.
4. To maintain tactical reconnaissance far inland so as to obtain information regarding the forward movements of German ground units.

The reaction of the Luftwaffe proved to be much as had been anticipated. It was slow in getting off the mark, and the number of planes eventually committed corresponded fairly closely to our estimates. Their fighters never succeeded in interfering effectively with the cover given to our troops on the ground. The R.A.F. was master of the skies over the beaches. This was indeed a triumph and a fore-warning of what the enemy might expect when we eventually launched our full-scale offensive across the Channel. The German bombers confined their attention to the ships at sea and here too their success was modest. Apart from a few hits on landing-craft the only success they scored was on the destroyer *Berkeley*, and that was almost accidental, being the result of an aircraft jettisoning her bombs at random.

Defensively it may be said that the R.A.F. won a considerable victory. They kept the German bombers and fighters off our troops and by the repeated laying of smoke-screens they certainly helped to keep down the number of casualties during the approach, during the period when the troops were on shore, and especially during the withdrawal. The manner in which smoke was employed was one of the most satisfactory aspects of the battle, and more use could profitably have been made of it had more been available.

A successful raid by Flying Fortresses escorted by Spitfires upon the German fighter aerodrome at Abbeville-Drucat destroyed a number of planes on the ground and certainly helped to blunt the vigour of the German *riposte*.

But the total cost to the R.A.F. was very heavy. We lost 106 aircraft, including 98 fighters, between dawn and dusk.

The withdrawal had been postponed to 11 a.m. to allow for the necessary shipping to be collected and for the R.A.F. to lay an adequate smoke-screen. It began almost exactly on time, and Colonel Labatt has recorded how just before the landing-craft arrived off White Beach a couple of Hurricanes swept overhead laying the most perfect smoke-screen that could be imagined from one end of the beach to the other. Without this and the similar smoking of the east and west headlands the losses of the Canadians must have been much higher. Even as it was, the re-embarkation was a desperate business. With the German machine-gun posts and snipers only 200 yards distant at many points there could be no proper beach control. The men just waded out and scrambled aboard as best they could. The tanks during this period performed an invaluable service by keeping up covering fire to the last. Most of them were by this time immobilised with broken tracks or other forms of damage but whenever the guns could be worked the gunners continued to fire. This determined resistance certainly prevented the German infantry from rushing the beaches while our men were actually being taken off. But as a result all the tanks had to be abandoned and the crews with them.

There is no need to describe the last scenes on the beaches, as the troops jostled their way aboard the landing-craft, overloading them until many capsized and the men were thrown into the water and picked off by snipers as they milled desperately around. The majority of the losses in the landing-craft occurred at this stage, for the enemy fire grew stronger as our resistance weakened.

Yet for over an hour craft after craft went in and evacuation continued under the direct fire of the German guns.

At 12.20 Commander McClintock, the naval officer directly in charge of the re-embarkation, signalled the Headquarters ship to the effect that he doubted whether any further evacuation were feasible. General Roberts, however, being naturally anxious that as many troops as possible should be withdrawn, asked that a further effort should be made. Accordingly, after consideration Captain Hughes-Hallett despatched the following signal:

'If no further evacuation possible withdraw.'

But owing to an error in transcription, easily comprehensible in view of the difficulties under which all concerned were working, the message as handed to Commander McClintock read:

'No further evacuation possible withdraw.'

In any case it is doubtful whether much more could have been done. Commander McClintock's motor launch was sunk at about this time and the Headquarters ship established no further signals contact with him. A despairing effort was made by H.M.S. *Calpe* at about 12.50 to close in to Red Beach to give covering fire from short range to any troops who might still be alive and free on shore. But as it drew in nothing could be observed but corpses on the beach and nothing but derelict landing-craft stranded in the surf just offshore. *Calpe*, coming under heavy fire, was compelled to draw off.

Even then a further effort was contemplated. Commander Ryder, who had won the V.C. at St. Nazaire, thought it might be possible to take H.M.S. *Locust* with her shallower draught closer in shore for a final reconnaissance. But even while the interchange of signals was in progress news was received that the greater number of the troops on the beaches had surrendered.

For at eight minutes past one, Brigadier Southam, commanding the 6th Canadian Brigade, who had been controlling the force ashore from the neighbourhood of the Casino, and had despatched frequent signals requesting the destruction or masking of the batteries on the west and east headlands, sent the following message, the last that was received from the shore:

'There seems to be a mass surrender of our troops to the Germans on the beach. Our people here have surrendered.'

Here must be mentioned the great courage and devotion displayed by Captain J. W. Foote, chaplain of the Royal Hamilton Light Infantry. Improvising an aid-post on the beach, he tended the wounded throughout the long ordeal; often he went out under heavy fire to bring in a wounded man; and, at the end, rather than embark, he preferred to remain and continue to serve his men as a prisoner of war. Captain Foote was the first Canadian chaplain to receive the Victoria Cross.

Colonel Labatt, describing the closing scenes on the beaches, has stated how, on coming ashore for the second time after his boat had been hit, he saw from 150 to 200 men sheltering behind the numerous wrecked vehicles on the shingle. Nearly all of them were wounded and in a terrible condition. He got the unwounded to work dragging their comrades who lay half in and half out of the water higher up the shore to save them from drowning. Then seeing that nothing further could be done with the spent force around him he sent off a captured German airman who had baled out on the beach to carry news that they were prepared to surrender.

A few minutes later the firing died down, and the next thing he noted was the abrupt appearance of thirty or forty Germans on the top of the sea-wall who covered the men below with their tommy-guns. The Canadians put up their hands. Then five or six of the Germans tossed a number of grenades among the wounded men. This incident, however, appears to have been exceptional. In general it must be said that the Germans treated our wounded well.

## 8

### *Losses and Gains*

In as much as its objectives were not achieved and our losses were so heavy the raid on Dieppe, viewed as a tactical operation, was a costly failure. Nearly 6,100 troops were embarked and of these no less than 3,648 were killed, wounded, missing or captured.

The Essex Scottish lost 30 officers and 501 other ranks: their embarkation strength was 32 officers and 521 other ranks. Two officers, neither of whom actually landed, and 20 other ranks returned unwounded, and one officer (Captain D. F. MacRae, who, though wounded, swam pushing a small boat containing a wounded man for two miles before he was picked up) and 28 other ranks returned wounded. There had been little cover for the battalion from the moment it landed, and during the evacuation very few landing-craft succeeded in touching down at Red Beach.

The Royal Hamilton Light Infantry on White Beach fared a little better, but out of 31 officers and 551 other ranks, their casualties amounted to all their officers and 449 other ranks. However, of the wounded 6 officers and 109 other ranks returned together with 102 other ranks who were unwounded, for the actual process of evacuation was a good deal more satisfactory from White Beach than from Red.

The Fusiliers Mont-Royal suffered very heavily, considering the comparatively short time they were ashore. In their case 31 officers and 552 other ranks were embarked and 28 officers and 484 others became casualties, of whom 2 officers and 52 other ranks returned wounded. Of the unwounded, 3 officers and 68 other ranks came back.

The tank battalion (The Calgary Regiment) brought back 15 officers and 232 other ranks, out of 32 officers and 385 other ranks, but with a single exception none of these men had actually been in action, for the later waves of tanks were never landed.

Every one of the twenty-seven tanks that went ashore had to be abandoned. Though they were unsuccessful in effecting a break-through into the town and beyond, the reports of the infantry are unanimous in paying tribute to the covering fire which they put up, particularly during the final stages, and also to the imperviousness of their armour to the German anti-tank fire. It has been asserted, though this seems difficult to substantiate, that not one of them was actually pierced by German anti-tank shells and that the losses suffered in action were due solely to broken or damaged tracks or to the failure of their engines. In consequence, not very many of their personnel were killed or wounded, though, as has been seen, nearly all were captured.

At Pourville the South Saskatchewan Regiment sustained the loss of 19 officers and 321 other ranks out of 25 and 498; and the Cameron Highlanders of Canada, 24 and 322 out of 32 and 471. At Puits the Royal Regiment of Canada which had embarked 26 officers and 528 other ranks, suffered still more grievously for the total casualties of this fine battalion included all the officers and 496 others.

The fatal casualties of the Canadian troops engaged amount to 56 officers and 851 other ranks. In all 1,945 officers and men, a great number of them wounded, became prisoners of war.

Casualties among the senior Canadian officers were very heavy. Of the two brigadiers, Brigadier Southam (6th Canadian Brigade) was wounded and taken prisoner and Brigadier Lett (4th Canadian Brigade) was wounded. Colonel Labatt (Royal Hamilton Light Infantry), Colonel Jasperson (Essex Scottish), Colonel Catto (Royal Regiment of Canada) and Colonel Merritt (South Saskatchewan Regiment), were all taken prisoner. Colonel Gostling, who led the Queen's Own Cameron Highlanders and Colonel Andrews of the Tank Regiment were killed; Colonel Ménard, commanding the Fusiliers Mont-Royal, was the only battalion commander to return to England, and he was wounded.

Considering the hazards of the expedition and the length of time that the ships were compelled to lie off a hostile shore, our naval losses were surprisingly light. The destroyer *Berkeley* was hit in the last minutes of the evacuation and had to be sunk by our own fire after the crew had been taken off, and thirty-three landing-craft in all were sunk or left derelict. The total loss in naval personnel was 81 officers and 469 other ranks. That naval losses were not higher is a striking tribute to the effectiveness of the air cover provided by the R.A.F., which was purchased, however, at heavy cost in pilots, air-crews, and aircraft.

To set against this what losses had we inflicted on the Germans? One coastal battery had been effectively destroyed; and German reports, which there is no particular reason to distrust, admit to two field guns, four anti-tank guns, and three light machine-guns completely written off.

As regards the number of killed or wounded, enemy losses were extremely low. We only succeeded in bringing back 37 prisoners, most of them naval ratings. The German official figures are 316 military casualties, 113 in the navy, 162 in the Luftwaffe; a total of 591, of whom 297 were actually killed.

In the air we claimed at the time 92 German planes destroyed with another 170 probables. The Germans admitted to 35. The actual figure is now established as 48 destroyed, with another 24 damaged. Here again, though far less decisively, the balance of losses was against us.

Dieppe, however, cannot be regarded merely as a tale of almost unrelieved disaster. Described by the Prime Minister as a 'reconnaissance in force' the raid was an experiment with combined operations by land, sea, and air. It was the logical development from the series of Commando raids that preceded it, the logical precursor of the future invasion of Europe from the west. It was not, of course, an attempt to open up a front in the West, although German propaganda, after some hesitation, proclaimed it as a genuine but unsuccessful endeavour to do so. This view, indeed, was actually held by many high German officers, including Keitel. Dr. Goebbels and his minions even asserted that the raid was the result of Stalin's personal insistence upon a 'Second Front'.

We went to Dieppe to gather essential experience in the mounting of a large-scale assault upon the German-defended coast of France. It had been assumed by our planners that such an operation would have good prospect of success if launched as a surprise attack: that is to say by ensuring that the assault-craft approached the beaches under cover of darkness and that the troops were put ashore rapidly in the first light of morning. No action of ours must forewarn the enemy, hence there could be no preliminary bombardment to 'soften up' the defences and no overwhelming fire support as the assault-craft closed the beaches. Surprise landings, it was also considered, might well be the best—perhaps the only—way of securing a port with most of its facilities intact, thereby obtaining an advantage which was difficult to over-estimate.

The raid on Dieppe put these tactics to the test. It was, by its very nature, a hazardous operation severely limited by the time factor, for the appointed tasks must be accomplished within a few stated hours. All depended upon the strict synchronisation in action of the land, sea, and air forces engaged; and each group of assault-craft must touch down at the right place at the right time. Here it should be remembered that the expedition sailed from four different ports, in thirteen groups, and that the assault-craft had a run-in of ten miles through the night.

While the gallantry and fighting powers of the troops command our heart-felt admiration, the plan of the raid, and certain decisions taken during its course, may invite criticism if only because our losses were so heavy and so few of the objectives were achieved. The reason for committing the whole of the tank battalion to the Dieppe beaches has already been explained. A detachment landed at Pourville, provided it could have been put ashore on the eastern bank of the river Scie, and could have negotiated the exits from the beach, might—or might not—have decided the issue at Four Winds Farm. Once battle was joined it was probably impossible to divert a number of L.C.Ts. from Dieppe to Pourville in time to be of use; and time was of all importance.

The Pourville landing, in retrospect, may seem to have promised much, but it is easy to see why it performed so little. The initial mistake of putting most of the stormers ashore with the river between them and their objectives was probably fatal to success; and the inland penetration of the Camerons, who were eventually confronted by a strongly defended river crossing, actually had little value.

Once they were committed to a surprise assault there was no chance of switching the leading units from their pre-determined tasks. The military commander's only means of influencing the fight was by the employment of his small—perhaps too small—reserve; and the inaccurate reports which reached the Headquarters ship were responsible for the decision to land the only remaining battalion and then the Marine commando on the beaches of Dieppe. It may be that a more elaborate system of liaison officers and better signal facilities were needed throughout.

We have seen that Captain Hughes-Hallett, who held the naval command, was of opinion, after all was over, that a capital ship could have been employed without undue risk to lend fire support to the assault. Naturally he was not alone among naval authorities in stressing the value, if not the necessity, of a heavy naval bombardment when landing operations were in question.[1] As has been said, we had no battleship available.

The raid on Dieppe was a small affair in comparison with the mighty effort put forth by the Allies in 1944; and it was followed by exercises and large-scale combined operations from which we continued to learn. But the complexities of the naval concentration for an assault from the sea; the difficulty of handling and controlling the diverse types of craft; the intricacies of signal communication, the wide range of special equipment required: all these and other factors were, to a considerable extent, revealed or at least indicated by our tragic experience at the beaches on August 19th, 1942. It is significant that on D-Day no attempt was made to seize a heavily defended port and that the assault, made in daylight, was preceded and covered by the heaviest naval and air bombardment that could be devised. To quote the official Canadian historian: 'The casualties sustained in the raid [Dieppe] were part of the price paid for the knowledge that enabled the great operation of 1944 to be carried out at a cost in blood smaller than even the most optimistic had ventured to hope for.'[2]

As for the Germans, there seems little doubt that their success, for it was a success, in repelling the raid on Dieppe induced them to persevere in the development of a system of coast defence which, in

[1] See Lord Keyes, *Amphibious Warfare and Combined Operations*, pp. 98–9.
[2] *The Canadian Army 1939–45: An Official Historical Summary*, p. 86.

1944, rendered our task of invasion easier than it might have been. At Dieppe we had attempted, by direct assault from the sea, to seize a port: therefore the defences of every port of consequence, receiving first consideration, were elaborated and strengthened. Yet when the Allied invaders came they brought their harbours with them. Again, the enemy grew over-confident of his ability to defeat assault landings on the open beaches of the intervening stretches of coast, where he never carried the linear system of defence to any considerable depth. So on June 6th, 1944, on the shores of Normandy, the full force of the Allied assault was able to open the way to final victory.

# GENERAL INDEX

# INDEX TO FORMATIONS AND UNITS